GIFT
&
COMMUNION

Jarosław Kupczak, OP

GIFT
&
COMMUNION

*John Paul II's
Theology of the Body*

TRANSLATED BY
Agata Rottkamp, Justyna Pawlak,
and Orest Pawlak

The Catholic University of America Press
Washington, D.C.

Copyright © 2014
The Catholic University of America Press
All rights reserved
The paper used in this publication meets the minimum
requirements of American National Standards for Information
Science—Permanence of Paper for Printed Library
Materials, ANSI Z39.48-1984.
∞

Design and typesetting by Kachergis Book Design

Library of Congress Cataloging-in-Publication Data
Kupczak, Jaroslaw, 1964– [Dar i komunia. English]
Gift and communion : John Paul II's Theology of the body /
Jaroslaw Kupczak, OP ; translated by Agata Rottkamp,
Justyna Pawlak, and Orest Pawlak.
pages cm
Includes bibliographical references and index.
ISBN 978-0-8132-3711-4 (pbk)
1. John Paul II, Pope, 1920–2005. Theology of the body.
2. Human body—Religious aspects—Catholic Church.
3. Sex—Religious aspects—Catholic Church.
I. Title.
BX1795.B63K8713 2014
233'.5—dc23   2014005422

*To Carl A. Anderson and the Knights of Columbus
In gratitude for their faith and work*

Contents

Foreword by Carl A. Anderson — ix
Acknowledgments — xv
Introduction — xvii
Abbreviations — xxiii

1. DISCOURSE ON METHOD — 1

An Adequate Anthropology — 5
Theological Hermeneutics — 18
Paul Ricoeur's Hermeneutics of Symbol and
John Paul II's Hermeneutical Circle — 29

2. THE BODY THAT REVEALS — 41

"The Beginning": The Body as Subject — 42
After the Fall: The Body as Object — 54
The Ethos of Redemption: An Affirmation of the
Dignity of the Human Body — 65
The Resurrection: The Virginal Meaning of
the Body — 75
Sacramentality of the Body — 83

3. THE GIFT THAT CREATES COMMUNION — 93

The Sources of Papal Thought — 97
    The Philosophical Anthropology of Karol Wojtyła — 98
    The Council's *Communio* Theology — 101
    Karol Wojtyła's Theology of Marriage and Family — 105
The Created and Uncreated Gift — 112

Gift and Communion in the Theology of the
Catecheses   116
Perspectives for Further Research   131

4. MAN AS THE IMAGE AND LIKENESS OF GOD   137

The "Philosophical Exegesis" of the Concept of *Imago Dei* in the Elohist and Yahwist Accounts of Creation   142
Gift Reveals the Human Likeness to God   147
The Communal Dimension of *Imago Dei*   149
The Body as a Sign of *Imago Dei*   152
The Influence of Sin on the Image of God in Man   156
The Christocentric Character of *Imago Dei*   159
Eschatological Fulfillment   163
The Synthetic Character of John Paul II's Theology of *Imago Dei*   165

5. THE LANGUAGE OF THE BODY   170

The Philosophical and Psychological Understanding of the Language of the Body   170
Sources of the Concept of "the Language of the Body" in the Philosophical Anthropology of Karol Wojtyła   178
The Song of Songs: An Unsuccessful Attempt to Return to the Innocence of Creation   186
The Book of Tobit: Love Strong through Hope   195
Ethical Consequences of the Language of the Body   199
    Humanae Vitae: On Nature as a Reflection of the Plan of God   199
    The Ontological and Phenomenological Truth of the Language of the Body   201

FINAL REMARKS   207

Bibliography   213
Index   227

Foreword

CARL A. ANDERSON

Speaking in 1978 of the newly elected John Paul I, Cardinal Karol Wojtyła once described the pope's role in post–Vatican II society as shouldering "the cross of contemporary man"—taking up and addressing the dangers, the wrongs that "can be righted only through justice and love."[1] Unknown to him at the time, he was describing the very task that would be laid upon his own shoulders less than a month later when he would be elected to the papacy and would declare "Do not be afraid. Open wide the doors to Christ."[2]

Today, millions cherish John Paul II's invitation to courage and truth. As much as this was an invitation to individuals, as his pontificate progressed it became clear that for him this was an invitation to families and even to entire cultures as well. Paul VI once wrote in *Evangelii nuntiandi*, "The split between the Gospel and culture is without doubt the drama of our time."[3] John Paul II made this drama a central focus of his pontificate, encouraging the introduction of the Gospel into cultures where the message of Christ was

---

1. Karol Wojtyła, "Sermon at Mogila for the Triumph of the Cross: September 16, 1978," in Adam Boniecki, *The Making of the Pope of the Millennium: Kalendarium of the Life of Karol Wojtyła* (Stockbridge, Mass.: Marian Press, 2000), 830-831.
2. John Paul II, "Homily for the Inauguration of the Pontificate: October 22, 1978." The text of the homilies of John Paul II as well as of all documents of the Catholic Church (unless otherwise noted) come from the official Vatican website: www.vatican.va.
3. Paul VI, *Evangelii nuntiandi*, 20.

unknown, and introducing it anew where it is now ignored or rejected. As he said in the United States, "The Gospel of Jesus Christ is at home in every people. It enriches, uplifts and purifies every culture."[4] It is a transformative gift, which those who have received it cannot withhold from others.

For John Paul II, the evangelization of contemporary culture depends upon witness and especially the witness of the Christian family, which he perceived to be the principal place of encounter between the Gospel and culture. Unfortunately, perhaps nowhere was the dichotomy of Gospel and culture more obvious, more imperative, for him than in the area of marriage and family life. And as marriage and family life are themselves dichotomized within secular culture, even pitted against each other and against the freedom of each person by contemporary notions of autonomy and association, the health of our contemporary culture may ultimately depend upon the ability of Christian families to witness in their own lives to the reality of their unique vocation.

This evangelization and renewing witness are possible; but for this, John Paul II maintained, married couples require an "adequate awareness of the individual Christian's vocation" as well as great "spiritual maturity."[5] Even as he was writing these words of his first encyclical, *Redemptor hominis,* he had already begun providing such a foundation in his general audiences. Beginning with the subject of man being made in the image of God and later exploring the Christian's vocation with the focus of the married couple, he gave us what is now known as the Wednesday Catecheses on the Theology of the Body. As John Paul II said in 1999, "The truth is that the sexual configuration of bodiliness is an integral part of God's original plan, in which man and woman are created in the image and likeness of God and are called to enact a faithful

---

4. John Paul II, "Address to the Native Peoples of the Americas: September 14, 1987."

5. John Paul II, *RH,* 21.

and free, indissoluble and fruitful communion that is a reflection of the richness of Trinitarian love."[6]

The way in which John Paul II introduces this theological approach alone suggests his concern to overcome the split of Gospel and culture identified by Paul VI, as the Wednesday catecheses examine the Gospel message with insights gained from contemporary philosophy and psychology infused with his own dramatic sense of life and faith. In his Wednesday catecheses, John Paul II presents some of the most familiar passages of sacred scripture with a freshness that makes one think of what it must have been like for the early Greek Christians steeped in the popular philosophies of their day as they began to read the Bible for the first time.

These catecheses are fundamental to the sustained witness of Christian married love required by the ever-increasing challenges presented to contemporary man. In the pages that follow, Jarosław Kupczak has made evident the importance of the pope's theology of the body to the recovery of a Catholic sense of married life and its renewal within the context of an increasingly secular and at times hostile society.

The Wednesday catecheses do not stand in isolation. They are an integral part of a lifetime devoted to the family. As a priest and philosopher, Karol Wojtyła published as one of his first works *Love and Responsibility*, and he continued these themes in his work as a playwright, in *The Jeweler's Shop* and *The Radiation of Fatherhood*, which show an early and deep contemplation of the vocation to love in marriage and parenthood. In reading these earlier works, one is struck by their concrete, existential context and by the corresponding absence of both abstraction and idealism. For John Paul II, the pastoral care of the family life was indispensible to the renewal of the Catholic Church and society sought by the Second Vatican Council. As part of his effort to imple-

---

6. John Paul II, "Address to the Participants in the International Study Week Promoted by the Pontifical Institute for Studies on Marriage and Family: August 27, 1999."

ment the process of conciliar renewal within the Archdiocese of Krakòw, he published *Sources of Renewal,* in which he described marriage and family as "the first, fundamental Christian community" for the laity and, like the council, recognized the importance of this community "for the building up of the Church."[7] Many years later, John Paul II would write that the Second Vatican Council was "the constant reference point of my every pastoral action."[8] Certainly, this is apparent in the pope's entire approach to marriage and family ministry. For the first time, *Gift and Communion* makes clear how this is true for the pope's Wednesday catecheses, highlighting not only John Paul II's theology of the body within the context of the pope's broader theological vision but also the ways this vision was shaped by the context of pastoral renewal sought by the Second Vatican Council.

It is truly remarkable that a pope would dedicate approximately four years to the exposition of a unique theological approach to understanding human love and sexuality. The Wednesday catecheses alone represents a level of personal commitment to furthering the renewal of married life unprecedented in the history of Christianity. Not even the assassination attempt against his life could deter him from this task. When considered as part of the broader context of magisterial teaching, which includes the apostolic exhortation *Familiaris consortio,* the *Letter to Families,* and the encyclical *Evangelium vitae,* the Wednesday catecheses constitute a legacy by which this great pope may be rightly considered the apostle of married and family life for the third millennium. It is also a testament to the dimensions of the pastoral task to prepare married couples for the "spiritual maturity" required to live an authentic Catholic married life in today's society.

Thus, *Gift and Communion* is an indispensible guide to un-

---

7. Karol Wojtyła, *Sources of Renewal: The Implementation of Vatican II,* translated by P. S. Falla (San Francisco: Ignatius Press, 1980), 392.

8. John Paul II, "Homily of January 25, 1985."

derstanding not only John Paul II's theological approach to marriage and family, but also his vision of the nature and dignity of the human person. In his first book, *The Human Person in the Philosophy of Karol Wojtyła*, Jarosław Kupczak gave invaluable examination of the influences of Wojtyła's writings on philosophical ethics, Christian anthropology, and phenomenology. Compromising neither clarity nor the intricacy of the individual in his examination, Kupczak's work provided an invaluable foundation for examining John Paul II's theology of the body. I believe *Gift and Communion* will likewise prove an invaluable insight into not only the message of John Paul II, but also the profound innovations that truly give hope and depth to marriage and family in a time when for too many habit and tradition seem to be the only surety of their importance.

We may hope that *Gift and Communion* will inaugurate new scholarly interest in the integral role of the Wednesday catecheses in the anthropological vision of John Paul II. In the past, some downplayed the Wednesday catecheses as a papal teaching not of the same authority as an encyclical or apostolic exhortation. Some of this can be attributed to what Kupczak recognizes as the view that the Wednesday catecheses are "inaccessible." Because of this, Kupczak suggests that "a detailed manual" is needed. However, he has provided us with much more than that in *Gift and Communion*. He has opened a window on the Wednesday catecheses through which we may see more clearly the richness of the catecheses and the profound depth of John Paul II's understanding of the human person. The theology of the body is a unique contribution to contemporary theology too important to be ignored. It becomes an insight into our vocation.

Pope Paul VI once remarked that the pope must see the world "with the eyes of Christ." Perhaps we would do well to attempt to see the world through the eyes of a great pope too. In the early years of his pontificate, John Paul II once confided to an associate that he did not think that history would remember much about his pontificate, but that if it did he hoped he would be remembered for what he had done to strengthen Christian married life. *Gift and Communion* provides ample evidence as to why this should be so.

Acknowledgments

Every book, although it may have but one author, is always made possible by the contributions of many. This English translation of my book, which was first published in Polish by Znak Publishing House in Kraków in 2006, would not have come to be without the inspiration, continual help, and financial support of Carl A. Anderson, the Supreme Knight of the Knights of Columbus. First and foremost I am grateful to him and to his wife, Dorian. The translators, Agata Rottkamp and Justyna and Orest Pawlak, have been immensely helpful in the whole process of preparing this book. The editors at the Catholic University of America Press, James C. Kruggel and Theresa B. Walker, have repeatedly proven to be professional, helpful, and forbearing.

I also wish to thank others who provided me with a necessary inspiration and many forms of practical support: George Weigel, Mary and Russel F. Hittinger, David L. Schindler, Michael Waldstein, Robert D. Wieckowski, and Adrian J. Reimers.

The most extensively used source in this book is John Paul II, "Man and Woman He Created Them: A Theology of the Body," trans., introduction, index, by M. Waldstein (Boston: Pauline Books and Media, 2006), ©Daughters of St. Paul, U.S.A., Boston, Mass. All rights reserved. Used with permission. Quotations on pages 29 through 39 from Paul Ricouer, *The Symbolism of Evil*, vol. 17, Religious Perspectives series, ©1967 by Paul Ricouer, © renewed 1995, reprinted by permission of HarperCollins Publishers.

Introduction

The goal of this book is to present that aspect of theological anthropology which John Paul II himself referred to as "the theology of the body."[1] The primary source for the presented reflections is the 129 catecheses John Paul II delivered during his Wednesday general audiences in the Vatican from 5 September 1979 to 28 November 1984.[2] From now on they will be referenced as the Wednesday catecheses on the theology of the body.[3]

The Wednesday catecheses were delivered in four cycles. Each of them reflects on a chosen Bible passage and concerns a related issue that is fundamental for the theology of the body. The first cycle, entitled "Christ appeals to the 'Beginning'" and consisting of twenty-three catecheses, was delivered from 5 September 1979 to 2 April 1980. Its biblical basis is Christ's teaching on the indissolubility of marriage, which hearkens back to Genesis: "Have you not read that the one who made them at the beginning 'made them male and female'?"[4]

The second cycle, entitled "Christ appeals to the human heart"

---

1. John Paul II, *Man and Woman He Created Them: A Theology of the Body*, translation, introduction, and index by Michael Waldstein (Boston: Pauline Books and Media, 2006). Hereafter quoted as *TB*.
2. George Weigel, *Witness to Hope: Biography of the Pope John Paul II* (New York: Cliff Street Books, 1999), 334–43.
3. The term "Wednesday catecheses," so long as it is not further specified, refers to the Wednesday Catecheses on the Theology of the Body.
4. Mt 19:4. All biblical quotations and references come from *New Revised Standard Version* (Oxford University Press, 1991).

and consisting of forty papal catecheses, began 16 April 1980 and ended 6 May 1981. The Sermon on the Mount is the inspiration for the papal reflections in this cycle,[5] especially the teaching that "everyone who looks at a woman with lust has already committed adultery with her in his heart."[6] The third cycle, entitled "Christ appeals to the resurrection" and consisting of twenty-three catecheses, began 11 November 1981 and finished on 21 July 1982. This cycle is based on Christ's discussion with the Sadducees regarding the levirate law and the resurrection to come.[7]

The fourth and last cycle of the papal catecheses on the theology of the body is devoted to the sacramentality of marriage and to deliberations on the encyclical *Humanae vitae* of Paul VI (1968). It consists of forty-three papal addresses and lasted exceptionally long; it began 28 July 1982, was interrupted for about one year (from 9 February 1983 to 23 May 1984) when during his general audiences the pope chose to focus on the meaning of the Holy Year of Redemption being celebrated that year, and was then completed on 28 November 1984. Two books of the Old Testament constitute the biblical sources for the papal deliberations in the fourth cycle of catecheses, the Song of Songs and the Book of Tobit, as well as a passage of the Letter to the Ephesians concerning the sacramentality of marriage.[8]

The papal theology of the body, as presented in the catecheses, has been widely praised. George Weigel considers the work "one of the boldest reconfigurations of Catholic theology in centuries" and writes that the papal theology of the body is "a theological time bomb" that will go off with dramatic and positive consequences for the Church. The Wednesday catecheses are thus "a decisive moment in exorcising the Manichaean demon and its deprecation of

---

5. Mt 5:1–7, 28; Lk 6:12–49.
6. Mt 5:28.
7. Mt 22:24–30; Mk 12:18–27; Lk 20:27–40.
8. Eph 5:21–33.

human sexuality from Catholic moral theology."⁹ Simultaneously, according to Weigel, the pope's theology of the body "is the most creative Christian response to the sexual revolution and its 'pulverization' of the human person ever articulated."¹⁰

Another commentator on the pope's thought, Walter Schu, writes that the theology of the body presented by John Paul II "truly opens a new horizon for all married persons and families."¹¹ Renowned Austrian moral theologian Bishop Andreas Laun states that the teaching of John Paul II about human sexuality and love "leaves behind everything which has been said about this issue thus far during the twenty centuries of the history of Christianity."¹²

Reading these favorable opinions about the papal theology of the body gives rise to a fundamental question: how is it possible that such significant writings of John Paul II are not more readily available as the object of serious theological studies nor as a theme of popular and public reflection or of homilies, sermons, or retreat talks.¹³ Undoubtedly, many Western theologians who were "infected" with the spirit of rebellion against the magisterium of the Church that was incited by Paul VI's encyclical *Humanae vitae* still hold to the ideological conviction that inspiration for one's creative work is not to be found in the documents of the magisterium, and especially not in the teaching on marriage and family of the "conservative" pope from Poland.

9. Weigel, *Witness to Hope*, 342.
10. George Weigel, "Introduction," in Walter J. Schu, LC, *The Splendor of Love: John Paul II's Vision for Marriage and Family* (Hartford, Ky.: New Hope Publications, 2004), 22–23.
11. Ibid., 27.
12. Andreas Laun, *Aktuelle Probleme der Moraltheologie* (Vienna: Herder Verlag, 1991), 70–71.
13. These critical remarks refer foremost to European theology; however, they may also apply to some extent in the American context. For example, in *The Splendor of Faith: Theological Vision of John Paul II*, an excellent book by renowned American theologian Avery Dulles, SJ, the catecheses are a mere mention (Avery Dulles, SJ, *The Splendor of Faith: Theological Vision of John Paul II* [New York: Crossroad Publishing, 1999], 103, 110–11). There are many similar examples.

However, another reason why the papal theology of the body is inaccessible is rooted in the catecheses themselves. Admittedly, the papal catecheses on the theology of the body are difficult and demanding, and require a good introduction and commentary. This "time bomb" needs a detailed instruction manual.

The difficulty in reading the catecheses results both from the language they are written in and from the method of their reflections. In a way that is similar to his philosophical texts written before 1978, John Paul II uses a very complicated style that requires engagement and focus of the reader. The issues in consideration are analyzed on several levels simultaneously.

On the one hand, the catecheses present a phenomenological description of human experience and subjectivity, which clearly reveals the poetic and linguistic creativity of the pope. On the other hand, the author of the catecheses is in constant dialogue with Western philosophical and theological traditions, as well as with contemporary achievements in biblical exegesis, philosophy, and theology. In a manner well known to the readers of the philosophical works of Karol Wojtyła, references to Paul Ricoeur and Mircea Eliade can be found alongside those to Aristotle and Plato; analyses drawn from the works of Max Scheler are interwoven with references to the thought of St. Augustine and St. Thomas Aquinas.

As already mentioned, the catecheses are an interpretation of biblical texts chosen by John Paul II himself. This interpretation is unique. Marian Grabowski rightly calls it a "philosophical exegesis" and "a translation of biblical imagery into philosophical notions and of biblical narration into philosophical narration."[14] In his biblical hermeneutics, John Paul II suggests a new and interesting interpretation of the relation between philosophy and theology, and explains biblical texts using notions taken from philosophical works of different thinkers, both contemporary and classical.

14. Marian Grabowski, "W stronę antropologii adekwatnej," in *O antropologii Jana Pawła II,* edited by Marian Grabowski (Toruń: Wydawnictwo UMK, 2004), 20.

The reader's difficulties in grappling with the catecheses are amplified by the fact that they do not contain sufficient scientific means such as footnotes, explanations, references, or a bibliography, which such works usually contain.[15] This present work intends to supplement this shortage.

This book consists of five chapters. The reflections in the first chapter present the theological method of the catecheses and focus on explaining two terms used by the pope himself to describe this very method: "adequate anthropology" and "hermeneutics." In particular, this chapter focuses on the similarities between John Paul II's hermeneutics and Paul Ricoeur's theory of symbols.

The second chapter takes on the task of a theological interpretation of the human body, a theme that is fundamental in the catecheses. The discussion of this subject takes into account three key ages in the theological history of man: the time of original innocence, the time after original sin, which is pervaded by God's initiative of salvation, and the eschatological time of the resurrection.[16] According to the pope, interpreting human life in light of these three theological ages is the key to theological anthropology, because each of the ages is in some way present in man's self-knowledge and experience. Following in the pope's footsteps, this analysis aims to create "a three-dimensional," integral image of man. The last part of the second chapter is devoted to the sacramentality of the body in the context of the sacramentality of marriage.

15. Kenneth Schmitz, in considering the difficulties of a pilgrim standing in St. Peter's Square or of a contemporary reader of the catecheses, is correct when he writes, "Indeed, it is no doubt true that the *Talks* would tax the ability of an audience hearing these ideas for the first time and in such a setting, for the talks make little concessions to their hearers. They bring to my mind a small puzzle that scholars of St. Augustine would surely solve for me: to what sort of an audience did the African saint address his magnificent sermons?" (Kenneth L. Schmitz, *At the Center of the Human Drama: The Philosophical Anthropology of Karol Wojtyla—Pope John Paul II* [Washington, D.C.: The Catholic University of America Press, 1993], 91).

16. This is why the first three cycles of the catecheses, which present these three theological stages of human history, are the key for the entire theology of the body.

I argue that the two terms "gift" and "communion" are the main pillars of the papal theology of the body; thus their prominent place in the title of this book. The third chapter treads the philosophical and theological paths that lead these two terms to rise to such prominent significance in the thought of John Paul II. A historical retrospective will aid us in examining the philosophical anthropology and ethics of Karol Wojtyła and the theology of the Second Vatican Council, as well as classical theories of Christian Trinitarian theology and ecclesiology. The papal reflections on gift and communion will be presented and evaluated inside a framework of some promising changes in contemporary anthropology and ecumenical theology.

A key concept for Christian theology, and especially for theological anthropology, is the concept of *imago Dei*, that is, the belief that man is created "in the image of God."[17] The Wednesday catecheses present an interesting reinterpretation of *imago Dei* theology, at the center of which are the notions of gift and communion. The fourth chapter of the book presents, analyzes, and critically evaluates this aspect of the pope's work.

One of the most interesting parts of the papal theology of the body concerns the theological category of "the language of the body." The fifth chapter presents psychological, philosophical, and theological sources of this theory as well as the way in which John Paul II uses the language of the body in his theological interpretation of Paul VI's encyclical *Humanae vitae*.

Certainly, philosophy and the theology of the body were of special interest for John Paul II both before 1978 and after he was elected pope. Therefore, an effort to understand and creatively interpret this part of his teaching is crucial to understanding his entire theological oeuvre as well as the many accomplishments of his great pontificate.

17. Gn 1:26–27.

Abbreviations

Abbreviations of the books of the Bible are according to the New Revised Standard Version (1989).

AS	*Acta Synodalia Sacrosancti Concilii Oecumenici Vaticani II*
ATA	*Augustine through the Ages: An Encyclopedia*
CCC	*Catechism of the Catholic Church*
CCSL	*Corpus Christianorum, Series Latina*
DBI	*Dictionary of Biblical Imagery*
DS	*Dictionnaire de spiritualité*
DTC	*Dictionnaire de théologie catholique*
DV	John Paul II, *Dominum et vivificantem*
ER	*Encyclopedia of Religion*
EV	John Paul II, *Evangelium vitae*
FC	John Paul II, *Familiaris consortio*
FR	John Paul II, *Fides et ratio*
GS	*Gaudium et spes*, the Pastoral Constitution on the Church in the Modern World of the Second Vatican Council
HV	Paul VI, *Humanae vitae*
L	John Paul II, *Letter to Families for the International Year of the Family*
LG	*Lumen gentium*, the Dogmatic Constitution on the Church of the Second Vatican Council
LTK	*Lexikon für Theologie und Kirche*
NA	*Nostra aetate*, the Declaration on the Relation of the Church to Non-Christian Religions of the Second Vatican Council
NIB	*The New Interpreter's Bible*
RC	John Paul II, *Redemptoris custos*

RH	John Paul II, *Redemptor hominis*
RM	John Paul II, *Redemptoris mater*
SC	*Sources Chrétiennes*
SCG	Thomas Aquinas, *Summa contra gentiles*
STh	Thomas Aquinas, *Summa theologiae*
TB	John Paul II, *Man and Woman He Created Them: A Theology of the Body*
TDNT	*Theological Dictionary of the New Testament*
TRE	*Theologische Realenzyklopädie*
VC	John Paul II, *Vita consecrata*
VS	John Paul II, *Veritatis splendor*

GIFT
&
COMMUNION

Chapter One

DISCOURSE ON METHOD

Using the title of the first philosophical publication of René Descartes, *Discours de la méthode* from 1637, as the name of this chapter is intentional.[1] It results from the conviction that the method of the theological anthropology of John Paul II is built in opposition to the Cartesian method, which has been considered paradigmatic for modern humanities and social sciences.[2] The papal reflections in the catecheses are theological; however, the fact that both thinkers intend to understand the real man living in history makes a comparison with Cartesian thought possible.

Undoubtedly, one of the most important events which defined the modern age at the transition from the sixteenth to the seventeenth century was the creation of a new model of science that gradually replaced the Aristotelian tradition in different

---

1. René Descartes, "Discourse on the Method," in *The Philosophical Writings of Descartes,* translated by John Cottingham, Robert Stoothoff, Dugald Murdoch (New York: Cambridge University Press, 1985), vol. 1, 111–51.

2. Edmund Husserl, *The Crisis of European Sciences and Transcendental Phenomenology: An Introduction to Phenomenological Philosophy* (Evanston, Ill.: Northwestern University Press, 1970).

fields of knowledge. Galileo's *Discorsi e dimostrazioni matematiche intorno a due nuove scienze* (*The discourses and mathematical demonstrations relating to two new sciences*) in 1638 marks the birth of modern science.[3] In lieu of the Aristotelian tradition, Galileo suggested a scientific model based on the mathematization of the results of experimentation and observation, in which the metaphysical penetration into the nature of things is replaced by an examination of phenomena and causal relationships.

After Galileo, science gradually gave up on a theological, "internal" understanding of natural phenomena that were previously considered the manifestation of hidden meaning and began to see them as mathematically analyzable sets of relations. A consequence of this mathematization of science was treating nature as a world of physical bodies, closed in on itself, and governed by natural causality, which unequivocally determined every event before it took place.[4] Such a "scientific" perception of the world necessarily led to dualism, because what was left outside this "mathematical universe" was man as a spiritual being, all cultural and social phenomena, and the whole sphere of life.[5]

At the same time as Galileo postulated a mathematization of science grounded on empirical experimentation in Italy, in England Francis Bacon formulated in a systematic concept of this new inductive and experimental science. In the book *Great Instauration* (1620) Bacon emphasizes that the goal and main criterion of true science consists in exercising human governance over nature: "a way must be opened for the human understanding entirely different from any hitherto known, and other helps provided, in order that the mind may exercise over the nature of things the

---

3. Amos Funkenstein, *Theology and the Scientific Imagination from the Middle Ages to the Seventeenth Century* (Princeton, N.J.: Princeton University Press, 1986), 12–18.

4. An excellent and concise description of this process one can find in Michael Waldstein's "Introduction" in John Paul II, *Man and Woman He Created Them*, 36–62.

5. Husserl, *The Crisis of European Sciences*, 48–53.

authority which properly belongs to it."⁶ In Bacon's project, the identification of knowledge with power is accompanied by a deep contempt toward classical metaphysics, which, according to Bacon, has been deceptive in its principles, futile in terms of concrete achievements, and harmful because it produced unnecessary and insolvable quarrels.

The new science of Galileo and Bacon found its continuation in the thought of "the father of modern philosophy," René Descartes.⁷ According to Descartes, there are two kinds of substances in the world: extended things (*res extensa*) and thinking things (*res cogitans*). Material things are characterized purely by extension; they have only geometrical properties and undergo only mechanical changes. Descartes classified all of nature—animate and inanimate—as *res extensa* and therefore subject to mechanistic movement; animal and human bodies are also mere machines.⁸

In Cartesian philosophy the borders between nature and the spiritual world were drawn in such a way that, on the one hand, mechanistically interpreted nature encompasses all phenomena of life and the "bodily" aspect of man, while on the other hand, psyche is completely devoid of such movements, and described as mind (*mens*), spirit (*animus*), intellect (*intellectus*), or reason (*ratio*). Therefore, in Cartesian philosophy, man too is cleft into

---

6. Francis Bacon, *The New Organon and Related Writings* (Indianapolis: Bobbs-Merrill, 1960), 4.

7. Benedict Ashley, *Theologies of the Body: Humanist and Christian* (Braintree: Pope John XXIII Medical-Moral Research and Education Center, 1985), 204–12; Charles Taylor, *Sources of the Self: The Making of the Modern Identity* (Cambridge, Mass.: Harvard University Press, 1989), 143–59.

8. At the very beginning of the *Treatise on Man,* Descartes states, "I suppose the body to be nothing but a statue or machine made of earth, which God forms with the explicit intention of making it as much as possible like us. Thus God not only gives it externally the colors and shapes of all the parts of our bodies, but also places inside it all the parts required to make it walk, eat, breathe, and indeed to imitate all those of our functions which can be imagined to proceed from matter and to depend solely on the disposition of our organs." (René Descartes, *Treatise on Man,* in *The Philosophical Writings of Descartes,* 1:99).

two parts. First, his body, which belongs to the sphere of extended things, *res extensa,* is only a complex mechanism, this being the case for other living creatures as well. Second, the spirit, the thinking part, *res cogitans,* constitutes our real nature. In Descartes, the application of the new scientific method—based on mathematical precision and clarity—in anthropological analyses led to a gross deformation of the *humanum.*

Cartesian anthropological dualism led to the establishment of false notions in the field of human cognition and understanding, which has had far-reaching and negative consequences in the history of humanist knowledge. Bremen University professor Zdzisław Krasnodębski describes these false notions as the "Cartesian paradigm." This paradigm is based on the conviction that "I myself can know myself directly by internal perception, or introspection, but know things in the world by external perception. Moreover, through introspection one grasps states of consciousness, 'psychological experiences,' to which no one else has direct access, whereas through external perception one grasps 'pure' facts, wrested from the shell of secondary qualities that are merely evaluative projects of consciousness."[9]

In the humanism built on the Cartesian paradigm, self-knowledge and knowledge of another person are the sum of two cognitive views regarding two different objects: movements of the human body, which do not differ from other types of motion in the natural sphere, and internal experiences learned through introspection. In Descartes's mistaken view, the subject in the process of cognition is an independent and neutral observer, and the fundamental type of cognition is the perception of "naked natural facts." Many contemporary philosophers emphasize that, in spite of such oversimplifications and anthropological deformations,

---

9. Zdzisław Krasnodębski, *Rozumienie ludzkiego zachowania: Rozważania o filozoficznych podstawach nauk humanistycznych i społecznych* (Warsaw: Państwowy Instytut Wydawniczy, 1986), 7.

"the Cartesian paradigm" thus understood decisively influenced the understanding of man in modern science and culture, especially in currents inspired by positivism and empiricism.[10] John Paul II's theological anthropology belongs to the tradition of critical reflection that tries to overcome this dualistic and reductionist way of approaching man.

An Adequate Anthropology

John Paul II describes the theological anthropology of his Wednesday catecheses as an "adequate anthropology," which is an "understanding and interpretation of man in what is essentially human.... 'Adequate' anthropology relies on essentially 'human' experience. It is opposed to reductionism of the 'naturalistic' kind."[11] Thus, the pope's adequate anthropology describes man in terms of what is "essentially human" and intends to search for such human elements through an exploration of "essentially human experience."

John Paul II argues that biblical revelation encourages and entitles us to create an adequate anthropology thus defined: "the absolute impossibility of reducing man to the 'world'"[12] is a consequence of the truth about the creation of man in the image of God.[13] In interpreting the account of the creation of man in Genesis, the pope argues that "in the light of the Bible's first sentences, man can neither be understood nor explained in his full depth with the categories taken from the 'world,' that is, from the visible totality of bodies."[14]

The pope notes that, in and of itself, the biblical language that describes the creation of man in the book of Genesis requires the

---

10. Leszek Kolakowski, *The Alienation of Reason: A History of Positivist Thought*, translated by Norbert Guterman (Garden City, N.Y.: Doubleday, 1968), 19–29.
11. *TB*, 178–79.   12. Ibid., 135.
13. Gn 1:27.   14. *TB*, 135.

use of special categories to describe man and woman in their corporeality:

> The "beginning" tells us relatively little about the human body in the naturalistic and contemporary sense of the word. From this point of view, we find ourselves in this study on a wholly prescientific level. We know almost nothing about the inner structures and regularities that reign in the human organism. Nevertheless, at the same time—perhaps exactly because the text is so ancient—the truth that is important for the integral vision of man reveals itself in a simpler and fuller way. This truth *concerns the meaning of the human body in the structure of the personal subject*. The reflection about these ancient texts allows us as a next step to extend this meaning to the whole sphere of human *intersubjectivity*, especially in the perennial relationship between man and woman.[15]

Using scholastic distinctions, then, we can say that the material object of John Paul II's adequate anthropology in the catecheses is man revealed in what is "essentially human," whereas the formal object is the phenomenon of corporeality—"the meaning of the human body in the structure of the personal subject." John Paul II's phenomenological description of the "essentially human" experience of man seems to be the starting point for such an anthropology. As noted above, a thus constituted theology of the body is intentionally opposed to the "Cartesian paradigm" that appeared in Western culture as a radical project to establish an adequate anthropology. The "Cartesian paradigm" also intended to present what is "essentially human," that is, the consciousness of the subject. However, the Cartesian project resulted in a deformed concept of man, and the description of human corporeality turned out to be its "weak point."[16]

---

15. Ibid., 221. The emphasis by italics in the quotations from John Paul II's theology of the body comes from the author himself (Waldstein, "Introduction," 6).

16. It is worth noting that the philosophical anthropology of Karol Wojtyła, the result of a phenomenological-metaphysical synthesis, was also created in opposition to the legacy of Cartesian thought. Wojtyła intended this anthropology to reconnect two currents that modern post-Cartesian philosophy had divided: the subjectivistic philosophy of the person

To describe the real meaning of John Paul II's adequate anthropology, we must show how the Wednesday catecheses touch on "what is fundamental and essentially personal, both in every individual, man or woman, and in their reciprocal relations."[17] Since it is theological in nature, the adequate anthropology of the catecheses searches for elements of the "essentially 'human' experience of man" in inspired biblical texts, especially in the Yahwist account of creation found in the second chapter of Genesis. This description is fundamental to the pope's thought, because it is "the oldest description and record of man's self-understanding"[18] and presents the creation of man primarily "in the aspect of his subjectivity."[19]

Without giving away too much of the discussion that follows, we can say that the inspired Yahwist author in his account of creation presents what John Paul II calls "original solitude" as part of the "essentially human experience of man." The Creator's words point to the "original solitude" of Adam: "It is not good that the man should be alone."[20] In what follows in the Yahwist text, we read that God "formed every animal of the field and every bird of the air, and brought them to the man to see what he would call them."[21] The process of naming the animals evokes the experience of solitude in Adam: "The man gave names to all cattle, and to the birds of the air, and to every animal of the field; but for the man there was not found a helper as his partner."[22] According to the pope, the exceptionality and superiority of Adam over all of nature reveals itself as solitude in man's subjective experience.

---

and the objectivistic philosophy of being. Wojtyła discussed this, inter alia, in the introduction to his *opus magnum*, *The Acting Person* (Karol Wojtyła, *The Acting Person*, trans. by Andrzej Potocki (Dordrecht: D. Reidel Publishing, 1979), 18–19; also: John Paul II, *Crossing the Threshold of Hope* [New York: Alfred A. Knopf, 1994], 50–53; L 19).

17. *TB*, 221. 18. Ibid., 137.

19. Ibid., 138–39. A deeper reflection on the place of biblical texts in the pope's adequate anthropology is presented in the later parts of this chapter, which will focus on the papal understanding of theological hermeneutics.

20. Gn 2:18. 21. Gn 2:19.

22. Gn 2:20.

John Paul II emphasizes that the Yahwist image of man giving names to the animals has an important anthropological meaning: "*the created man* finds himself from the first moment of his existence *before God* in search of his own being, as it were; one could say, in search of his own definition; today one would say, in search of his own 'identity.'"[23] Man, searching for his identity, finds that he is radically different from the world of animals: "but for the man there was not found a helper as his partner."[24] John Paul II notes that man "cannot be put on a par with any other species of living beings on the earth."[25] The process of man distinguishing himself from all other creatures leads to the "delineation of the human being as a human person"[26] and is, at the same time, a process that reveals man's self-knowledge:

Self-knowledge goes hand in hand with knowledge of the world, of all visible creatures, of all living beings to which man has given their names to affirm his own dissimilarity before them. Thus, consciousness reveals man as the one who *possesses the power of knowing* with respect to *the visible world*. With this knowledge, which makes him go in some way outside of his own being, *man* at the same time *reveals himself to himself in all the distinctiveness of his being.*[27]

The Yahwist narration, notes the pope, emphasizes the role of human corporeality in man's growth in self-consciousness as a subject and a person. Man experiences original solitude when he learns that he "belongs to the visible world; he is a body among bodies": "the body, by which man shares in the visible created world, makes him at the same time aware of being 'alone.'"[28] A few pages later, John Paul II emphasizes this anti-Cartesian definition of human subjectivity through the body even more strongly: "Man is a subject not only by his self-consciousness and by self-determination, but also based on his own body. *The structure of*

---

23. *TB*, 149.
25. *TB*, 148.
27. Ibid.
24. Gn 2:20.
26. Ibid., 150.
28. Ibid., 152.

this body is such that it permits him to be the author of genuinely human activity. In this activity, the body expresses the person."²⁹

From John Paul II's description of the phenomenon of "original solitude" we can now delineate the fundamental elements of the pope's method of adequate anthropology. This anthropology is characterized by an interpretation of biblical texts that searches for elements of "the essentially human experiences of man," that is, those elements that differentiate man from the natural world, and particularly from the world of animals (*animalia*). Accepting the inspired character of the biblical texts, the pope claims that the truth about man revealed in scripture refers, in some way, to every human being. We can therefore talk about a unity of Adam's experience with the experience of the inspired author of the creation account as well as with the experience of today's reader of the Bible.³⁰

It is worth noting that, in the process of interpreting biblical texts, John Paul II uses the achievements of modern philosophy. The assumed unity of Adam's experiences with those of today's readers allows the pope, for the aim of his exegesis, to use characteristically modern terms such as "self-consciousness" and "subjectivity." Yet, because the unity of human experience transcends history, these modern concepts are not extrinsically imposed on Genesis, and they in no way distort the meaning of the biblical texts.

29. Ibid., 154.
30. It is worth emphasizing that the theological truth about the unity of the biblical Adam with every human being has always been present in the poetic works of Karol Wojtyła. In his play *The Jeweler's Shop* (1960), the mysterious figure of Adam was described as "a common denominator of us all, at the same time a spokesman and a judge" (Karol Wojtyła, *The Jeweler's Shop*, in *Collected Plays and Writings on Theater*, translated by Bolesław Taborski [Berkeley: University of California Press, 1987], 321). Kenneth Schmitz claims that Adam represents in this way a "modern Everyman," or the "human nature common to every one of us" (Schmitz, *At the Center of the Human Drama*, 21). Also, in two of Wojtyła's important poetic works from 1964, *Reflections on Fatherhood* and the play *Radiation of Fatherhood*, Adam describes himself as "a man who can be placed apart and then made a common denominator for all men" (Wojtyła, *Collected Plays*, 365–66; also, Schmitz, *At the Center of the Human Drama*, 23).

Marian Grabowski emphasizes the positive and constructive role of modern philosophy in the papal interpretation of the Bible, especially in the interpretation of such anthropological notions as shame and nakedness. Grabowski points out that the catecheses contain both a "philosophical exegesis of the Genesis" and a "translation of biblical images into philosophical concepts and a translation of biblical narration into philosophical narration."[31] The intriguing issues connected with a "philosophical exegesis" of the Bible will be discussed in the next chapter along with the papal understanding of theological hermeneutics.

John Paul II's adequate anthropology corresponds to the methodological proposals of Marian Jaworski, a philosopher who closely cooperated with Cardinal Wojtyła. A few years before the catecheses were written, Jaworski outlined a method of Christian anthropology in his article "Teologia a antropologia: Aspekt filozoficzny" (Theology and anthropology: the philosophical aspect).[32] His article can help us to understand the method for establishing an adequate anthropology, especially the role of phenomenology in discovering "what is fundamental and essentially personal."[33]

Jaworski argues that Christian anthropology, inspired by revelation, should focus particularly on the fundamental modern category of the subject, which he contrasts with the category of things or objects. A Christian reflection on man should therefore assume a phenomenological-existential character, which is, after all, assumed by the language of biblical revelation. The fundamental element that characterizes the phenomenological-existential method

31. Grabowski, "W stronę antropologii adekwatnej," 20.
32. Marian Jaworski, "Teologia a antropologia: Aspekt filozoficzny," in *Teologia a antropologia: Kongres teologów polskich 21–23 IX 1971,* edited by Marian Jaworski and Adam Kubiś (Kraków: Wydawnictwo Papieskiej Akademii Teologicznej, 1971), 68–96.
33. Chronologically, Jaworski's article precedes the Wednesday catecheses by several years. I analyze it here in order to indicate that the method of catecheses has its sources and precedents in the style of thought of some Polish personalistic philosophers, especially from Lublin and Kraków.

is that reflections on man begin with the reality given directly to the subject: *prius quoad nos,* in other words, with a complete description and analysis of human experience.

According to Jaworski, such an integral and phenomenological description, which includes both the external and internal experiences of man, is not in opposition to a metaphysical theory of man. Just the opposite is true. Such description requires metaphenomenological justification and clarification. Jaworski bases the justification for the phenomenological-metaphysical synthesis in Christian anthropology on two grounds. The first is the dynamic of the human mind itself, which "moves from the question, what are things for us (a phenomenological, functional, or economical problem) to the more fundamental issue, what are things in themselves (an ontological problem). The human mind moves from description to definition."[34] The second, Jaworski notes, is that the truths of the faith concerning God and creation, for example, the Christological term *"homoousion"* (consubstantial), which was introduced by the Nicene Council, have not only existential and functional significance, but also an ontological meaning.

In the Wednesday catecheses, phenomenology and metaphysics are also not opposed to one other. Rather, the attentive reader will note that these two methodological approaches complement each other and that John Paul II constantly seeks points of contact between them.[35] Reflecting on the first chapter of Genesis, John Paul II notes that the biblical account of creation inspired not only the theory of transcendentals but also metaphysical re-

---

34. Jaworski, "Teologia a antropologia," 81. The encyclical *Fides et Ratio* (1997) is the most important text of John Paul II that presents the phenomenological-metaphysical method of Christian anthropology. There, we find a philosophical postulate summarizing these reflections of Jaworski: "from phenomenon to fundament" (*FR* 83). We will return to *Fides et Ratio* later.

35. Undoubtedly, an important source of methodological synthesis of phenomenology and metaphysics is to be found in the philosophical research of Karol Wojtyła done before 1978. This research resulted in the mature reflection in Wojtyła's introduction to the book *The Acting Person* (3–22).

flection on contingent being (*ens contingens*).³⁶ One of the most inspiring elements of the catecheses is the pope's phenomenological description of the language of the body; moreover, the pope emphasizes that the language of the body is rooted in the nature of the person metaphysically understood—in man's ontological structure.³⁷ Similarly, in his reflection on the human condition before original sin, John Paul II maintains that while the traditional teaching of the Church uses the metaphysical language of original justice (*iustitia originalis*), the theology of the body explores revelation by means of another language, that of human subjectivity.³⁸

Clearly, then, John Paul II's adequate anthropology, while giving methodological primacy to the phenomenological description of human experience, does not exclude the metaphysical perspective. Rather, the pope's approach excludes various forms of anthropological reductionism:

> We are, in fact, the children of an age in which, due to the development of various disciplines, this integral vision of man [presented in the holy scriptures, especially the New Testament] can easily be rejected and replaced by many *partial conceptions* that dwell on one or another aspect of the *compositum humanum* but do not reach man's *integrum* or leave it outside their field of vision. Various cultural tendencies then insert themselves here that are based on these partial truths and on this basis make their proposals and practical suggestions for human behavior and, even more often, about *ways of relating to "man."*³⁹

The pope insists that the most frequent forms of anthropological reductionism absolutize partial knowledge about man—knowledge that is derived from the natural sciences, especially modern biology. In a particular way, this type of anthropological reductionism concerns the truth about human corporeality. In the catecheses, the pope issues a philosophical warning about the inadequacy of such scientific knowledge:

36. *TB*, 136–37.
37. Ibid., 642.
38. Ibid., 198.
39. Ibid., 220.

But in and of itself such *science does not yet develop* the consciousness of the body as a sign of the person, as a manifestation of the spirit. The whole development of contemporary science of the body as organism has rather the character of biological knowledge, because it is based on the disjunction between what is bodily and what is spiritual in man. When one uses such one-sided knowledge of the body's functions as an organism, it is not difficult to reach the point of treating the body more or less systematically as an *object of manipulations;* in this case, man no longer identifies himself subjectively, so to speak, with his own body, because it is deprived of the meaning and dignity that stem from the fact that this body is proper to the person.[40]

In this passage the pope criticizes the tendency to make absolute what is rendered partial by the Cartesian distinction between *res cogitans* and *res extensa*. John Paul II argues that an anthropological reductionism that consists in absolutizing a partial knowledge of man, derived from the natural sciences, leads to dualism; that is, it questions the spiritual and corporeal unity of man. This error in describing man has far-reaching consequences for ethical judgments regarding human behavior, ranging from sexuality to bioethics.[41] Ultimately, anthropological dualism leads to the manipulation of the human body, or to the practice of "using" the human body.[42]

John Paul II uses the concept of the "sexual urge" to show how anthropological reductionism unlawfully transfers terms from the natural sciences to a philosophy of man. In his interpretation of the creation account in Genesis, the pope emphasizes that biblical revelation draws "a clear and unambiguous boundary" between the world of animals (*animalia*) and man, who is created in the image of God. The existence of this boundary should warn the an-

40. Ibid., 361.
41. See: *VS* 48–50; *EV* 22. Also: Germain Grisez, *Christian Moral Principles* (Chicago: Franciscan Herald Press, 1983), 137–39; idem: "Dualism and the New Morality," in *Atti del Congresso Internazionale Tommaso d'Aquino nel Suo Settimo Centenario* (Rome: Pontificia Accademia Romana di San Tommaso d'Aquino, 1977), 5:323–30.
42. *L,* 19.

thropologist against too hastily moving terms from one discipline to another:

> Thus, *the application to man* of this *category*, a substantially naturalistic one, which is contained in the concept and expression of *"sexual instinct," is not entirely appropriate and adequate*. Of course, one can apply this term on the basis of a certain analogy; in fact, man's particularity in comparison with the whole world of living beings (*animalia*) is not such that, understood from the point of view of species, he cannot be qualified in a fundamental way as an *animal* as well, but as an *animal rationale* [rational animal]. For this reason, despite this analogy, the application of the concept of "sexual instinct" to man—given the dual nature in which he exists as male and female—nevertheless greatly limits and in some sense "diminishes" what the same masculinity-femininity is in the personal dimension of human subjectivity.[43]

At this juncture, it is helpful to point out some similarities between the reflection on anthropological reductionism in the catecheses and Wojtyła's book *Love and Responsibility* (1960), where Wojtyła grounds his deliberations on the distinction between object and subject. While the person is an object, as well as a subject, it is subjectivity that distinguishes the person from the world of things, as well as from the world of animals. The subject differs therefore from things and from the animal world "by a specific inner self, an inner life, characteristic only of persons."[44]

Essential to the anthropology in Karol Wojtyła's *Love and Responsibility* is a clear contrast between the person and the world of animals, a contrast based on Wojtyła's object–subject distinction: "The person's contact with the objective world, with reality, is not merely "natural," physical, as is the case with all other creations of nature, nor is it merely sensual as in the case of animals. A human

---

43. *TB*, 438.
44. Karol Wojtyła, *Love and Responsibility*, translated by H. T. Willetts (San Francisco: Ignatius Press, 1981), 22.

person, as a distinctly defined subject, establishes contact with all other entities precisely through the inner self."⁴⁵

Wojtyła stresses that in order to defend the philosophy of man against anthropological reductionism, one should clearly maintain the difference between the world of persons and the world of animals in those disciplines where the same terms are used to discuss both realities. The "sexual urge" is one such term: "The sexual urge in man functions differently from the urge in animals, where it is the source of instinctive actions governed by nature alone. In man it is naturally subordinate to the will, and *ipso facto* subject to the specific dynamics of that freedom which the will possesses. The sexual urge can transcend the determinism of the natural order by an act of love."⁴⁶

The sexual urge is therefore "a specific force of nature,"⁴⁷ but its meaning transcends biology toward the world of persons, which is governed by ethical norms. Fertility and the richness of human love transcend the biological drive of sexual instinct characteristic of animals. According to Wojtyła, this is most clearly evident in the most perfect form of human love—betrothed love, the essence of which is "self-giving, the surrender of one's 'I,'" and which is not realizable in a purely physical order bereft of reason.⁴⁸

Karol Wojtyła/John Paul II's polemics with anthropological reductionism make him a part of a major current in contemporary philosophical and theological anthropology. In the book *Zarys filozofii człowieka* (An outline of the philosophy of man) Stanisław

---

45. Ibid., 23.
46. Ibid., 50.
47. Ibid., 52.
48. Ibid., 95–100. Already in his early works, Wojtyła undertook the problem of the necessity of having a personalistic understanding of the sexual urge in a series of scientific and press articles ("Instynkt, miłość, małżeństwo," in *Aby Chrystus się nami posługiwał* [Kraków: Znak, 1979], 36–50; "Religijne przeżywanie czystości," *Tygodnik Powszechny* 9, no. 6 [1953]: 1–2; "Myśli o małżeństwie," *Znak* 9, no. 7 [1957]: 595–604; "Propedeutyka sakramentu małżeństwa," in *Rola kobiety w Kościele* [Lublin: Wydawnictwo Naukowe Katolickiego Uniwersytetu Katolickiego, 1958], 87–92).

Kowalczyk, an important contemporary representative of Lublin's school of philosophy, differentiates five forms of anthropological reductionism and identifies their major representatives: physicism (Claude Lévi-Strauss, Tadeusz Kotarbiński); biologism (Friedrich Nietzsche); psychologism (Sigmund Freud); sociologism (Karl Marx); and logical pragmatism (Bertrand Russell).[49] Kowalczyk emphasizes that these various forms of anthropological reductionism originate from an epistemological monism, that is, the conviction that one can construct a theory of man based exclusively on the empirical sciences.[50] He summarizes his reflections as follows: "The scientific model of man (physical, biological, sociological, etc.) leaves out that aspect of man's personality which constitutes his *differentia specifica* from the rest of the world. The natural and econo-sociological sciences, while focusing on quantitative aspects, cannot explain personal-spiritual existence. That is why these forms of anthropological reductionism are a false way of searching for the solution to the mystery of man."[51]

Kowalczyk's critical reflection on the contemporary forms of anthropological reductionism highlights the need for an adequate anthropology that addresses what John Paul II describes as the "fundamental and essentially personal."[52] Kowalczyk maintains that no empirical science can replace philosophy in creating a theory of man. Kowalczyk also agrees with John Paul II that a truly adequate anthropology should be the result of a synthesis of phenomenology and metaphysics.

As noted earlier, already in his pre-1978 thinking Karol Wojtyła

---

49. Stanisław Kowalczyk, *Zarys filozofii człowieka* (Sandomierz: Wydawnictwo Diecezjalne, 1990), 7–12.

50. Kowalczyk argues that such methodological exclusivism is usually connected with philosophical materialism, or with a belief that scientific knowledge is limited to matter perceptible through sensory cognition and that all of the reality, including man's psychophysical singularity, ought to be explained by means of categories proper to matter.

51. Kowalczyk, *Zarys filozofii*, 12.

52. *TB*, 221.

maintained that man should be described by categories characteristic of his subjectivity, and not by those that emphasize his similarity to the world of things. Wojtyła called the first kind of definition "personalistic" and the second "cosmological." For Wojtyła, the personalistic definition touched on his own project, whereas typical examples of the cosmological approach are definitions from the anthropologies of Aristotle and Boethius.[53] It is worth noting that the distinction between the "personalistic" and the "cosmological" understandings of man concerns the different descriptive tasks of each category rather than a radical philosophical difference. For instance, in the "cosmological" Aristotelian definition of man, "man is a rational animal," the term "rational" indicates the personalistic dimension. Also, in the Boethian definition, "*rationalis naturae individua substantia*," the first part of the definition points to the personalistic dimension of man.[54] Arguably, various philosophies of man perceive and describe in a different manner this element, which is constitutive of "an adequate anthropology." Certainly, in many contemporary anthropological theories, the phenomenon of human freedom, as opposed to natural determinism, constitutes such an element.

Accepting the main postulate of the pope's "adequate anthropology," which concerns a description of man based on what is "essentially human," is a necessary condition (*sine qua non*) for the truth of any anthropology. Therefore, the originality of the method of the papal reflections in the Wednesday catecheses is not to be found solely in this methodological postulate. Rather, the uniqueness of John Paul II's work is also closely tied to the

53. Karol Wojtyła, "Subjectivity and the Irreducible in the Human Being," in idem, *Person and Community: Selected Essays*, translated by Theresa Sadok, OSM (New York: Peter Lang, 1993), 210–12; also: Jarosław Kupczak, *Destined for Liberty: The Human Person in the Philosophy of Karol Wojtyła/John Paul II* (Washington, D.C.: The Catholic University of America Press, 2000), 103–4.

54. Aristotle, *On the Soul* III, 3. 427a19–b9, www.classics.mit.edu/Aristotle; Boethius, *Contra Eutychen et Nestorium*, ch. 3, www.gutenberg.org.

hermeneutical dimension of his theology, which we will discuss in the following section.

Theological Hermeneutics

In addition to the term "adequate anthropology," John Paul II uses the term "hermeneutics" to describe his method of catechetical reflection. The pope uses this term in several different contexts, though its use in the phrase "hermeneutics of the gift" seems to be the most significant. Interpreting the statement of Christ in his discussion with the Pharisees on the indissolubility of marriage,[55] the pope remarks: "We should now turn anew to those fundamental words that Christ used, that is, to the word 'created' and to the subject, 'Creator,' introducing into the considerations carried out so far *a new dimension, a new criterion of understanding and of interpretation that we will call 'hermeneutics of the gift.'*"[56] The hermeneutics of the gift is an essential point of the pope's theological anthropology. This hermeneutical approach is, as the pope defines it, "a criterion of understanding and interpretation" of the inspired biblical text, which allows the said text to reveal man in his subjectivity, in the dimension of gift.[57]

The hermeneutics of the gift points first of all to the presence of love:

Only Love creates the good, and in the end it alone can be perceived in all its dimensions and its contours in created things and, above all, in

---

55. Mt 19:3–9.   56. *TB*, 179.

57. In a similar way, John Paul II speaks of "the anthropological hermeneutics of the Gospel" which he also calls "the anthropology of the Gospel" (*TB*, 545). In this context, he also writes about those who are representatives of the modern "hermeneutics of man" (ibid.). In his analysis of chosen passages from the New Testament, the pope notes that the question about the human "meaning of 'being a body'" is a fundamental issue for "anthropological hermeneutics" (*TB*, 457), and also for "*the hermeneutics of man* in general: for the fundamental problem of understanding him and for the self-understanding of his being in the world" (*TB*, 527).

man. Its presence is the final result, as it were, of the hermeneutics of the gift we are carrying out here.... This consistent giving, which goes back to the deep roots of consciousness and the subconscious and to the final levels of the subjective existence of both man and woman and which is reflected in their reciprocal *"experience of the body," bears witness to rootedness in Love.*[58]

The hermeneutics of the gift thus reaches into the most personal dimensions of the subject, into the deepest roots of consciousness and subconsciousness, to "levels of subjective existence" that are involved in experiencing the body.[59]

John Paul II also uses the term "hermeneutics" in another context, when he writes about "the hermeneutics of the sacrament of marriage." The pope states: "The dimension of the sign, which is proper to marriage as a sacrament, confirms the specific theological anthropology, the specific hermeneutics of man, which in this case could also be called *"hermeneutics of the sacrament," because it allows us to understand man on the basis of the analysis of the sacramental sign.*"[60] The hermeneutics of sacrament is, therefore, once again understood as "a criterion of understanding and interpretation" of man, which is revealed in a specific liturgical practice, in the celebration of the sacrament of marriage.[61] Hermeneutics thus understood gives meaning to a specific theological vision of man.

58. Ibid., 190.
59. A separate chapter of this book is devoted to the theological issue of gift.
60. *TB*, 546–47.
61. This method of constructing a theory of man clearly reminds us of the hermeneutics used by Mircea Eliade, who, through the analysis of human symbols and religious rituals, tries to obtain the descriptions of structures of human self-consciousness and of the human experience of the *sacrum*. In the preface to his well-known book *A History of Religious Ideas*, Eliade presents his hermeneutical research program in the following way: "For the historian of religions, every manifestation of the sacred is important: every rite, every myth, every belief or divine figure reflects the experience of the sacred and hence implies the notions of being, of meaning, and of truth" (Mircea Eliade, *A History of Religious Ideas* [Chicago: University of Chicago Press, 1979], 1:xiii. John Paul II writes about his recognition of Eliade's philosophy of religion in *Crossing the Threshold of Hope*, 35–36).

Keeping in mind the analyses in the previous part of this chapter that concerned the notion of an adequate anthropology, we may point to several fundamental features of the pope's hermeneutics. First and foremost, the hermeneutics of the catecheses is an interpretation of biblical texts, which intends to explain man through "what is essentially human."[62] Using this hermeneutics in his interpretation of biblical texts, John Paul II creates a theological anthropology that "relies on essentially 'human' experience,"[63] revealing, above all, the dimension of human subjectivity, and, in particular, the dimension of the human experience of the body.

As was already alluded to in our deliberations on adequate anthropology, John Paul II uses the achievements of contemporary philosophy of consciousness in his interpretations of biblical texts, which allows us to define his hermeneutics by the term "philosophical exegesis." This "translation of biblical images to philosophical concepts," characteristic of papal hermeneutics, is possible due to John Paul II's conviction about the unity of experience of the inspired author of the creation accounts and of today's readers of the Bible. As will be shown in the following analyses, the pope's understanding of the relation between philosophy and theology has its sources in his conception of three ages of human nature, or in other words, of the three theological periods in the economy of salvation.[64]

A general reflection on modern hermeneutics may help us to garner a deeper understanding of John Paul II's use of the hermeneutical method in the papal catecheses. The notion of hermeneutics is notoriously difficult to define with precision, because of the diverse usage of this concept in different fields of knowledge. Thomas M. Seebohm differentiates four fundamental meanings of

---

62. *TB*, 178.
63. Ibid., 179.
64. These three periods in the economy of salvation have been identified in the prologue to this book and will be further analyzed in chapter 2.

the term.⁶⁵ In its oldest meaning, hermeneutics refers to a specific methodology of text interpretation. In its second meaning, hermeneutics is a general theory of understanding. Martin Heidegger introduced a third means of understanding hermeneutics to philosophy, where the term is understood as an ontological interpretation of human existence. The fourth definition, connected especially with the work of Paul Ricoeur, emphasizes the existential interpretation of symbols and myths. This book does not intend to present a detailed analysis of each of the four definitions of hermeneutics, though some clarification of them will help us reveal essential aspects of the hermeneutical method used by John Paul II.

Historians emphasize that hermeneutics in the first meaning was known in antiquity. In Greek mythology, the word *hermenein* referred to Hermes, whose role consisted of "explaining the commands of the gods, i.e. translating them into language understood by mortals."⁶⁶ For Plato and Aristotle *hermeneia* meant explaining and translating, and *hermeneus* referred to the one who explains, the interpreter. Hermeneutical practices existed in every ancient culture. The development of hermeneutics in Western culture is closely connected with Jewish and Christian interpretations of holy scripture.⁶⁷

Friedrich Schleiermacher (1768–1834) is considered the founder of the first and oldest type of modern hermeneutics, textual hermeneutics. As a Protestant pastor and theologian, he was convinced that the creation of a philosophical theory of understanding texts might help to answer questions asked by biblical exegetes.

65. Thomas M. Seebohm, "Hermeneutics," in *Encyclopedia of Phenomenology*, edited by Lester Ambree and others (Dordrecht: Kluwer Academic Publishers, 1997), 308.
66. Hans-Georg Gadamer, "Hermeneutyka," in Andrzej Bronk, *Zrozumieć świat współczesny* (Lublin: Wydawnictwo Naukowe Katolickiego Uniwersytetu Lubelskiego, 1998), 283.
67. Werner G. Jeanrond rightly notices that the "history of hermeneutics is not identical with the history of the term 'hermeneutics'" (Werner G. Jeanrond, *Theological Hermeneutics: Development and Significance* [New York: Crossroad, 1991], 12). For the history of Jewish and Christian biblical hermeneutics see Jeanrond, 12–43, 120–58.

Seebohm writes that the first canon of Schleiermacher's hermeneutics requires that "the text has to be understood in the context of its contemporary readers and not in the context of the interpreter, because the meaning of the text, originally clear for contemporary readers, can be darkened and corrupted by tradition."[68] The understanding of a text should therefore begin with a grammatical analysis of the structure and language forms in which the original author expresses his views. According to Schleiermacher the interpretation of the Bible should be subjected to the general rules of hermeneutics, and the biblical text should be treated as any other literary work at the early stage of language analysis.[69]

The philosophical foundations of textual hermeneutics, as outlined by Schleiermacher, greatly contributed to the development of the historical-critical method in biblical studies.[70] It is not the intent of this work to discuss the history of this method, nor its achievements and limitations, since many others have already addressed these topics. For our purposes, I want to point out that John Paul II used the historical-critical method in the Wednesday catecheses to interpret Old and New Testament texts in order to formulate the theological anthropology contained in them. In the catecheses, John Paul II's interpretation of the biblical texts is based on the analysis of original Hebrew and Greek meanings, interpreted in accord with their time and culture.[71] The

---

68. Seebohm, "Hermeneutics," 308.

69. "Neither its language nor its genre requires that there be a special hermeneutics for the Bible, nor does its double layer of meaning.... Inspiration, as an infusion into the mind (*Gesinnung*), should not influence the work of interpretation. If in the case of the Bible, as in every other case, the goal of hermeneutics is to understand the text as their original readers understood them, the fact that they are inspired does not affect the interpretation at all. Therefore, there is no special hermeneutics for the New Testament, because it is inspired, and the only remaining possible justification for one is its complex use of language" (Friedrich Schleiermacher, *Hermeneutics: The Handwritten Manuscripts,* edited by Heinz Kimmerle, and translated by James Duke and Jack Forstman [Missoula, Mont.: Scholars Press, 1977], 215–16).

70. See Franz Mussner, *Histoire de l'herméneutique de Schleiermacher à nos jours* (Paris: Editions du Cerf, 1972).

71. For example, see exegetic analysis of Hebrew terms: *adam* (136, 158), *elohim*

pope frequently refers to contemporary biblical dictionaries and other scientific works throughout.[72]

Summarizing and concluding the long debate on the language and literary genre of the first three chapters of Genesis, John Paul II identifies the said genre as "myth," understanding this concept in accord with modern hermeneutics, especially in the works of Mircea Eliade and Paul Ricoeur.[73] The pope notes that modern man should not interpret the biblical myths about creation and the fall literally, because their authors did not intend to furnish a scientific description of events according to today's biology, physics, history, or cosmology; rather the authors of Genesis meant to present a religious and metaphysical interpretation of creation and the fall. In his remarks on the method for establishing an "adequate anthropology," John Paul II notes that Genesis "tells us relatively little about the human body, in the naturalistic and modern sense of the word," because the biblical author wants "to arrive at what is fundamental and essentially personal."[74]

---

(237), *goel* (498); and Greek: *sklerokardia* (264), *sarx* and *soma* (330), *eusebeia* (352–53), *psyche* (409), *mysterion* (489–90), etc.

72. It is worth noting that the papal reflections in the Wednesday catecheses, delivered during general audiences, have a pastoral character. As a result, with the exception of a few passages, they do not include any scientific apparatus, such as: bibliographies, footnotes, or suggestions for further studies. Nevertheless, the depth of papal thought seems to result from a very reliable, scientifically conscientious, and precise theological reflection. Some themes in the catecheses were also enriched by references to available works from scientific exegesis and biblical theology, for example: the biblical understanding of the heart (231), the problem of monogamy in the Old Testament (270–73), the views of Sadducees and Essenes (380–86), the biblical understanding of immortality (395), the problem of Pauline authorship of the Letter to Ephesians (466), the issue of "headship" in St. Paul's writings (499), etc. The papal reflection on the theology of the Song of Songs is enriched by impressive scientific data on the history of the exegesis of this book (548–51); a similar reference can be found in case of Johannine theology (234).

73. See *TB*, 137–42 (includes papal references to the understanding of myth by Mircea Eliade, Paul Ricoeur, Paul Tillich, Henri Schlier, and others). The authors indicated by John Paul II argue that myth is an important source of historical truth, and a justified way of relating history and its meaning (Mircea Eliade, *Myth and Reality* [New York: Harper Torchbooks, 1963]; Paul Ricoeur, "Myth and History," in *ER*, 10:273–82).

74. *TB*, 221. In the book of Juliusz Synowiec, *Na początku: Wybrane zagadnienia Pięcioksięgu* (Warsaw: Akademia Teologii Katolickiej, 1987), we find a concise summary

Modern hermeneutics strongly emphasizes the historical dimension of human cognition and the understanding of texts. Wilhelm Dilthey (1833–1911) was one of the first thinkers who reflected philosophically on the historical distance between the author and the reader of a text. Dilthey argues that understanding in the humanities consists in recognizing the intention of the author of a text, or the subject of historical events, by identifying with him. This identification, which transcends historical distance, is possible due to the unity of experiences, or a psychological bond, between the author and the reader of a text, and is ultimately due to the nature common to all men: it is finding the "me" of the reader in the "you" of the author.[75]

At a later stage in the development of hermeneutics, Dilthey's views on human historical consciousness and the historical conditioning of cognition were significantly deepened and modified by Martin Heidegger and Hans-Georg Gadamer, among others.[76] The achievements of hermeneutical philosophy made modern man aware that his own experiences are a part of history, and that his own self-understanding is a necessary point of reference for

---

of the debate on the question whether the literary genre of the account of creation and other passages of the Pentateuch may be defined as myth. The author, among many contemporary exegetes, answers in the affirmative, and defines, after Henri Cazelles, the monotheistic myth as a "literary genre which expresses the human need to know divinity not in an abstract way, but in a personal and concrete way." (ibid., 144) Synowiec emphasizes that "myth being at the same time theology, philosophy, history, epic, novel and poem, aspires to express the whole of human life" (ibid.; also, 68–71).

75. Kuderowicz writes that Dilthey sees the ultimate guarantee of understanding in culture in the existence of a psychological community between the author and the interpreter. The understanding of the other is possible only due to a reference to one's own experience in this *Lebensphilosophie*. Kuderowicz illustrates this hermeneutical circle by quoting Dilthey: "Because of the content, the following relationship is formed: what I understand in the other I can find in myself as an experience, and thanks to this understanding I can find in the other what I experience" (quoted in: Zbigniew Kuderowicz, *Dilthey* [Warszawa: Wiedza Powszechna, 1987], 100).

76. On the historical dimension of hermeneutics: Hans-Georg Gadamer, *Truth and Method*, translated by Joel Weinsheimer and Donald G. Marshall (New York: Crossroad, 1990), 171–264.

other opinions and points of view, particularly those of ages past. From this perspective, reflection on one's own self-understanding is revealed as a condition for understanding others.

John Paul II's theology of the body is based on the hermeneutical assumption that everyone who reads the Bible and interprets God's revelation as it relates to the three ages of man—original innocence, the period that follows original sin, marked as it is by God's salvific initiative, and the time of the resurrection—will always appeal to his own experience when trying to understand the presented truths. Modern human experience, as the pope knows, appears radically different from the human condition before original sin, as well as from the experience of the life to come. However, John Paul II emphasizes that "in this case, *our human experience is in some way a legitimate means for theological interpretation* and that, in a certain sense, it is an indispensable point of reference to which we must appeal in the interpretation of the 'beginning.'"[77] Based on temporal and historical human experience, the pope argues, we can reach a certain "theological approximation" of who man was "in the beginning" and who man will be "in the future life."

Describing man in the state of original innocence, before original sin, John Paul II undertakes on the basis of biblical data (mostly from Gn 1–3) "to reconstruct the constitutive elements of man's original experience."[78] "Man's original experience" of himself, of his own body, and of another man and woman is not defined primarily by the pope on the basis of the first man's remoteness in time. Rather, the pope emphasizes the constitutive and foundational character of the "original experience" for the man of each historical age: "The important thing, therefore, is not that these experi-

---

77. *TB*, 145.
78. Ibid., 169. These "constitutive elements of man's original experience" will be analyzed mainly in chapter 2. Here we can only point to the most important of them: solitude, nakedness, the experience of mutual gift, etc.

ences belong to man's prehistory (to his 'theological prehistory'), but that they are always at the root of every human experience."[79]

John Paul II writes that we do not pay attention to such "essential experiences" in our everyday life: "they are so interwoven with the ordinary things of life that we generally do not realize their extraordinary character."[80] However, despite the fact that essential experience is concealed, it is "certainly located on the threshold of all later 'historical' experience. Nevertheless, this experience also seems to rest on an ontological depth that is so great that man does not perceive it in his own daily life, even if at the same time he presupposes it in some way and postulates it as part of the process of the formation of his own image."[81]

Analogically to the pope's claim that "every man carries in himself the mystery of his 'beginning,'"[82] we may extrapolate the thought of the catecheses: every man also bears in himself the mystery of the eschatological fulfillment of his existence in the life to come. Commenting on Christ's statement on the levirate law,[83] John Paul II emphasizes that when

Christ explains that in the "other world" ... "they will take neither wife nor husband"—then it is clear that here we are dealing with a development of the *truth about the same man*. Christ points out man's identity, although this identity *is realized in a different way in eschatological experience than* in the experience of the very "beginning" and of all history. And nevertheless, man will always be the same, just as he came forth from the hand of his Creator and Father.[84]

Only when we take into account these two trans-historical dimensions of human experience—the "beginning" and the life to come— are we able to create a consistent and complete "three-dimensional" image of man.[85] This theological image includes the truths about

---

79. Ibid., 169–70.
80. Ibid., 170.
81. Ibid.
82. Ibid., 217.
83. Mt 22:24–30.
84. *TB*, 398.
85. Stanisław Grygiel defines these temporal dimensions of adequate anthropology

the three stages of the economy of salvation: the original innocence, the time after the original sin marked by God's initiative of salvation, and the resurrection. This "reconstruction" of human experience, to use papal terms, reveals the "perennial meaning of the human body" and the "perennial meaning of the human person,"[86] and thus enables the construction of an adequate anthropology.

At this juncture, it is worth asking: how does man have access to these trans-historical dimensions of his existence, and how he can know them? In John Paul II's theological anthropology, the fundamental source of knowledge about the three dimensions of human existence is revelation, which enlightens and explains man's experience of himself, God, other men, and the world. Our reflections must probe further, however: can man know the truth about the "eternal meanings of the human person," concerning his original solitude and nakedness, the dynamics of mutual gift, and the call to eschatological fulfillment in *communio personarum*, in an exclusively natural way, without God's revelation? John Paul II does not directly ask this question in the catecheses, nor does he offer a clear answer, which may actually be different in the case of various truths about human prehistory and posthistory. It is unlikely that this epistemological question can be answered unambiguously. Rather, we should emphasize that the historical experience of man necessarily points to the human roots in the prehistory of "the beginning," as well as to completion in the posthistory of the Resurrection.

To summarize, the pope treats the two trans-historical dimensions of human existence—the beginning and the Resurrection—as "the first principles" that make human experience understandable. In the catecheses the pope writes:

---

of the catecheses as prehistory, history and posthistory. These apt terms will be employed throughout this work (Stanisław Grygiel, "Od samotności do daru," *Znak* 34, no. 5 [1982]: 363–84).

86. *TB*, 229–31, 400.

Neither the truth about this "beginning" about which Christ speaks, nor the eschatological truth can be reached by empirical and rationalist methods alone. Yet, is it not possible to affirm that man carries these two dimensions in some way in the depth of the experience of his being, or, rather, that he is in some way on the way toward them as toward dimensions that fully justify the very meaning of his being body, that is, of his being "carnal" man? ... The experience of humanity and especially the experience of the body allow the listener to unite with these words the image of the new existence in the "future world," for which earthly experience provides the substratum and basis.[87]

Before moving to the fourth meaning of hermeneutics, as suggested in the previous analyses, and its relation to the Wednesday catecheses, it is worth pondering the language John Paul II uses to discuss the three dimensions of human existence. According to the principles of an adequate anthropology, the pope focuses on establishing a description of human experience. When discussing the prehistory of "the beginning," John Paul II reconstructs the "original human experiences" that "are always at the root of every human experience."[88] Similarly, in reflecting on the eschatological fulfillment of man in the future life, as revealed in the Word of God, John Paul II describes this fulfillment using language that touches on human subjectivity.

John Paul II is well aware that, in the last few centuries, traditional theology, in discussing the three ages of human existence, has used metaphysical terms that refer to the concept of human nature: integral nature (*natura integra*), fallen nature (*natura corupta*), redeemed nature (*natura redempta*).[89] Consciously using different vocabulary and language that focuses on the description of the internal experiences and the subjectivity of the person, the pope seems to be returning to the original intuitions of a biblical way of thinking. As a result, he avoids the problems and misunderstand-

---

87. Ibid., 398.
88. Ibid., 169–70.
89. Ibid., 140–41.

ings that have arisen in the last few centuries around terms such as "integral nature" (*natura integra*) or "pure nature" (*natura pura*).[90]

Paul Ricoeur's Hermeneutics of Symbol and John Paul II's Hermeneutical Circle

In order to better understand the hermeneutical method in John Paul II's theological anthropology, the previous subchapter outlined the four fundamental definitions of modern hermeneutics. It seems that John Paul II's hermeneutical method embraces some elements from every one of these four definitions. In this section we will reflect on the fourth understanding of hermeneutics.

The aforementioned fourth meaning of hermeneutics is connected with the French thinker Paul Ricoeur.[91] Ricoeur argues that the fundamental task of philosophical hermeneutics is the analysis of symbols and myths, which allow man access to the deepest and most essential layers of human existence. Ricoeur devotes a significant part of his book *The Symbolism of Evil* (1960) to the interpretation of the Adam myth from Genesis.[92] The similarity of Ricoeur's thought on the myth of Adam to the first part of John Paul II's reflections on Adam in the Wednesday catecheses allows us to compare these two ways of approaching "the beginning." In turn, this comparison allows for a more precise probing into John Paul II's hermeneutical method.

---

90. See Henri de Lubac, *Augustianism and Modern Theology* (New York: Herder and Herder, 1968).

91. Many commentators on papal thought emphasize the similarity of the hermeneutical deliberations of John Paul II with those of Paul Ricoeur (Stanisław Grygiel, "Czyn objawieniem osoby?" *Znak* 23, no. 2–3 [1971]: 200–208). It is important to note that we are interested here mainly in the early works of Ricoeur, such as *La symbolique du mal* (1960) and *Le conflit des interpretations. Essais d'herméneutique* (1969).

92. The first edition of this work in French was entitled: *Finitude et culpabilité, II. La symbolique du mal* (Paris: Editions Montaigne, 1960). Here, we will use the English translation: Paul Ricoeur, *The Symbolism of Evil*, translated by Emerson Buchanan (New York: Harper and Row, 1967).

Ricoeur ranks the myth of Adam among the four most important myths about the beginning. The other three, says Ricoeur, are the myth of chaos, the myth of the tragedy, and the myth of the expelled soul.[93] While we do not intend to discuss each of these myths in detail, it is worth considering each briefly to better understand Ricoeur's interpretation of the myth of Adam. The myth of chaos combines cosmology with theogony, and the creation of the world with the creation of the gods. Ricoeur emphasizes that in this myth chaos precedes order and that the principle of evil is primary, inscribed in the essence of things. In the myth of tragedy, developed most exhaustively in ancient Greek tragedy, the cause of evil as experienced by man is to be found in the sphere of the gods: god tempts, blinds, and leads man to doom. Thirdly, Ricoeur calls the myth of the expelled soul a "philosophical justification of anthropological dualism." [94] In it, the human body is considered a place of exile for the soul, which belongs to spiritual sphere. The divine soul in cast into a material body as penance for the evil committed in a different, spiritual world.

Paul Ricoeur and John Paul II both agree and diverge in their understanding of the essence of myth. Ricoeur defines myth as "a traditional narration which relates to events that happened at the beginning of time and which has the purpose of providing grounds for the ritual actions of men of today and, in a general manner, establishing all the forms of action and thought by which man understands himself in his world."[95] Ricoeur shares with modern linguistic philosophy and structuralism the conviction that man can access his most fundamental experiences only through language.[96] As a result, in the process of humanity's growth in self-understanding, myth, which is the development of

---

93. Ricoeur, *The Symbolism of Evil,* 171–74.
94. Ibid., 279.   95. Ibid., 5.
96. Paul Ricoeur, "Structure and hermeneutics," in Ricoeur, *The Conflict of Interpretations: Essays in Hermeneutics,* edited by Don Ihde (Evanston, Ill.: Northwestern University Press, 1974), 27–61.

an even more simple and fundamental form—the symbol—functions as an access code to humanity's own experiences.

Ricoeur differentiates three fundamental functions of myths. First, the myth represents the history of every human being by using a model story, where a concrete time "represents all times."[97] Second, in myths every human life is presented inside a universe where a tension exists between the Beginning and the End, the Origin and the Apocalypse. Third, the myth, by telling a story, intends to come closer to "the enigma of human experience, namely, the discordance between the fundamental reality—the state of innocence, the status of a creature, or essential being—and the actual modality of man, as defiled, sinful, guilty."[98]

Of course, for both Ricoeur and John Paul II myth is not a chronicle of real events in human history. That said, however, myth concerns human history because it uses timeless symbols and motifs to express truths about man immersed in history.[99] It is worth noting that Ricoeur consistently and radically cleanses myth of any references to real historical events, and, in using this hermeneutical methodology to understand the myth of Adam, he goes much further than John Paul II. Both thinkers agree, for example, that the story about the fruit of the tree of the knowledge of good and evil is a symbolical representation of the theological essence of original sin. However, for Ricoeur, Adam and Eve are only symbolic figures without any reference to human history. Moreover, according to Ricoeur, the story of Adam and Eve is not about the relation between man and woman, but, rather, sheds light on the two dimensions within every human being. There is an Adam and an Eve in every one of us, where Eve refers to passivity and submissiveness before external temptation, and Adam signifies initiative and conscious choice.[100]

97. Ricoeur, *The Symbolism of Evil*, 162.
98. Ibid., 163.
99. Ricoeur, "Myth and History," 273–82.
100. "Eve, then, does not stand for woman in the sense of 'second sex.' Every woman

In his analysis of the myth of Adam, John Paul II does not go as far as Ricoeur in emphasizing the difference between myth and history. In the Wednesday catecheses, John Paul II neither rejects the historicity of Adam and Eve nor does he take a clear stand in the dispute between polygenesis and monogenesis regarding the beginnings of humankind. The difference in understanding of Old Testament myths between Ricoeur and John Paul II stems from diverging epistemological attitudes the two thinkers have toward biblical texts. In answer to the question "Why is looking at myths worthwhile?" Ricoeur, as a philosopher, responds that myths enable man to gain greater self-understanding, which, in his view, is the main criterion enabling man to verify the authenticity of a myth.[101] For this reason Ricoeur admits no epistemological difference between the myths of Genesis, the myths of ancient Greece and Rome, and the Babylonian story about Gilgamesh. For John Paul II, however, such an epistemological difference exists between the myth of Adam and the others, because the Genesis text is the inspired Word of God. According to the Christian point of view, inspired texts, read in faith, have important hermeneutical significance. They convey the endless depth of the Word of God, whose authenticity always exceeds the capabilities of the human mind to approach the divine truth by means of literary, philosophical, and theological methods.

Another significant difference between Ricoeur and John Paul II regarding the myth of Adam concerns their attitudes toward the theological concept of original sin. Ricoeur holds that the theory of original sin, which was initiated by St. Augustine and constitutes an important part of Catholic teaching, is merely a false rationalization that distorts the text of Genesis.[102] However, in criticizing the theory of *peccatum originale*, Ricoeur does not object so much to

---

and every man are Adam; every man and every woman are Eve; every woman sins 'in Adam', every man is seduced 'in' Eve" (Ricoeur, *The Symbolism of Evil*, 255).

101. Ibid., 355.

102. "In particular, it is essential to be convinced from the start that the concept

individual elements of Augustinian thought as to the whole project of Augustine's speculative interpretation. Augustine's theory of original sin, according to Ricoeur, changes *mythos* to *logos* as part of a consistent philosophical and theological system and, as a result, deprives the story of Adam of its symbolical and mythical depth. The symbol, Ricoeur, believes, is abandoned and "invalidated" the moment it is explained theologically.

Ricoeur's criticism of the Augustinian theology of original sin certainly suffers from some inconsistencies. Ricoeur differentiates between three levels of hermeneutical thinking.[103] The most fundamental and original symbols constitute the first level. The second consists in putting symbols together in mythical stories, and the third appears when we attempt to reflect speculatively on a myth, that is, when *mythos* is confronted with *logos*. Even while preserving the absolute primacy of the inspired biblical texts, the Church's reflections on *peccatum originale* throughout the ages can be understood as applying the third level of hermeneutics to the myth of Adam. Such reflection neither "invalidates" nor abandons the symbol or myth as Ricoeur claims. We can see John Paul II's interpretation of the myth of original sin as an example of the third level of hermeneutics as understood by Ricoeur.[104]

The "third level" of hermeneutics is exemplified in the cateche-

---

of original sin is not at the beginning but at the end of a cycle of living experience, the Christian experience of sin. Moreover, the interpretation that it gives of this experience is only one of the possible rationalizations of the root of evil according to Christianity. Finally and above all, this rationalization, which is embalmed by tradition and has become the cornerstone of Christian anthropology, belongs to a period of thought marked by Gnostic pretensions to 'know' the mysteries of God and human destiny" (ibid., 4; also, Ricoeur, "The Hermeneutics of Symbols I," in *The Conflict of Interpretations*, 304–9).

103. Ricoeur, *The Symbolism of Evil*, 7–8, 236–38.

104. It is worth noting that the centuries-old hermeneutical tradition of theological reflection of the Church verifies the statements and theories of individual theologians. During the development of the reflection on *peccatum originale* some historical theses regarding Adam and Eve's sin were rejected (e.g., the conviction that original sin may be identified with sexual desire), others only questioned (the necessity of accepting monogenesis as the theory explaining the origins of man), while others yet became a part of the Church's teaching (the conviction that every man is born in the state of original sin).

ses in two ways. First, the pope accepts in faith the teaching of the Church concerning issues he discusses in the catecheses. This acceptance in faith is for the pope an internal criterion of interpretation of biblical texts, though it is never discussed in the catecheses *expressis verbis*. Second, this third level of ecclesial hermeneutics, that is, the teaching of the Church, is embedded in footnotes to the catecheses, indicating possible directions for the speculative interpretation of biblical texts.[105]

Another concept important to the thought of Ricoeur and John Paul II—allowing for a comparison of the thinkers' interpretation of the story of Adam, and of biblical texts in general—is that of the hermeneutical circle, which addresses the starting point of philosophical reflection and undermines the possibility of philosophy without presuppositions. In his famous essay "The Symbol Gives Rise to Thought," Ricoeur criticizes the model of modern philosophy that, in search for a starting point, attempts to be a philosophy without presuppositions:

> The illusion is not in looking for a point of departure, but in looking for it without presuppositions. There is no philosophy without presuppositions. A meditation on symbols starts from speech that has already taken place, and in which everything has already been said in some fashion; it wishes to be thought with its presuppositions. For it, the first task is not to begin but, from the midst of speech, to remember; to remember with a view to beginning.[106]

Ricoeur suggests an alternative to the modern project of philosophy without presuppositions: a philosophy that speaks "from the fullness of being" and "from the fullness of speech." Ricoeur's frequently quoted saying "the symbol gives rise to thought" expresses a "third philosophical path" between, on the one hand, a

---

105. *TB*, 198–99, 238–40. The instantiation in John Paul II's reflections of two kinds of theological hermeneutics at the third level is discussed later in this chapter when we focus on the encyclical *Fides et Ratio*.

106. Ricoeur, *The Symbolism of Evil*, 348–49.

passive repetition of symbol and myth and, on the other hand, the annulment and invalidation of the symbol through critical explanation. This "third way" of Ricoeur's hermeneutics consists in "a creative interpretation of meaning, faithful to the gift of meaning that comes from the symbol, and faithful also to the philosopher's oath to seek understanding."[107]

Consequently, philosophical and theological hermeneutics intends not to invalidate, but to rebuild and revive myth. Though modern man has irretrievably lost the "original naiveté" through which he could directly experience the hierophany of original sacred symbolism, hermeneutics may give him "a second naiveté and immediacy," or a new contact with existence through symbol.[108] The synthesis of critical philosophical reflection and direct experience of the "sense radiating from a symbol" is expressed by Ricoeur in his famous formula, which is called in the hermeneutical tradition the hermeneutical circle: "we must understand in order to believe, but we must believe in order to understand."[109] It is worthwhile to examine briefly Ricoeur's understanding of the hermeneutical circle, for it is close to John Paul II's theological hermeneutics.

First, Ricoeur illustrates the necessity of faith for understanding in the hermeneutical circle using Rudolf Bultmann's well-known statement, which presents the problem of pre-understanding in philosophical thinking: "All understanding, like all interpretation, is ... continually oriented by the manner of posing the ques-

107. Ibid. Such philosophy is even more important because of Ricoeur's view that contemporary language, subject to the criteria of pragmatism, utilitarianism, and technical effectiveness, is threatened by the phenomenon of the "emptying of language" that consists in a loss of words, meanings, and symbols that truly allow man to name himself and reality as well as approach that which really exists (ibid., 348).

108. In his classic work, Don Ihde emphasizes that in Ricoeur's thought "a new naiveté" differentiates between two basic kinds of hermeneutics, i.e., the "hermeneutics of suspicion" and the "hermeneutics of faith" (Don Ihde, *Hermeneutic Phenomenology: The Philosophy of Paul Ricoeur* [Evanston, Ill.: Northwestern University Press, 1971], 141–42). Jan Snijders argues that the idea of a lost and regained naiveté comes from Karl Jaspers (Jan Snijders, *The Early Works of Paul Ricoeur* [Nijmegen: n.p., 1982], 53–54).

109. Ricoeur, *The Symbolism of Evil*, 351.

tion and by what it aims at (by its *Woraufhin*). Consequently, it is never without presuppositions; that is to say, it is always directed by a prior understanding of the thing it interrogates in the text. It is only on the basis of that prior understanding that it can, in general, interrogate and interpret."[110]

Therefore, one of the conditions for understanding is the consciousness that the critical reflection of the philosopher or theologian does not begin in a void, but originates in some often unconscious pre-understanding, in faith, in a worldview, or in certain convictions. The reflections of the subject are not indifferent to these presuppositions or to the way we ask questions or search for answers.[111]

Ricoeur also emphasizes that the horizon of faith and the pre-understanding of the subject should be recognized, brought out from the shadows, and discussed: "we must understand in order to believe." Writing about the need to understand in order to have faith, Ricoeur spells out an important epistemological and existential postulate, that is, that a consistent interpreter of symbols and myths cannot remain a neutral spectator. Since the hierophantic element cannot be removed from an integral discussion of the symbol, the symbol leads not so much to "a simple augmentation of self-awareness, a simple extension of reflexive consciousness," as to an ontological and qualitative change of consciousness and life.[112]

In *The Symbolism of Evil*, Ricoeur emphasizes that the hermeneutics of the symbol must not stop at the neutral ground of un-engaged reflection, but should lead to the development of existential structures, "since existence is the being of man."[113] Ricoeur's

---

110. Quoted in ibid., 351.
111. The theme of pre-understanding is also key for the question of the possibility of the existence of Christian philosophy (Kenneth L. Schmitz, *What Has Clio to Do with Athena? Etienne Gilson: Historian and Philosopher* [Toronto: Pontifical Institute of Mediaeval Studies, 1987]).
112. Ricoeur, *The Symbolism of Evil*, 356.
113. Ibid., 357.

concept of the hermeneutics of the symbol, much like the papal theological hermeneutics of the body, is a polemic against the post-Cartesian vision of man as pure consciousness: "The symbol gives reason to think that the *Cogito* is within being, and not vice versa. Thus the second naiveté would be a second Copernican revolution: the being which posits itself in the *Cogito* has still to discover that the very act by which it abstracts itself from the whole does not cease to share in the being that challenges it in every symbol."[114]

John Paul II's theological concept of the hermeneutical circle is similar to Paul Ricoeur's thought on the latter. John Paul II builds the encyclical *Fides et ratio* (1998) on the two pillars—*Credo ut intelligam* and *Intelligo ut credam*—that, as we have seen in Ricoeur's thought, can serve as the simplest definition of the hermeneutical circle. *Fides et ratio* is worth a closer look, as it helps illuminate the hermeneutical method of the Wednesday catecheses.

In *Fides et ratio,* John Paul II argues that the formula *Credo ut intelligam* (I believe in order to understand) indicates the importance of faith for the process of human understanding. Writing about the great contributions of Christian thinkers in the history of philosophy and theology, he emphasizes that they were able to attain the highest forms of speculation precisely due to an encounter with God in the depth of their minds.[115] Their achievements were possible through faith, which elevates the whole human person, directs his freedom, and thus facilitates the process of human cognition. For theological faith leads to the acceptance of the fact that human knowledge is a continuous journey and that its path is accessible only to the humble, who accept the truth that the transcendent God cares for the whole world.[116] Faith also purifies human reason and enables it to undertake "truths which might never have been discovered by reason unaided."[117] Thanks

114. Ibid., 356.
115. *FR,* 41.
116. Ibid., 18.
117. Ibid., 76.

to faith, "reason is offered guidance and is warned" and "is stirred to explore paths which of itself it would not even have suspected it could take," where it "discovers new and unsuspected horizons."[118]

Though *Fides et ratio* does not reflect on a longing for a philosophy without presuppositions, as criticized by Ricoeur, it does dwell on the concept of pre-understanding, which is the starting point of every human reflection, be it philosophical or theological. The previously noted existential attitude of supernatural faith is an instantiation of such pre-understanding that influences the believing subject's way of thinking in a significant and, as the pope emphasizes, positive manner. The encyclical argues that people without supernatural faith also have pre-understanding. John Paul II writes that "everyday life shows well enough how each one of us is preoccupied by the pressure of a few fundamental questions and how in the soul of each of us there is at least an outline of the answers."[119] He observes that "all men and women are in some sense philosophers and have their own philosophical conceptions with which they direct their lives."[120]

John Paul II points out that in the process of maturation, human beings accept many important truths on the basis of their intuition, of their trust in their parents or moral authorities, or just based on common knowledge: "there are in the life of a human being many more truths which are simply believed than truths which are acquired by way of personal verification."[121] Pointing to existential pre-understanding, the pope summarizes his thought thus: "the human being, the one who seeks the truth, is also *the one who lives by belief.*"[122]

The encyclical *Fides et ratio* likewise emphasizes the impor-

---

118. Ibid., 73.
119. Ibid., 29. It seems that this "outline of the answers" to fundamental human questions, carried in every man's heart, are the same as the "original human experiences," which John Paul II discusses in his catecheses (*TB*, 169).
120. *FR*, 30. 121. Ibid., 31.
122. Ibid., 31.

tance of speculative and systematic reflection in the human cognitive process: "Through philosophy's work, the ability to speculate, which is proper to the human intellect, produces a rigorous mode of thought; then in turn, through the logical coherence of the affirmations made and the organic unity of their content, it produces a systematic body of knowledge. In different cultural contexts and at different times, this process has yielded results which have produced genuine systems of thought."[123]

Concerning the need for philosophy in theological reflection, John Paul II observes that the basis and condition of philosophical research consists in the existence of reason formed and properly educated in the sphere of concepts and arguments:

> For its part, dogmatic theology must be able to articulate the universal meaning of the mystery of the One and Triune God and of the economy of salvation, both as a narrative and, above all, in the form of argument. It must do so, in other words, through concepts formulated in a critical and universally communicable way. Without philosophy's contribution, it would in fact be impossible to discuss theological issues such as, for example, the use of language to speak about God, the personal relations within the Trinity, God's creative activity in the world.[124]

In accord with the most authentic currents of Christian Tradition, *Fides et ratio* presents an outline of a Christian hermeneutics of "the third level," to use Ricoeur's term. This hermeneutics neither abolishes nor invalidates the symbols and myths present in the scriptures, because it cannot completely exhaust the inspired Word of God. Simultaneously, because of its trust in the strength of human reason, Christian hermeneutics confronts *mythos* with *logos,* myth "gives rise to thought."[125]

To summarize, the mutual relationship of faith and critical reflection, theology and philosophy, outlined in the encyclical *Fides*

---

123. Ibid., 4.   124. Ibid., 66.
125. Ricoeur, *The Symbolism of Evil,* 347–57.

et ratio, resembles the hermeneutical circle: "Although faith, a gift of God, is not based on reason; it can certainly not dispense with it. At the same time, it becomes apparent that reason needs to be reinforced by faith, in order to discover horizons it cannot reach on its own."[126]

The hermeneutical circle, as John Paul II understands it, also operates in his interpretation of biblical texts in the Wednesday catecheses. In the papal "hermeneutics of gift," the Word of God is accepted in faith, and then undergoes "philosophical exegesis," and its "biblical images are translated to philosophical notions,"[127] so that the Word can shine with all the radiance of its truth (*Veritatis splendor*).

---

126. *FR*, 67.
127. Grabowski, "W stronę antropologii," 20.

Chapter Two

THE BODY THAT REVEALS

In the Wednesday catecheses, John Paul II describes and analyzes the human body according to the principles of an adequate anthropology. As shown in the previous chapter, the pope explains the concept of an adequate anthropology as "an understanding and interpretation of man in what is essentially human."[1] Through a phenomenological concentration on what is characteristic to man—subjectivity, an experience of self, and self-reflection—an adequate anthropology opposes empiricist anthropological reductionism that "reduces man to 'the world'" and understands man only "with the categories taken from the 'world,' that is, from the visible totality of bodies."[2]

The papal theology of the body, therefore, considers the human body both in the structure of the personal subject and within the web of interpersonal relations. It is key to point out that this description of the body is not merely a description of the somatic structure of the human organism, but, primarily, a description of

1. *TB*, 178.
2. Ibid., 135.

"man who expresses himself by means of that body, and in this sense... 'is' that body."³

"The Beginning": The Body as Subject

John Paul II's theological hermeneutics take into account two fundamental aspects of the body: its reality as object, and its place in the structure of the subject. The pope notes that "practically all *the problems of the 'ethos of the body' are* at the same time *linked with the body's ontological identification* as the body of the person and with the content and quality of subjective *experience,* that is, at the same time *'living' both one's own body* and in interhuman relations, particularly in the perennial 'man-woman' relation."⁴

According to John Paul II, the subjective experience of the body is two-sided: there is the personal and intimate experience of one's own body, and also the bodily experience that is born of an encounter with others. In the pope's reflection, "the meaning of the body" points to man's subjective experience of the body: "*The 'meaning of the body' is at the same time what shapes the attitude: it is the way of living the body. It is the measure that the inner man— that is, that heart,* to which Christ appeals in the Sermon on the Mount—applies to the human body with regard to its masculinity and femininity (and thus with regard to its sexuality)."⁵

Therefore, the meaning of the body, according to John Paul II, concerns the meaning of the body for the subject, and also the way the subject experiences this meaning of the body. The catecheses use the term "the meaning of the body" in two fundamental ways: the spousal and parental meanings of the body.⁶ Before explaining

---

3. Ibid., 346. Due to the character of the method peculiar to an adequate anthropology, the description of the human body that we owe to the natural sciences is omitted in this work, similarly as in the papal catecheses on the theology of the body. Such a description may be found in Ashley, *Theologies of the Body,* 19–51.

4. *TB,* 365.   5. Ibid., 255.

6. One can also find the terms "the beatifying meaning of the body" (*TB,* 194) and

these terms, it is worthwhile to emphasize the anti-Cartesian and anti-dualistic epistemology of the pope's theology of the body.

In the philosophical current beginning with René Descartes, man's most fundamental experience is his experience of the "self," articulated in the famous Cartesian formula *cogito, ergo sum*.[7] In his book *Crossing the Threshold of Hope* (1994), John Paul II describes modern philosophy's Cartesian turn as the absolutization of subjective consciousness and the divorce of thinking from the total existence of the subject.[8] Many historians of philosophy agree with the pope's evaluation of this development. For instance, a Polish philosopher, Władysław Tatarkiewicz, in his classic *History of Philosophy*, writes:

> Descartes found in reason, and in self-knowledge, an "Archimedean point" for philosophy, sufficient to base on it the existence of "self," and indirectly the existence of God and other bodies. The existence of "self" resulted directly from the existence of thought; if there is thought, then there must also be somebody who is thinking: "I think, therefore I am" (*cogito, ergo sum*). Who am I?—a being who thinks. The thinking self, or soul, exists, even if the body is an illusion; existence, which is independent of the body, is an independent substance.[9]

Another renowned historian of philosophy, Frederick Copleston, emphasizes that the establishment of subjectivity as the starting point of philosophy has become a staple of post-Cartesian thought, which has significantly influenced such thinkers as Friedrich Hegel, Edmund Husserl, and Jean Paul Sartre.[10]

John Paul II's theology of the body explores a characteristic

---

"the personal meaning of the body" (*TB*, 288) in the catecheses. Both terms will be discussed in a later part of this work.

7. Descartes, *Discourse on the Method*, 127.

8. John Paul II, *Crossing the Threshold of Hope*, 37–38, 50–53.

9. Władysław Tatarkiewicz, *Historia filozofii* (Warszawa: Wydawnictwo Naukowe PWN, 2001), 48.

10. Frederick Copleston, SJ, *A History of Philosophy* (Westminster: Newman Press, 1959), 4:150–52.

theme of the post-Cartesian tradition, that is, the subjectivity and consciousness of man. John Paul II's approach, however, precludes any anthropological dualism or diminishment of the role of the body in human cognition. Moreover, John Paul II holds that human beings know and experience their own subjectivity not through a subjective concentration on their own experience and their "I," but through their own corporeality. This truth comes to the fore in the first pages of the catecheses, which are devoted, as we have observed, to analyzing the creation account of man in the first two chapters of Genesis.

John Paul II's interest in the Yahwist account of man's creation,[11] which is chronologically prior to the Elohist account,[12] narrows in on the text's concentration on the subjectivity and consciousness of man, especially as these elements correspond to the sensitivities of modern post-Cartesian anthropology.[13] The Yahwist narrative, according to the catecheses, differentiates five stages in the formation of human subjectivity, paying special attention to the role of the human body in this process. These stages are as follows: covenantal relation with God, the vocation to work, Adam's freedom of choice, original solitude, and creation of Eve.

As outlined in the Yahwist account in Genesis, the first stage of man's awareness of his own subjectivity is based on his first, and primeval, covenant with God: from the beginning of his existence, as John Paul II says, "the words of the first command of God-Yahweh (Gn 2:16–17), which speak directly about the submission and dependence of man-creature on his Creator, indirectly reveal precisely this level of humanity as subject of the covenant and 'partner of the Absolute.'"[14] Since God speaks to man, man is not only a passive object of God's activity, but also a subject.

The second stage of revealing the subjectivity of created man is related to his call to work. According to the Yahwist account,

11. Gn 2:5–25.
12. Gn 1:1–2, 4.
13. *TB*, 134–37.
14. Ibid., 151.

"The Lord God took the man and put him in the garden of Eden to till it and keep it."[15] Among all beings created by God, John Paul II notes, only man is called "to cultivate and take care" of the garden. This task indicates man's unique place in the created world: "One can say that from the very beginning the awareness of 'superiority' inscribed in the definition of humanity has originated in a typically human praxis."[16]

The pope emphasizes that human "superiority" to the natural world is closely tied to the material reality of the human body, which enables man "to cultivate and take care" of the garden. Man's discovery of his own subjectivity corresponds to God's call for man to subdue the earth, found in the Elohist account of creation: "Be fruitful and multiply, and fill the earth and subdue it; and have dominion over the fish of the sea and over the birds of the air and over every living thing that moves upon the earth."[17]

The third stage of the formation of human subjectivity appears when God commands man to eat of all the trees in the garden of Eden, but not of the fruit of the tree of the knowledge of good and evil: "but of the tree of the knowledge of good and evil you shall not eat, for in the day that you eat of it you shall die."[18] John Paul II observes that the mere fact of God's commandment reveals in man "the aspect of choice and self-determination (that is, of free will)."[19] Human self-determination and freedom are accentuated in Genesis by the threat of death, which appears as "*a radical*

---

15. Gn 2:15.   16. *TB*, 154.

17. Gn 1:28. The issue of human domination (Hebrew *radah*) over nature, which God commands in Genesis 1:28, is one of the most important problems of modern ecological thought (see John T. Pawlikowski, OSM, "Theological Dimensions of an Ecological Ethics," in *The Ecological Challenge. Ethical, Liturgical, and Spiritual Responses*, edited by R. N. Fragomeni and J. T. Pawlikowski, OSM [Collegeville, Minn.: Liturgical Press, 1994], 43–46). This problem is not discussed by John Paul II in his Wednesday catecheses.

18. Gn 2:17.

19. *TB*, 151. On the philosophical concept of self-determination and its relation to free will see Wojtyła, *The Acting Person*, 105–86.

antithesis of all that man had been endowed with."[20] The fact that man can live or die, says the pope, reveals the consequences of human choice and the meaning of personal freedom, but also shows the fragility of the human body.[21]

Another element of man's subjectivity revealed in the Yahwist account—the fourth stage—is connected to the phenomenon that John Paul II dubs "man's original solitude." These words of the Creator point to this phenomenon: "It is not good that the man should be alone."[22] Further confirmation and development can be found in a continuation of the Yahwist narrative: God "formed every animal of the field and every bird of the air, and brought them to the man" for the man to give them names.[23] John Paul II emphasizes that the process of man naming the animals has an important anthropological meaning: "*the created man finds himself from the first moment of his existence before God* in search of his own being, as it were; one could say, in search of his own definition; today one would say, in search of his own 'identity.'"[24] In searching for his identity man discovers or knows that he is different from every animal. In fact, the pope speaks of man's essential dissimilarity from "the visible world, ... from the whole world of living beings (*animalia*)."[25]

For Adam, naming the animals leads him to an experience of solitude: "The man gave names to all cattle, and to the birds of the air, and to every animal of the field; but for the man there was not found a helper as his partner."[26] Man's exceptionality and his

---

20. *TB*, 155.
21. In the introduction to the Polish original version of the catecheses, John Paul II emphasizes the aspectual character of the theological anthropology presented therein. Undoubtedly, one of the issues that is key for the theology of the body and that is dealt with in a limited way is the question of human suffering and death (John Paul [Jan Paweł] II, *Mężczyzną i niewiastą stworzył ich: Odkupienie ciała a sakramentalność małżeństwa* [Vatican City: Libreria Editrice Vaticana, 1986], 6).
22. Gn 2:18. 23. Gn 2:19.
24. *TB*, 149. 25. Ibid., 150.
26. Gn 2:20.

superiority over the world of nature are revealed in his subjective experience as solitude.[27]

Adam's discovery—the realization of being different from the animals—is "the first and fundamental manifestation of humanity."[28] The pope asserts that man's

self-knowledge goes hand in hand with knowledge of the world, of all visible creatures, of all living beings to which man has given their names to affirm his own dissimilarity before them. Thus, consciousness reveals man as the one who *possesses the power of knowing* with respect to *the visible world*. With this knowledge, which makes him go in some way outside of his own being, *man* at the same time *reveals himself to himself in all the distinctiveness of his being*.[29]

In analyzing the formation of human subjectivity, John Paul II, in his adequate anthropology, acknowledges the insights of classical metaphysics.[30] According to the pope, the formation of man's subjectivity in the Yahwist account corresponds to the Aristotelian definition of man as a "rational animal" (*animal rationale*).[31] Ac-

---

27. It seems that the notion of "transcendence"—one of the most fundamental philosophical terms describing the phenomenon of the human person in Karol Wojtyła's *opus magnum*, *The Acting Person*—points to this same phenomenon of exceptionality and superiority (Wojtyła, *The Acting Person*, 105–86). Moreover, as stated in the introduction, this book originated as a philosophical explanation of human transcendence, which was spoken of in documents of the Second Vatican Council. Consequently, the epigraph to the Polish version of *The Acting Person* is a passage from *Gaudium et spes*: "The Church, by reason of her role and competence, is not identified in any way with the political community nor bound to any political system. She is at once a sign and a safeguard of the transcendent character of the human person" (*GS*, 76). Therefore, we may consider John Paul II's reflection on original solitude, as presented in the catecheses, as a theological supplement or continuation of his philosophy of human transcendence. Another philosophical term used by Wojtyła that indicates the phenomenon of original solitude is *incomunicabilitas* (Wojtyła, *The Acting Person*, 107; also: Schmitz, *At the Center of the Human Drama*, 21–29, 99–102; Mary Shivanandan, *Crossing the Threshold of Love: A New Vision of Marriage in the Light of John Paul II's Anthropology* [Washington, D.C.: The Catholic University of America Press, 1999], 141–49).

28. *TB*, 150.   29. Ibid., 150.

30. Ibid., 151–53.

31. Aristotle, *Politics* I, 2. 1253a5–a39. When John Paul II refers to the Aristotelian

cording to Aristotelian logic, this definition consists of two parts: the first points to the closest species (*genus proximum*) and the second to a specific difference (*differentia specifica*).³²

The animal world is the closest species (*genus proximum*) to man. Man shares with animals their nature as living and feeling material substances; thus the term "animal" in the Aristotelian definition. Reason constitutes the specific difference (*differentia specifica*) that differentiates man from the animal world; thus the term "rational" in the definition. John Paul II holds that, in a way, the Yahwist narration "justifies" the Aristotelian definition of man because it presents created man first as "a body among bodies": here, man, by virtue of his corporeality, belongs to the visible world of nature. Next, through a clearly outlined presentation of the formation of man's subjectivity, the Yahwist account shows how man is differentiated from the animal world and what the basis is for his privileged place in creation.³³

Finally, John Paul II observes regarding the fourth stage that the Yahwist author assigns the key role to human corporeality in Adam's knowledge and experience of himself: "the body, by which man shares in the visible created world, makes him at the same time aware of being 'alone.'"³⁴ By comparing John Paul II's theological treatment of the formation of human subjectivity, as outlined in the Yahwist account of creation, with Karol Wojtyła's philosophical analysis of subjectivity in *The Acting Person* (1969), we see the significance of corporeality in the structure of the hu-

---

definition of man, he quotes it in Latin in the same form under which it appeared in medieval interpretations (*STh* I, 29, 4; 85, 3).

32. Aristotle, *Categories* V, 2a11–4a10; *Metaphysics* III, 3. 998b14–99a23.

33. At this point, it is worth emphasizing the synthetic character of John Paul II's thought and his capability of describing man in parallel ways using terminology and notions originating in different philosophical theories. Here, the Aristotelian concept of rationality as a specifically human difference is used to define the phenomenon that, in the Wednesday catecheses, is usually described by means of the language of modern phenomenology as subjectivity.

34. *TB*, 152.

man subject. In Wojtyła's philosophical anthropology, the importance of the human body for the person is particularly emphasized in his theory of "an integration of the person in the act."[35]

The fifth and last stage of the Yahwist description of the formation of man's subjectivity through the body is related to the creation of woman. John Paul II stresses that God's formation of woman from Adam's rib indicates that the unity of man and woman is based on a sharing of the same humanity.[36] Only because she is created from Adam's flesh can woman fulfill the original solitude of man. Man, therefore, expresses his joy in a "wedding" song[37] when he sees the woman's humanity and femininity: "This at last is bone of my bones and flesh of my flesh."[38] As man realized in his experience of original solitude that he is different from the animals, so the creation of woman, in whom man found "a helper,"[39] reveals the relational dimension of human nature and the fact that man becomes a complete person and finds fulfillment only in relation with the woman.

John Paul II asserts that describing the relationship between the man and woman as a "community" is insufficient. There is a need for a "stronger" term, drawn from the documents of the Second Vatican Council, namely "a communion of persons" (*communio personarum*).[40] Man and woman, as a communion of persons created in love, become the image of the Holy Trinity: "Man becomes an image of God not so much in the moment of solitude as in the moment of communion. He is, in fact, 'from the beginning'

---

35. Wojtyła, *The Acting Person*, 189–259; also Kupczak, *Destined for Liberty*, 102–4, 115–18, 134–36.

36. Gn 2:21–22. Bruce Vawter writes in a similar way about the meaning of woman being created from Adam's rib (Hebrew *sela*): "This may seem obvious to us, but it was very important to the author to insist, against contemporary opinions to the contrary, that woman was not inferior to man. Rather, man and woman complement one another in the same human species." (Bruce Vawter, "Genesis," in *A New Catholic Commentary on Holy Scripture,* edited by R. C. Fuller [Melbourne: Nelson, 1969], 178).

37. *TB*, 160.
38. Gn 2:23.
39. Gn 2:18.
40. *TB*, 162–63.

not only an image in which the solitude of one Person, who rules the world, mirrors itself, but also and essentially the image of an inscrutable divine communion of Persons."[41]

The pope writes that, in the first joyful meeting of man and woman, the key role is played by the spousal meaning of the body. When the man sees the woman who was created from his own body he recognizes another person, equal to him in dignity and humanity, though with a body different in its somatic sexual structure. The woman's appearance makes man aware that if he is to be himself, he must be in a communion of persons: "femininity in some way finds itself before masculinity, while masculinity confirms itself through femininity."[42] The pope emphasizes that the man can only recognize himself once he sees the woman: "The man speaks these words ["flesh from my flesh and bone from my bones"] as if it were only at the sight of the woman that he could identify and call by name *that which makes them in a visible way similar, the one to the other,* and at the same time *that in which humanity is manifested."[43]* For both, man and woman, self-discovery through an encounter with the other occurs through the human body: "the body reveals man."[44]

The original unity of man and woman, as described in the Yahwist narration, is expressed and realized in their marital unity: "Therefore a man leaves his father and his mother and clings to his wife, and they become one flesh."[45] Biblical scholars point out that the Yahwist account of creation developed in a world that approved of polygamy and divorce, and considered the inferior status of women as self-apparent and affirmed by long-standing tradition. Counter to the cultures of the time, the Yahwist author

---

41. Ibid., 163. The fourth chapter of this work is devoted to a reflection on *imago Dei*.
42. *TB*, 166.
43. Ibid., 164. Many commentators emphasize that the papal theology of the body can be seen as a part of relational anthropology (Shivanandan, *Crossing the Threshold of Love*, 141–70). We will return to this discussion in the next chapter.
44. *TB*, 164.
45. Gn 2:24.

proposes that, in the creation of man and woman, Yahweh desired human marriage to be monogamous. One exegete remarks: "There is no doubt that the inspired author, though he lived in a society that permitted both polygamy and divorce, taught that monogamous, indissoluble marriage was what Yahweh had intended in the creation of man and woman.... Just like the inferior status of women in human society, polygamy and its attendant evils were the result of sin and its consequences, and not of divine intervention."[46]

According to John Paul II, the biblical "becoming one flesh" of man and woman signifies much more than mere sexual unity. Rather, it concerns a mutual knowledge and an encounter of man and woman that takes place at a much deeper level than the sphere of human sensuality alone:

> Sex, however, is something more than the mysterious power of human bodiliness, which acts, as it were, by virtue of instinct. On the level of man and in the reciprocal relationship of persons, sex expresses an ever-new surpassing of the limit of man's solitude, which lies within the makeup of his body and determines its original meaning. This surpassing always implies that in a certain way one takes upon oneself the solitude of the body of the second "I" as one's own.[47]

John Paul II points out that the common terms that describe the biblical meaning of "becoming one flesh" are impoverished and inadequate. For instance, the term "sexual instinct" suggests a biological determinism or an internal compulsion to the sexual act "analogous to the instinct that stimulates fruitfulness and procreation in the whole world of living beings (*animalia*)."[48] Another term, "sexual intercourse," seems to neglect the fact that it is two persons that come together in love.

---

46. Vawter, "Genesis," 178.
47. *TB*, 167–68.
48. Ibid., 184. On the reductionist character of the term "sexual desire," see above, 17–20.

The pope considers as deeply authentic the biblical description of sexual intercourse as "knowing."[49] This term introduces the marital intercourse of man and woman into *"the specific dimension of the persons"*:[50] "Thus, they reveal themselves to one another with *that specific depth of their own human 'I,' which precisely reveals itself also through their sex,* their masculinity and femininity. And thus, in a singular way, the woman 'is given' in the mode of knowledge to the man, and he to her."[51] "Becoming one flesh," thus understood, also reveals the parental meaning of the body: "Consequently, 'knowledge' in the biblical sense signifies that man's 'biological' determination, on the part of his body and his sex, is no longer something passive but reaches a level and content specific to self-conscious and self-determining persons; therefore, it brings with it a particular consciousness of the meaning of the human body bound to fatherhood and motherhood."[52]

John Paul II finds another important insight revealing the meaning of the human body in the last line of the second chapter of Genesis: "And the man and his wife were both naked, and were not ashamed."[53] The pope notes that this statement of the Yahwist account justifies in a particular way the method of adequate anthropology adopted in the catecheses, because it links the reflection on the human body (i.e., they "were naked") with the description of the consciousness of the first human couple (i.e., they "were not ashamed").[54] Therefore, in the context of this discussion

---

49. In biblical language sexual intercourse is defined as "knowing" (Hebrew *jada*). Ephraim Speiser notes that "knowing" in the Old Testament is never merely intellectual, but, rather, signifies an existential experience of the known thing (Ephraim A. Speiser, *Genesis: Introduction, Translation, and Notes* [Garden City, N.Y.: Doubleday, 1986], 31–32). Consequently, in his translation, the verse discussed here reads as follows: "The man had experience of his wife"; ibid., 29).

50. *TB*, 206. 51. Ibid., 207.
52. Ibid., 212. 53. Gn 2:25.

54. In the culture of the ancient Middle East, nakedness was considered unnatural and negative, and indicated the humiliation of defeated slaves (2 Sm 10:4; Is 20:1–6), a punishment for sin (Mi 1:8; Neh 3:5), and especially adultery (Is 47:2–3; Jr 13:22; Ez 16:36–37).

on man's discovery of his subjectivity through the body, this biblical text "describes ... their reciprocal experience of the body, that is, the man's experience of the femininity that reveals itself in the nakedness of the body and, reciprocally, the analogous experience of masculinity by the woman."[55]

John Paul II suggests that to fully understand the Yahwist author's statement about man and woman's lack of shame in the state of original innocence, one has to consider what happened somewhat later, when Adam and Eve ate of the fruit from the tree of the knowledge of good and evil: "Then the eyes of both were opened, and they knew that they were naked; and they sewed fig leaves together and made loincloths for themselves."[56] According to the pope, the statement "they knew that they were naked" concerns not only the sense of sight, since prior to their first act of disobedience toward God, man and woman looked at each other's naked bodies. Rather, it involves *"a radical change in the meaning of the original nakedness* of the woman before the man and of the man before the woman. This change emerges from their consciousness as a fruit of the tree of the knowledge of good and evil."[57] Shame appears as a kind of a "boundary" experience, which marks the beginning of a new age in human history, the age after original sin.

The lack of shame in the state of original innocence does not indicate a lack or underdevelopment in man and woman's con-

---

As a result, Jesus, because he was seen as a transgressor in the eyes of his persecutors, was stripped of his clothes before the crucifixion (Mt 27:35; also: "Naked, Nakedness," in *DBI*, 581–82). Similarly, in the biblical world, shame indicates the humiliation of a defeated enemy (Ps 83:17–19), the emotions of a rejected sinner (Mi 3:7; Lv 20:17). Finally, shame is "seen objectively as that moral state which exhibits the reprehensible and degrading nature of sin, and subjectively as a psychological or emotional consequence that flows from guilt and sin" ("Shame," in *DBI*, edited by Leland Ryken and others (Downers Grove, Ill.: InterVarsity Press, 1998), 780; also, David W. Cotter, *Genesis* [Collegeville, Minn.: Liturgical Press, 2003], 33).

55. *TB*, 171.   56. Gn 3:7.
57. *TB*, 172.

sciousness, but, rather, the opposite. "The words of Genesis 2:25, 'they did not feel shame,' do not express a lack but, on the contrary, they serve to indicate a particular fullness of consciousness and experience, above all the fullness of understanding the meaning of the body connected with the fact that 'they were naked.'"[58]

The original nakedness of man and woman therefore symbolizes a completeness and an innocence of knowing another person through the body, "the particular fullness of interpersonal communion," in which the body expresses "the person in his or her ontological and essential concreteness, which is something more than 'individual,' and thus expresses the human, personal 'I,' which grounds its 'exterior' perception from within."[59] The lack of shame makes the communion of persons (*communio personarum*) possible.

In John Paul II's thought, the original nakedness of man and woman signifies a certain transparency of their bodies before the advent of sin. Their ability to see the internal and spiritual reality of the other person in what is external and corporeal springs from a purity of spirit. Seeing the nakedness of another person without shame means "an original depth in affirming what is inherent in the person, that is, what is "visibly" feminine and masculine, through which the 'personal intimacy' of reciprocal communication is constituted in all its radical simplicity and purity."[60] Thus, the original nakedness of man and woman, free from shame, reveals the spousal meaning of the body.

After the Fall: The Body as Object

John Paul II's theology of the body refrains from analyzing original sin or the process of temptation that precedes it.[61] Instead, the pope points out that the Tempter recasts the image of

58. Ibid., 174.
60. Ibid.
59. Ibid., 176.
61. Gn 3:1–5.

God, which is revealed in the mystery of creation as Love, in the image of a jealous rival, who vigilantly guards his privileges: "God knows that when you eat of it [the fruit of the tree of the knowledge of good and evil] your eyes will be opened, and you will be like God, knowing good and evil."[62]

By eating the fruit of "the tree of the knowledge of good and evil," man accepts the Tempter's false image of God. "By casting doubt in his heart on the deepest meaning of the gift, that is, on love as the specific motive of creation and of the original covenant (see Gn 3:5), man turns his back on God-Love, on the 'Father.' He in some sense casts him from his heart."[63]

John Paul II emphasizes that the shame of man and woman after they sin is connected with the fear of God. By hiding among the trees of the garden, they show that "*the shame they feel before each other* [is] the immediate fruit of the tree of the knowledge of good and evil, *a sense of fear before God has matured: a fear previously unknown.*"[64] Man himself speaks in the Yahwist text of this fear: when God asks "Where are you?" the man replies, "I heard the sound of you in the garden, and I was afraid, because I was naked; and I hid myself."[65] Adam's fear of meeting Yahweh is a consequence of a transformation of the image of God in the eyes of men. Yahweh is now perceived as somebody from whom one flees and hides, someone to fear.

The pope notes that man does not tell God the truth when he

---

62. Gn 3:5. The Tempter uses a lie to distort the commands God gave to Adam and Eve and, ultimately, to undermine their trust in the Creator (Cotter, 33–34). As a result, Christ says of the Devil that "he is a liar and the father of lies" (ψεύστης ἐστὶν καὶ ὁ πατὴρ αὐτοῦ; Jn 8, 44).

63. *TB*, 237. John Paul II also writes thus in the encyclical *Dominum et vivificantem* on the distortion of the image of God in the first temptation: "God the Creator is placed in a state of suspicion, indeed of accusation, in the mind of the creature. For the first time in human history there appears the perverse 'genius of suspicion.' He seeks to 'falsify' Good itself; the absolute Good, which precisely in the work of creation has manifested itself as the Good which gives in an inexpressible way: as *bonum diffusivum sui*, as creative love" (*DV*, 37).

64. *TB*, 238.   65. Gn 3:9–10.

points to nakedness as the cause of his fear; he is afraid for a much more serious reason. For man discovers that after his sin, he is deprived of the manifold gifts of God's grace that he had received at creation: "In reality, what shows itself through 'nakedness' is man deprived of participation in the Gift, man alienated from the Love that was the source of the original gift, the source of the fullness of good intended for the creature."[66]

In accord with the traditional teaching of the Church, John Paul II defines the effects of original sin as the deprivation in man of supernatural and preternatural gifts and "damage in what belongs to nature itself, to humanity."[67] The pope does not reflect at length on this teaching of the Church, but, rather—with the intent of realizing his project of "philosophical exegesis"—carefully explores the words of man directed to God from the Yahwist account: "I was afraid, because I was naked; and I hid myself."[68] According to the pope, this statement signifies a radical change in the meaning of nakedness after original sin. This change can be analyzed in its four fundamental dimensions that concern man's relationships: to God, to one's self, to nature, and to other persons.

First, man's fear is an unquestionable sign of the change of his relation to God. It leads to the attempt to hide from Yahweh among the trees of the garden. This fear is characteristic of man who has already lost the grace of original innocence.[69]

---

66. *TB*, 239.

67. Ibid., 240. On effects of original sin see.: *STh* I-II, q. 85; *CCC* 399–401; Thomas C. O'Brien, OP, "Fallen Nature," in St. Thomas Aquinas, *Summa Theologiae: Latin Text and English Translation, Introductions, Notes, Appendices, and Glossaries* (Oxford: Blackfriars, 1964–1981), 26:154–61; Auguste-Joseph Gaudel, "Péché originel," in *DTC*, vol. 12–1, col. 479–81, 591–602.

68. Gn 3:10.

69. Umberto Cassuto argues that Adam and Eve's behavior after sin clearly indicates a new anxiety of their consciences. Cassuto notes that the biblical text emphasizes that Adam and Eve "heard" God's steps in the garden only after their sin: "It is possible that the Lord God had already been walking in the garden prior to this; Scripture tells us only that the man and his wife, now that their conscience was uneasy, became aware of One who could demand from them an account of their deeds" (Umberto Cassuto, *A Com-*

Secondly, John Paul II emphasizes that the sacramental dimension of the body in the mystery of creation is diminished after original sin. Before original sin, the human body had been a visible and transparent sign of the person. It had been marked "as the visible factor of transcendence, in virtue of which man, as a person, surpasses the visible world of living beings (*animalia*)."[70] After original sin, however, the body loses its transparency as an expression of the person and, simultaneously, as the image and likeness to God.[71]

Moreover, the relation of man to nature is deeply disrupted after original sin. God's words "foretell the hostility, as it were, of the world, the resistance of nature against man and his tasks; they foretell the toil that the human body was then to suffer in contact with the earth subdued by him":[72]

Cursed is the ground because of you; in toil you shall eat of it all the days of your life; thorns and thistles it shall bring forth for you; and you shall eat the plants of the field. By the sweat of your face you shall eat bread until you return to the ground, for out of it you were taken; you are dust, and to dust you shall return.[73]

Man's nakedness and fear after original sin express "*the awareness of being defenseless,* and the sense of *insecurity* about his somatic structure *in the face of the processes of nature that operate with an inevitable determinism.*"[74] John Paul II calls man's experience of his sinful nature "cosmic shame."[75]

---

mentary on the Book of Genesis [Jerusalem: Magness Press, Hebrew University, 1989], 151). Also, the Yahwist's comment that Adam and Eve hid before God not among bushes or rocks, but "among the trees of the garden" seems to indicate that "though the sinner was trying to forget his sin and cause others to forget it, he is unable to silence the voice of his conscience and to obliterate the traces of his misdeeds; at every step he encounters objects that remind him and others of the transgressions that he has committed" (ibid., 155).

70. *TB,* 241.

71. We continue this analysis of the change in the meaning of the body in a later part of this chapter.

72. *TB,* 242.   73. Gn 3:17–19.

74. *TB,* 242.

75. Ibid. Bruce Vawter writes about the change in man's attitude to nature after sin:

John Paul II notes that the relational dimension of shame reveals itself first in the "boundary experience" of sexual shame of the man and the woman: "Then the eyes of both were opened, and they knew that they were naked; and they sewed fig leaves together and made loincloths for themselves."[76] The relational dimension of shame—the fourth element in the change of the meaning of original nakedness—is the mutual shame of man before woman and woman before man. It is what urges them to cover their naked bodies and particularly their sexual differences, before the gaze of the other person.

The catecheses emphasize that a deeper reflection on the relational character of sexual shame leads to a discovery of revealing its deeper source, which John Paul II calls "immanent shame."[77] The pope describes this shame experienced by man and woman as "*a specific difficulty in sensing the human essentiality of one's own body,*" or "a certain constitutive fracture in the human person's interior, *a breakup, as it were, of man's original spiritual and somatic unity.*"[78] The man who experiences immanent shame "realizes for the first time that his body has ceased drawing on the power of the spirit, which raised him to the level of the image of God."[79] Experiencing lust and other weaknesses of the body, this man also suffers from the pangs of an uneasy conscience that informs him of a threat to the ethical value of his conduct and to personal dignity itself.[80]

In the history of theology, the phenomenon indicated by the

"The condemnation of the man in vs. 17–19 is the lengthiest of all, but it is the simplest in import: it is the Yahwist's etiology of the paradox that the kindly earth from which man was taken and which he was set to till is so niggardly in return for all his labor.... Man is set at variance with his natural environment.... What now occurs is that enmity is put between man and the soil, just as enmity was put between the offspring of the woman and the serpent" (Bruce Vawter, *On Genesis: A New Reading* [Garden City, N.Y.: Doubleday, 1977], 85).

76. Gn 3:7.
78. Ibid., 243–44.
80. Ibid., 247–48.

77. *TB*, 242–43.
79. Ibid., 244.

THE BODY THAT REVEALS 59

experience of immanent shame has been defined as "concupiscence" (ἡ ἐπιθυμία, *concupiscentia*). It is worth remembering that already prior to Christianity, Greek philosophers were aware of this tension and division in man. They argued that the evil of some sensual desires is a consequence of their irrationality, a result of their refusal to submit to reason.[81] We owe to biblical revelation the knowledge that this tension and division in man is a result of the original sin of Adam and Eve and that this sinfulness is passed down to every descendant of Adam as lust.[82] In Western theology, it was St. Augustine who systematically explored the biblical data regarding *concupiscentia*, which he defined as a disorder of human nature and a result of the original sin of Adam and Eve.[83] This disorder, which primarily concerns human sensuality, persists in every descendent of Adam even after baptism, which cleanses the soul of the guilt of original sin. Fighting concupiscence is the spiritual task of every Christian, with the support of the grace of redemption.

The appearance of shame as described in the Yahwist account of creation causes a radical and negative transformation of the mutual relationship between man and woman, which John Paul II calls "the insatiability of the union."[84] In accord with the pope's anthropology, this negative change first concerns the meaning of the nakedness of the body, and then deeply penetrates the consciousness of man and woman. After the first sin, the sexual difference between man and woman ceases to be a certain means of achieving a communion of persons, "as if the body in its masculinity and

---

81. Hermann M.-F. Büchsel, "θιμος, ἡ ἐπιθυμία," in *TDNT*, 3:168–69.

82. "For all that is in the world [ἐν τῷ κόσμῳ]—the desire of the flesh [ἡ ἐπιθυμία τῆς σαρκὸς], the desire of the eyes [ἡ ἐπιθυμία τῶν ὀφθαλμῶν], the pride in riches [ἡ ἀλαζονεία τοῦ βίου]—comes not from the Father [ἐκ τοῦ πατρὸς] but from the world [ἐκ τοῦ κόσμου]. And the world and its desire [ἡ ἐπιθυμία αὐτοῦ] are passing away" (1 Jn 2: 16–17; see Büchsel, "θιμος, ἡ ἐπιθυμία," 167–72).

83. "Concupiscence," in *ATA*, 224–27; Alfred Vanneste, *The Dogma of Original Sin* (Brussels: Vander, 1975), 73–111.

84. *TB*, 247.

femininity ceased to be 'free from suspicion' as the substratum of the communion of persons, as if its original function were 'called into doubt' in the consciousness of the man and the woman. What disappears is the simplicity and 'purity' of their original experience, which helped to bring about a singular fullness of mutual self-communication."[85]

The negative transformation of the man-woman relation also deeply imbues human consciousness: "Almost unexpectedly, an insurmountable threshold appeared in their consciousness that limited the original 'self-donation' to the other with full trust in all that constituted one's own identity and at the same time diversity, female on the one side, male on the other. The diversity, or the difference between the male and female sexes, was abruptly sensed and understood as an element of the mutual opposition of persons."[86] After sin, the sexual dimension of the body becomes a problem; the body, which in the state of original innocence was obvious clear sign of the union of persons, becomes for historical man a sign of a rupture of communion and of a permanent division between man and woman brought about by sin.[87]

John Paul II argues that "the insatiability of the union" breaks and limits the spousal meaning of the body: "the human body in its masculinity and femininity has almost lost the power of expressing this love in which the human person becomes a gift."[88] The pope notes that the bodies of man and woman, having lost the natural ability to express the dimension of a gift that calls to communion and the ability to reveal a subjectivity that is open to the other person, become mere objects of attraction and desire:

---

85. Ibid. 86. Ibid., 247–48.

87. In the catecheses, the pope calls attention to the fact that the insatiability of the union thus understood "neither destroys nor excludes the conjugal union willed by the Creator (see Gn 2:24), nor its procreative effects" (*TB*, 252). Rather, it makes its realization more difficult and moves it to another dimension, the dimension of fight against sin and of concern for the culture of chastity.

88. *TB*, 258.

"the subjectivity of the person gives way in some sense to the objectivity of the body."[89] We read in the catecheses as follows:

> Because of the body, man becomes an object for man: the female for the male and vice versa. Concupiscence signifies, so to speak, that the personal relations of man and woman are one-sidedly and reductively tied to the body and to sex, in the sense that these relations become almost incapable of welcoming the reciprocal gift of the person. They neither contain nor treat femininity and masculinity according to the full dimension of personal subjectivity; they do not constitute the expression of communion, but remain one-sidedly determined "by sex."[90]

This process, described above, of treating the other person as an object, creates a threat of mutual "appropriation" that consists in using the other person for one's own ends: "*The relationship of the gift changes into a relationship of appropriation.*"[91] According to John Paul II, the words of God spoken to the woman after the sin indicate the mutual treatment of the other person as an object, which leads to appropriation: "your desire shall be for your husband, and he shall rule over you."[92] These ominous words predict multiple forms of discrimination against women in human history and reveal lust, which leads to the treatment of the other person as an object, as the source of these unjust inequalities.[93]

Indeed, terms such as "treating the other person as an object" and "using the other person" have important sources in Western culture. The *frui-uti* distinction occupies a central place in the thought of St. Augustine; it concerns the attitude to a good that man desires. *Frui* is an attitude of experiencing first of all the highest good—God, whom man should desire and seek for his own sake.[94] *Uti* concerns using all other goods in order to achieve the highest good.

---

89. Ibid., 259.
90. Ibid.
91. Ibid., 260.
92. Gn 3:16.
93. See note 70 above.
94. St. Augustine, *On Christian Doctrine* I, 20–22; also: "Uti/Frui," in *ATA*, 859–61.

In the thought of Immanuel Kant, an important representative of the European Enlightenment, the terms "aims" and "means" obtain their proper meanings in the anthropocentric context of his ethics. The Kantian understanding of these terms is expressed by his formulation of the practical imperative: "So act that you use humanity, whether in your own person or in the person of any other, always at the same time as an end, never merely as a means."[95] Kant's practical imperative seems to be the source of the so-called personalistic norm, central to the philosophical deliberations of Karol Wojtyła's *Love and Responsibility:* "The person is the kind of good, which does not admit of use and cannot be treated as an object of use and as such the means to an end."[96]

The negative moral judgment, repeatedly expressed in the catecheses, of using and treating the person as an object has its roots in the personalistic norm formulated by the then thirty-eight-year-old Karol Wojtyła. Simultaneously, it is worth emphasizing that in the papal theology of the body, Wojtyła's understanding of "aims" and "means," rooted as it is in Kant's thought, is set in a theological context. In accordance with the principles of Christocentric humanism, however, these terms do not thereby lose their anthropocentric character.[97]

As indicated in the introduction to this work, in the Wednesday catecheses John Paul II considers the situation of historical man affected by sin through the prism of Christ's Sermon on the Mount: "You have heard that it was said, 'You shall not commit

95. Immanuel Kant, "Groundwork of the Metaphysics of Morals," in Kant, *Practical Philosophy,* translated by Mary J. Gregor (Cambridge: Cambridge University Press, 1996), 80.

96. Wojtyła, *Love and Responsibility,* 41. The Kantian influence on Wojtyła should not obliterate the fact of Wojtyła's strong criticism of Kant (Karol Wojtyła, *Wykłady lubelskie* [Lublin: Wydawnictwo Naukowe Katolickiego Uniwersytetu Lubelskiego, 1986], 39–57, 144–55; also, Kevin Rickert, "Wojtyła's Personalistic Norm: A Thomistic Analysis," *Nova et vetera* 7, no. 3 (2009): 653–78).

97. John Saward, *Christ Is the Answer: The Christ-Centered Teaching of Pope John Paul II* (Staten Island, N.Y.: Alba House, 1995).

adultery.' But I say to you that everyone who looks at a woman with lust has already committed adultery with her in his heart."[98] According to the pope, a proper interpretation of the words "looks with lust" is most essential to understanding Christ's statement.[99] Christ's words by no means refer to a psychological understanding of lust, which may be described as "an intense orientation toward the object caused by its characteristic value."[100] Rather, the term "lust" used by Christ already contains a negative ethical qualification.

John Paul II clarifies this negative understanding of the term "lust" by differentiating between a subject and object: "It is, in fact, one thing to be aware that the value of sex is part of the whole richness of values with which a feminine being appears to a man; it is quite another thing to 'reduce' the whole personal richness of femininity to this one value, that is, to sex as the fitting object of the satisfaction of one's own sexuality."[101] Lust does not recognize the spousal meaning of the body, but treats the body of the other person as an object and "aims directly toward one and only one end as its precise object: *to satisfy only the body's sexual urge.*"[102] Sexual lust, of which Christ speaks in the Sermon on the Mount, therefore impairs the value of the other person and intentionally reduces the fascination with the other person's sex to one value.[103]

John Paul II writes that when Christ speaks of looking lustfully in the Sermon on the Mount, he draws attention to the re-

---

98. Mt 5:27-28.

99. Michael Waldstein, whose translation of John Paul II's Wednesday catecheses is being used in this book, translates Matthew 5:28 as "But I say to you: Whoever looks at a woman to desire her [in a reductive way] has already committed adultery with her *in his heart*" (*TB*, 225). In his translation of John Paul II's theology of the body, Waldstein decides to use the word "desire" with some qualifiers: lustful, concupiscent, and reductive. In this book, we keep the New Revised Standard Version translation of Matthew 5:28. In John Paul II's theology, the essence of the "lustful look" consists in an improper, sinful, reductive desire. Similarly to Waldstein, therefore, the word "lust" will be exchanged with "concupiscence."

100. *TB*, 286.
101. Ibid., 287-88.
102. Ibid., 288.
103. Ibid., 287-88.

lationship between knowing or looking at the body of the other person and "wanting," which creates the human attitude of sexual lust. "The lustful look" may derive merely from lust, which is an interior disposition, but it may also strengthen and constitute this disposition: "the intentionality of knowledge determines and defines the intentionality of existence itself."[104] In accord with the traditional teaching of the Church on sin, the pope emphasizes that the turning point for intentional and axiological reduction of the fascination with the sex of the other person is the consent of the human will to treat the other person as a mere object to fulfill one's own sexual desire.[105] Then, using biblical language, it can be said that lust overcame the heart of man.

Continuing his analysis of Christ's words from the Sermon on the Mount, John Paul II points to the term "adultery in the heart" as another important expression requiring a more detailed analysis. The key question regarding Christ's statement that "everyone who looks at a woman with lust has already committed adultery with her in his heart"[106] concerns the relation between "adultery in the heart" and the external activity that constitutes the essence of the sin of adultery. The pope specifies that "adultery can only be identified 'in the flesh,' that is, when the two, the man and the woman, who unite with each other in such a way that they become one flesh (see Gn 2:24), are not spouses, that is, husband and wife in the legal sense."[107] There is also no doubt that, according to the commandment of the Decalogue, "you shall not covet your neighbor's wife,"[108] the lustful look at a woman who is not the wife of the one looking is sinful. It seems then, muses John Paul II, that "lustful looks" can only be permitted between spouses. But this interpretation corresponds neither to the internal logic of Christ's

---

104. Ibid., 290.
105. On human free will as a principal source of sin, see *STh* I-II, q. 74; *CCC* 1853, 1856–63.
106. Mt 5:28. 107. *TB*, 295.
108. Ex 20:17.

words, nor to the reflections on the spousal meaning of the body in the catecheses thus far.

John Paul II points out that Christ does not say that the lustful look is evil only when it happens outside of marriage, or when, for example, a man looks in this way at a woman who is not his wife. Rather, the lustful look is always evil, even when the husband looks lustfully at his wife, and the wife at her husband. The truth of this statement presents itself in the light of the above analyses:

> Concupiscence ... changes the very intentionality of the woman's existence "for" the man by reducing the wealth of the perennial call to the communion of persons, the wealth of the deep attraction of masculinity and femininity, to the mere satisfaction of the body's sexual "urge" (which is closely related to the concept of "instinct"). Such a reduction has the effect that the person (in this case the woman) becomes for the other person (the man) above all an object for the possible satisfaction of his own sexual "urge." *In this way, a deformation takes place in the reciprocal "for," which loses its character as a communion of persons in favor of the utilitarian function.*[109]

The essence of the biblical understanding of "lust" and "adultery in the heart" is the reduction of the other person—the subject of the communion of persons achieved through love—to an object used to fulfill a sexual desire. "Adultery in the heart" threatens the spousal meaning of the body of the other person, that is, the person who is being looked at with lust.

The Ethos of Redemption: An Affirmation of the Dignity of the Human Body

John Paul II emphasizes that the truth of Christ's words about "looking with lust" and "committing adultery in the heart" is revealed fully in the context of the ethos of the whole Sermon on

---

109. *TB*, 298.

the Mount.[110] According to the pope, the essence of the unique character of this ethos is the concentration on the human heart. In the light of Christ's Sermon on the Mount, Christian morality is not merely a set of commandments and external deeds, but is a call and strength to change and renew the human heart. The catecheses say that "the new dimension of ethos is always linked with the revelation of the depth that is called 'heart' and with the liberation of the heart from 'concupiscence' *so that man can shine more fully in this heart:* male and female in all the inner truth of the reciprocal 'for.'"[111]

The pope asserts that the internal character of the ethos of the New Testament, most clearly expressed in the Sermon on the Mount, has a fundamental meaning for the Christian theology of the body. The focus on the heart liberates Christian ethics from a Manichean understanding of the human body, which sees corporeality as the source of evil: "The implicit judgment about 'desire' as an act of the concupiscence of the flesh contains in itself, not the negation, but rather the affirmation of the body as an element that, together with the spirit, determines man's ontological subjectivity and participates in his dignity as a person."[112] It is not the body that is responsible for human sin, but the reason and will of the subject. The pope emphasizes that "while for the Manichaean mentality, the body and sexuality constitute, so to speak, an 'anti-value,' for Christianity, on the contrary, they always remain 'a value not sufficiently appreciated.'"[113]

For John Paul II, the focus on the human heart, so characteristic of the New Testament, does not only mean an accusation of the heart: "*In the Bible the threefold concupiscence does not consti-*

---

110. Mt 5:1–7, 29.
111. *TB*, 300. Using a quotation from a classic exegetical work, John Paul II reminds the reader that in its biblical meaning "heart" (καρδία) means the "*centre of man*" and the "*source of will, emotion, thoughts and affections*" (*TB*, 231; Robert Jewett, *Paul's Anthropological Terms: A Study of their Use in Conflict Settings* [Leiden: Brill, 1971], 448).
112. *TB*, 306. 113. Ibid., 307.

tute the fundamental and certainly not the only and absolute *criterion* of anthropology and ethics, although it is without doubt *an important coefficient for understanding man, his actions, and their moral value.*"[114] As a result, the ethics of the New Testament differ radically from the hermeneutics of the three "masters of suspicion": Karl Marx, Sigmund Freud, and Friedrich Nietzsche.[115]

In his unique reflection on this question, the pope points out that to some extent each of these three contemporary thinkers based his anthropology on one component of John's threefold concupiscence: the desires of the flesh, the desires of the eyes, and the pride of life.[116] Moreover, while analyzing, or even deconstructing, the phenomenon of false consciousness, each of the three "masters of suspicion" explained that, in fact, more fundamental mechanisms connected with human libido, and the fight for possession and power, operate beneath the surface of noble values, culture, and education. A precise explanation of this aspect of John Paul II's thesis as based on the analyses of the works of the "masters of suspicion" is beyond the scope of this work; however, using the thought of Friedrich Nietzsche, we may illustrate briefly what such an interpretation of the "hermeneutics of suspicion" would look like in the light of the theology of the First Letter of John.

---

114. Ibid., 311.

115. The pope uses the description of the three thinkers as "masters of suspicion" (*maîtres de soupçon*) after Paul Ricoeur. The relevant passage of Ricoeur's book *Le Conflit des interprétations*, quoted in the catecheses, reads as follows: "The philosopher trained in the school of Descartes knows that things are doubtful, that they are not what they appear to be. Be he never doubts that consciousness is as it appears to itself. In consciousness, meaning and the consciousness of meaning coincide. Since Marx, Nietzsche, and Freud, however, we doubt even this. After doubting the thing, we have begun to doubt consciousness. These three masters of suspicion, however, are not three masters of skepticism. They are surely three great 'destroyers.' ... All three free our horizon for a more authentic speaking, a new reign of truth, not only by means of a 'destructive' critique but by the invention of an art of interpreting.... For the first time comprehension is hermeneutics. Henceforth seeking meaning no longer means spelling out the consciousness of meaning but, rather, *deciphering its expressions*" (Ricoeur, "Psychoanalysis and Contemporary Culture," in Ricoeur, *The Conflict of Interpretations*, 148–49; *TB*, 310).

116. 1 Jn 2, 16–17; also see note 33 above.

In the traditional exegesis of the First Letter of John, the term "pride of life" (ἡ ἀλαζονεία τοῦ βίου) means a disordered and fatal tendency to self-aggrandize and think oneself superior to others, vainly seeking praise, popularity, and fame.[117] Traditionally, the Christian virtue of humility was understood as the opposite of the sin of pride. In the Nietzschean philosophy, however, Christian humility was "unmasked" as a characteristic of the weak and helpless; yet the psychological mechanism of resentment allows humility to be presented by "slaves" as something positive.[118] Therefore, it is the "pride of life," so depreciated by Christianity, that must become the positive characteristic distinguishing the Nietzschean "superman" as the source of his vital force, creativity, and "the will to power."[119]

117. St. Augustine, *Confessions* X, 36–41, translated by E. B. Pusey (Oxford: Parker, 1943), 215–20.
118. "There is nothing in life of any value except for power, assuming that life in itself is a will of power. Morality guarded losers against nihilism, for it ascribed infinite value to everyone, metaphysical value, and gave them a place in the order of things that was at variance with the order of the world's power and hierarchy: morality taught devotion, humility etc. If faith in this morality really dies, then losers will not be able to find solace any longer—and will be lost" (Friedrich Nietzsche, *Pisma pozostałe*, translated by Bogdan Baran [Kraków: Inter-esse, 1994], 208).
119. "One either obeys as a slave and a weakling, or one gives orders. The latter is the way of any proud natures, who interpret every obligation as law which one imposes upon oneself and others, even if it is imposed upon one externally. This is a great thing in morality—'I should do what I want to,' is its formula" (Nietzsche, *Pisma pozostałe*, 37). In the traditional exegesis of the first letter of St. John "the desire of the eyes" (ἡ ἐπιθυμία τῶν ὀφθαλμῶν) means man's disordered and sinful turning toward the possession of goods, both material and spiritual (St. Augustine, *Confessions* X, 34–35, 205–7; *CCSL* 27, 182–86). In this context the papal metaphor points to Karl Marx, who sees in man primarily the dimension of *homo oeconomicus*, for whom the most important thing is the possession and production of goods (Leszek Kolakowski, *Main Currents of Marxism: Its Origins, Growth, and Dissolution*, translated by P.S. Falla [Oxford: Oxford University Press, 1981], vol. 1, 132–44). John's "desire of the flesh" (ἡ ἐπιθυμία τῆς σαρκὸς) concerns the disordered, sinful turning toward sensual pleasures, among others, toward sexual pleasure (St. Augustine, *Confessions* X, 30–33, 199–205; *CCSL* 27, 176–82). Without going into detailed justification for this reference, John Paul II points to Sigmund Freud, who sees in man primarily desires suppressed by culture, mainly the sexual *libido* (Sigmund Freud, *The Future of an Illusion*, trans. by W. D. Robson—Scott [Garden City, N.Y.: Doubleday, 1961]).

John Paul II emphasizes that the ethos of the Sermon on the Mount, unlike the "masters of suspicion," does not accuse the human heart, but rather calls it to accept the gift of redemption. For Christ, the truth about "threefold concupiscence" is only a partial truth about the human heart. The ethos of "redemption of the body" calls man to *"rediscover,* or even better, to realize, the spousal meaning of the body and to express in this way the interior freedom of the gift, that is, the freedom of that spiritual state and power that derive from mastery over the concupiscence of the flesh."[120] Man, therefore, is not engulfed completely by threefold concupiscence, as the grace of redemption helps man and woman reread anew the spousal and parental meaning of the human body, inscribed in them in the mystery of creation.

The term "redemption of the body," frequently used in the Wednesday catecheses, is taken from a passage of the Letter to the Romans, which shows the cosmic dimension of Christ's redemption:

I consider that the sufferings of this present time are not worth comparing with the glory about to be revealed to us. For the creation waits with eager longing for the revealing of the children of God; for the creation was subjected to futility, not of its own will but by the will of the one who subjected it, in hope that the creation itself will be set free from its bondage to decay and will obtain the freedom of the glory of the children of God. We know that the whole creation has been groaning in labor pains until now; and not only the creation, but we ourselves, who have the first fruits of the Spirit, groan inwardly while we wait for adoption, the redemption of our bodies [τὴν ἀπολύτρωσιν τοῦ σώματος ἡμῶν].[121]

In this fragment of the Letter to the Romans, Paul examines human suffering in relation to the "vanity" and "corruption" of creation. According to Joseph Fitzmyer, the author of the letter draws here upon two Old Testament theological themes; he

120. *TB,* 313.   121. Rom 8:18–23.

presents the "vanity" and "corruption" of creation as effects of the original sin of Adam and Eve and speaks of the eschatological wait for the "new heavens and a new earth" promised by God.[122] In order to connect the idea of the salvation of man by Christ with the renewal of the whole of creation, the author of the letter speaks of the "redemption of the body." Fitzmyer insists that this eschatological salvation "is no longer considered from an anthropological point of view; it is now recast in cosmic terms. Human bodies that are said to await such redemption (8:23) are merely part of the entire material creation, which is itself groaning in travail until such redemption occurs. For the Christ-event is expected to affect not only human beings, but all the material or physical creation as well."[123]

In the Letter to the Romans, the redemption of the body means the workings of grace in human corporeality, which is especially marked by the threefold concupiscence spoken of in the First Letter of John. John Paul II's apt formulation "the ethos of the redemption of the body" calls attention to the fact that Christ's grace touches the human body by transforming the spirit and the human heart. In the language of the New Testament, this transformation happens first of all through a purity of heart, as spoken of in the Beatitudes: "Blessed are the pure in heart [οἱ καθαροὶ τῇ καρδίᾳ], for they will see God."[124]

The pope observes that the notion of purity in the theology of the New Testament has two meanings: general and specific. The general meaning identifies impurity with sin and purity with holiness. In the specific meaning, purity is seen as the opposite of sexual impurity. The pope's interpretation of certain biblical texts is worthy of lengthier examination because of the light it casts

---

122. Is 66:17, 66:22. Joseph A. Fitzmyer, SJ, *Romans: A New Translation with Introduction and Commentary* (New York: Doubleday, 1993), 505.

123. Fitzmyer, *Romans*, 505–6.

124. Mt 5: 8.

on anthropological notions fundamental for the theology of the body.

To illustrate the general, more universal meaning of purity, John Paul II analyzes two important passages from the New Testament: Christ's words referring to ritual purity[125] and Paul's statements about life according to the flesh and life according to the Spirit.[126] In the first passage, Christ explains the meaning of true purity in answer to the Pharisees' surprised question as to why his disciples do not wash their hands before eating: "But what comes out of the mouth proceeds from the heart [ἐκ τῆς καρδίας] and this is what defiles. For out of the heart come evil intentions, murder, adultery [μοιχεῖαι], fornication [πορνεῖαι], theft, false witness, slander. These are what defile a person, but to eat with unwashed hands does not defile."[127]

In accord with the ethos of the Sermon on the Mount, Jesus reinterprets in these words the ritual notion of purity by emphasizing that both moral purity and impurity have their source in the human heart. In this general view "every moral good is a manifestation of purity and every moral evil a manifestation of impurity."[128]

Significantly, in first-century Judaism, inspired as it was by the Old Testament, the fundamental meaning of purity had a ritual character and was connected with cultic practice. Impurity referred to persons (lepers, the dead), to animals (impure animals, carrion), or to things, and could be transferred by touch, or even by the presence of the impure person or thing in a given place, for example, in a home, or on board a ship. The impure person was not to appear in the temple, or even to pray, before cleansing, which was usually

---

125. Mt 15:18–20.
126. Gal 5:16–23.
127. Mt 15:18–20.
128. *TB*, 328. John Paul II refers very briefly to the basic semantic source of purity, which is washing of the human body of physical dirt (*TB*, 327). This reference appears in the catecheses only in the context of a distortion of the meaning of purity by its ritual meaning. Paul Ricoeur analyzes these semantic sources of religious purity as washing from dirt more extensively (Ricoeur, *The Symbolism of Evil*, 25–46).

done by means of water and which at times also required making special sacrifices.¹²⁹ Given this context, Friedrich Hauck is correct to state that "it is of the essence of the New Testament religion that the older ritual concept of purity is not merely transcended, but rejected as non-obligatory. The idea of material impurity drops away. Religious and moral purity replaces ritual and cultic."¹³⁰

In Pauline theology the general understanding of purity appears in the context of the opposition of "flesh" and "Spirit" as well as "works that spring from the flesh" and "works of the Spirit." It is the opposition of "flesh" and "Spirit" that undergirds, for instance, the theology of the Letter to the Galatians: "Live by the Spirit [πνεύματι περιπατεῖτε], I say, and do not gratify the desires of the flesh [ἐπιθυμίαν σαρκὸς]. For what the flesh [ἡ σὰρξ] desires is opposed to the Spirit, and what the Spirit [τὸ πνεῦμα] desires is opposed to the flesh; for these are opposed to each other, to prevent you from doing what you want."¹³¹

The opposition between "works that spring from the flesh" and "works of the Spirit" can also be seen in the Letter to the Romans: "For those who live according to the flesh [κατὰ σάρκα] set their minds on the things of the flesh, but those who live according to the Spirit [κατὰ πνεῦμα] set their minds on the things of the Spirit."¹³²

John Paul II strongly excludes the possibility of a Manichean interpretation of these quotations from Paul's letters: "The issue is not just the body (matter) and spirit (the soul) as two essentially distinct anthropological components that have from the 'beginning' constituted man's very essence. What is presupposed is, rather, that disposition of powers formed in man together with original sin, the sin in which every 'historical' human being shares."¹³³

---

129. Rudolf Meyer, "καθαρός: Clean and Unclean outside the NT: Judaism," in *TDNT*, 3:418–21.
130. Friedrich Hauck, "καθαρός: Clean and Unclean in the NT," in *TDNT*, 3:423–24.
131. Gal 5:16–17. 132. Rom 8:5.
133. *TB*, 330.

Clearly, "the body" in the above statements is not so much the external physical human body, but, rather, that part of internal human life that is subject to sin. Moreover, the expression "life according to the flesh" points to John's "threefold concupiscence."[134] This Pauline understanding of the body is confirmed by the opposition between "works of the flesh" and "the fruit of the Spirit," as it is presented, for instance, in the Letter to the Galatians: "Now the works of the flesh [τὰ ἔργα τῆς σαρκός] are obvious: fornication [πορνεία], impurity [ἀκαθαρσία], licentiousness [ἀσέλγεια], idolatry, sorcery; enmities, strife, jealousy, anger, quarrels, dissensions, factions, envy, drunkenness, carousing, and things like these ... the fruit of the Spirit is love, joy, peace, patience, kindness, generosity, faithfulness, gentleness, and self-control [ἐγκράτεια]. There is no law against such things."[135]

John Paul II notes that among the works of the flesh that Paul lists are also the sins that have a spiritual and internal character, that is, antagonisms, rivalry, bad temper, and jealousy. This is justified, because in Pauline thought "all sins are expressions of life 'according to the flesh' in contrast to 'life according to the Spirit.'"[136] The general understanding of "works of the flesh" is thus analogical to the general understanding of impurity in Christ's words concerning ritual purity.[137] According to the New Testament

---

134. 1 Jn 2:16–17. Udo Schnelle writes about St. Paul's understanding of the body (σάρξ) thus: "Those who live by their own devices and rely on themselves are assigned by Paul to the realm of the flesh. He calls the Corinthians 'people of the flesh' (σαρκίνοις), infants in Christ (1 Cor 3, 1) who live in human ways and thus according to the flesh (1 Cor 3, 3). They are oriented toward what is in the foreground and external, they let themselves be blinded by the visible, and they cannot press forward to the hidden but all-determining reality of God.... The 'people of the flesh' are characterized by self-involvement and self-sufficiency; they build on their own abilities and make their knowledge the measure of what is rational and real. In so doing, however, they are not aware that they are the ones who are delivered up helplessly to the dominating power of sin. A life κατὰ σάρκα means a life without access to God, a life that is captive to what is earthly and perishable" (Udo Schnelle, *The Human Condition. Anthropology in the Teachings of Jesus, Paul and John* [Minneapolis: Fortress Press, 1996], 60–61).

135. Gal 5:19–23.   136. *TB*, 337.
137. Mt 15:18–20.

ethos, then, every sin is an impurity and a work of the flesh because it opposes the spiritual energy that is derived from the Holy Spirit who transforms man.

The passage from the First Letter to the Galatians cited earlier also includes a more detailed and specific understanding of purity and impurity.[138] Therefore, "the works of the flesh," that is, impure sins in the general meaning, also include fornication (πορνεία), impurity (ἀκαθαρσία), and licentiousness (ἀσέλγεια). These impure deeds are contrasted in the Letter to the Galatians with "the fruit of the Spirit," that is, mastery (ἐγκράτεια), which, as the pope emphasizes, was defined as continence or moderation (*temperantia*) according to classical Christian ethics: "One can recognize this 'mastery' as a virtue that concerns continence in the area of all desires of the senses, above all in the sexual sphere, and thus in antithesis to 'fornication, impurity, licentiousness' and also to 'drunkenness' and 'orgies.'"[139]

According to John Paul II, the following passage from the First Letter of St. Paul to the Thessalonians sheds light on clearly the specific understanding of purity in the theology of St. Paul:

For this is the will of God, your sanctification [ὁ ἁγιασμὸς]: that you abstain from fornication [ἀπὸ τῆς πορνείας]; that each one of you know how to control your own body in holiness and honor [ἐν ἁγιασμῷ καὶ τιμῇ], not with lustful passion [μὴ ἐν πάθει ἐπιθυμίας], like the Gentiles who do not know God.... For God did not call us to impurity [ἐπὶ ἀκαθαρσίᾳ] but in holiness [ἐν ἁγιασμῷ].[140]

The pope points to two dimensions of the virtue of purity, as recommended by St. Paul to Christians: one negative and the other positive. The first dimension is "to abstain from fornication,"

---

138. Gal 5:19–23.
139. *TB*, 341. Walter Grundmann, "ἐγκράτεια," in *TDNT*, 3:339–42; Ulrich Luck, "σώφρον," in *TDNT*, 7:1097–103; Raymond Saint-Jean, "Tempérance," in *DS*, vol. 15, col. 142–49.
140. 1 Thes 4:3–5.7.

which consists in "holding back the impulses of sense-desire."[141] The positive dimension of purity is keeping the body "in holiness and honor," which is a return to perceiving the whole of the human body in the light of the mystery of creation, where everything "was good."[142] As a result, purity focuses on *"the dignity of the body, that is, on the dignity of the person* in relation to his or her own body, to the masculinity or femininity that shows itself in that body."[143]

John Paul II notes that purity may be understood in two ways: as a virtue and as a gift of the Holy Spirit. In the first meaning, purity is the effect of man's spiritual effort, which, as noted above, has negative and positive dimensions. In the second meaning, purity has a charismatic character. The pope emphasizes that in the traditional teaching of the Church about the seven gifts of the Holy Spirit the gift of piety (*pietas*) is the closest to the virtue of purity: "piety as a gift of the Holy Spirit seems to serve purity in a particular way by making the human subject sensitive to the dignity that belongs to the human body in virtue of the mystery of creation and of redemption."[144]

The Resurrection: The Virginal Meaning of the Body

The next statement Christ makes in reference to the meaning of the human body that is fundamental for John Paul II's "three-

---

141. *TB*, 343.
142. Gn 1:12.
143. *TB*, 349.
144. Ibid., 353. In his classic formulation, St. Thomas Aquinas argues that the gift of piety (*pietas*) perfects the cardinal virtue of justice. A just man shows proper reverence to God but a man enriched by the gift of piety sees God, first of all, as a loving Father and may enter into a relationship with him based on trust and love. *Pietas* also changes one's way of treating others, because it enables one to see in them daughters and sons of the Heavenly Father. John Paul II refers to this meaning of the gift of piety in his catecheses (*STh* I-II 68, 4; II-II 121, 1–2; also: Ambrose Gardeil, OP, *The Holy Spirit in Christian Life* [St. Louis: Herder Book 1953], 50–60; Irénée Noye, "Piété," in *DS*, vol. 12–2, col. 1694–1743).

dimensional vision of man" appears in the context of the discussion about the levirate law.[145] In their discussion with Christ, which is related by all three Synoptics, the Sadducees attempt to demonstrate the impossibility of the resurrection of the dead:

Teacher, Moses wrote for us that if a man's brother dies, leaving a wife but no child, the man shall marry the widow and raise up children for his brother. There were seven brothers; the first married and, when he died, left no children; and the second married her and died, leaving no children; and the third likewise; none of the seven left children. Last of all the woman herself died. In the resurrection whose wife will she be? For the seven had married her.[146]

Referring to the authority of Moses, which was greatly valued by the Sadducees, Christ refutes their conclusion: "And as for the dead being raised, have you not read in the book of Moses, in the story about the bush, how God said to him, 'I am the God of Abraham, the God of Isaac, and the God of Jacob'? He is God not of the dead, but of the living; you are quite wrong."[147]

John Paul II comments on Christ's statement that God "is not God of the dead, but of the living": "One can only understand this key statement, in which Christ interprets the words addressed to Moses from the burning bush, if *one admits the reality of a life that does not end with death*. Moses' fathers in the faith, Abraham, Isaac, and Jacob, are living persons for God ('for all live for him,' Lk 20:38), although according to human criteria they should be numbered among the dead."[148]

Even more significant for John Paul II's theology of the body are other statements made by Christ during his discussion with the Sadducees, which are recorded thus in the Gospel according to Luke: "Those who belong to this age marry and are given in

145. Mt 22:24–30; Mk 12:18–27; Lk 20:27–40.
146. Mk 12:19–23.   147. Mk 12:26–27.
148. *TB*, 384.

marriage; but those who are considered worthy of a place in that age and in the resurrection from the dead neither marry nor are given in marriage. Indeed they cannot die anymore, because they are like angels [ἰσάγγελοι], and are children of God [υἱοί εἰσιν θεοῦ], being children of the resurrection."[149]

John Paul II observes that for the Sadducees, who do not accept an anthropological soul-body dualism, Christ's words about "the future world" also unambiguously indicate the resurrection of human bodies: the resurrection of bodies in their masculinity and femininity. Nonetheless, Christ states: "Marriage and procreation do not constitute man's eschatological future. In the resurrection they lose, so to speak, their *raison d'être*. That 'other world' about which Luke speaks (20:35) means the definitive fulfillment of the human race, the quantitative closure of that circle of beings created in the image and likeness of God."[150] Therefore, John Paul II asserts that the resurrected human body may be defined as "virginal";[151] the new meaning of this human body no longer expresses the procreative dimension of marital life.

As John Paul II sees it, Christ's words that men and women will be "like angels" (ἰσάγγελοι) and will be "children of God" (υἱοί θεοῦ) in the world to come reveal important information about the eschatological state of man.[152] Without a doubt, being "like angels" cannot mean that human nature will be made akin to angelic nature through a loss of the body after the Resurrection. Rather, Christ speaks of a new "spiritualization of man,"[153] that is, a new entrusting of the body to the spirit, which will put an end to the painful tension between flesh and spirit experienced by historical man. Biblical revelation points to this tension and conflict: "For what the flesh desires [ἡ γὰρ σὰρξ] is opposed to the Spirit, and what the Spirit (τὸ πνεῦμα) desires is opposed to the flesh."[154]

149. Lk 20:34–36.
151. Ibid., 393.
153. *TB*, 389.
150. *TB*, 387–88.
152. Lk 20:36.
154. Gal 5:17.

John Paul II notes that while in the present life the harmony of the body and spirit is the effect of a spiritual effort on the part of man, in the future life it will be the result of a new outpouring of grace onto man.[155]

According to John Paul II, Christ's words that speak of men and women becoming "children of God" foretell this new grace in the future life (the pope uses the term "divinization of man"). Another term used in the catecheses to describe the state of eschatological man is a formulation taken from classical Christian eschatology: the vision of God "face to face" and "the beatific vision of the Divine Being."[156] The pope also adds that the beatific vision of God cannot be understood as mere intellectual knowledge, at least not according to the meaning bestowed on this term by modern epistemology. Rather, this term means that the whole man, body and soul, experiences the Trinity by virtue of grace.

The primary object of man's eschatological *visio beatifica* will be the Love in the communion of the three divine Persons. This beatific vision will "reveal to him [man] in a living and experiential way the '*self-communication*' of God to everything created and, in particular, *to man, [a self-communication] that is God's most personal 'self-giving': in his very divinity to man,* to that being who has from the beginning borne his image and likeness within himself."[157]

The pope writes that the human experience of Trinitarian Love in the future life will consist of man's participation in this

---

155. The pope recalls that St. Paul also writes about a new spiritualization of man after the resurrection in the First Letter to the Corinthians: "It is sown a physical body, it is raised a spiritual body. If there is a physical body, there is also a spiritual body. Thus it is written, 'The first man, Adam, became a living being'; the last Adam became a life-giving spirit. But it is not the spiritual that is first, but the physical, and then the spiritual" (1 Cor 15:44–46). We will return to St. Paul's statements about "the first Adam" and "the last Adam," important as these are for papal anthropology, in the reflections on the image of God in man.

156. *TB*, 393.

157. Ibid., 393.

Love and, simultaneously, of man's reciprocation of this Love. For the proper human response to God's self-giving to man—one that corresponds to the "logic of love"—will be man's complete and beatifying self-giving to God. This response will absorb "the person's whole psychosomatic subjectivity," and in it man "will concentrate and express all the energies of his own personal and at the same time psychosomatic subjectivity."[158] Man's self-giving to God and his sharing in God's love can be described as a participation in the communion of the Holy Trinity.

John Paul II points to two fundamental consequences of man's participation in God's love. The first will be the happiness and fulfillment of man, which the pope refers to as "a perfectly mature subjectivity."[159] The eschatological reality "will confirm the law of the integral order of the person, according to which the perfection of communion is not only conditioned by the spiritual perfection or maturity of the subject, but also in turn determines it."[160]

The truth of the faith about "the communion of saints" (*communio sanctorum*) indicates the second fruit of eschatological unity with God. In accord with John Paul II's anthropology, which deems interpersonal relations as constitutive for the person, the human community will also find its perfect fulfillment in God.[161] Moreover, "this concentration of knowledge ('vision') and love on God himself—a concentration that cannot be anything but full participation in God's inner life, that is, in trinitarian Reality itself—will at the same time be the discovery in God of the whole "world" of relations that are constitutive of the world's perennial order ('cosmos')."[162]

---

158. Ibid., 395.
159. Ibid., 394.
160. Ibid.
161. On the relational character of papal anthropology see note 105 above.
162. *TB*, 395. Cardinal Joseph Ratzinger writes about an eschatological "finding the whole world in God" in the context of the theological differentiation between individual judgment, which in the case of every man happens at the moment of death, and the Last Judgment, which will happen at the end of time (Joseph Ratzinger, *Death and Eternal*

John Paul II emphasizes that the eschatological state of man makes it possible to look in a new way at the spousal meaning of the human body. As stated earlier, the spousal meaning of the body is realized in history in marital and parental terms. However, "marriage and procreation do not definitively determine the original and fundamental meaning of being a body nor of being, as a body, male and female. Marriage and procreation only give concrete reality to that meaning in the dimensions of history. The resurrection indicates the closure of the historical dimension."[163] In the life to come, the spousal meaning of the body will be realized in a different way than in history. Nonetheless, it will retain its two fundamental meanings: being the manifestation of the person, and being a sign of the call for the person to be fulfilled in a communion of persons. Because in the future life the spousal meaning of the body will be fulfilled, above all, through love between eschatological man and God, it may also be described as the virginal meaning of the body.

Before reflecting further on the virginal meaning of the body, we should recall that the structure of John Paul II's catecheses on the theology of the body is based on the distinction between the three theological ages of human history, that is, the beginning, the time of the man of threefold concupiscence, and the time of the resurrection. These historical periods, however, are interrelated. The place where these ages meet, permeate one another, and "fight" against one another is in the heart of every man living in history.

According to John Paul II, the beginning is present in some way in the memory and heart of every historical man; it is present "at the root of every human experience."[164] Similarly, the reality

---

Life, translated by Michael Waldstein [Washington, D.C.: The Catholic University of America Press, 1988], 181–91).

163. *TB*, 399.
164. *TB*, 171.

of redemption and of the resurrection is, to some extent, an object of longing and hope for sinful man. After original sin, every man bears this reality "in the depth of the experience of his being, or, rather, that he is in some way on the way toward them as toward dimensions that fully justify the very meaning of his being body."[165]

Only by taking into consideration this three-dimensional, integral theory of human experience can we understand the meaning of the papal reflection on the special calling that concerns some of the descendents of Adam and Eve, the calling to devote oneself solely to God in virginity and celibacy.

John Paul II bases his reflection on continence for the kingdom of heaven first of all on Christ's discussion with the Pharisees on the indissolubility of marriage in the context of a writ of dismissal.[166] In the course of this discussion, when the disciples reply to the teaching of Christ that "if such is the case of a man with his wife, it is better not to marry," the Teacher explains that "not everyone can accept this teaching, but only those to whom it is given. For there are eunuchs who have been so from birth, and there are eunuchs who have been made eunuchs by others, and there are eunuchs who have made themselves eunuchs [εὐνοῦχοι], for the sake of the kingdom of heaven [διὰ τὴν βασιλείαν]. Let anyone accept this who can."[167]

John Paul II concentrates his analysis on the third group indicated by Christ: "one can say that the choice of continence for the kingdom of heaven is a charismatic orientation toward that eschatological state in which human beings 'take neither wife nor husband.'"[168] In the future life, continence will be the proper state of life of men and women, who will be "like angels." For historical man, however, continence is an anticipation of the future life and

---

165. Ibid., 398.
167. Mt 19:10–12.
166. Mt 19:3–9.
168. *TB*, 414.

an eschatological sign. The pope explains this reality of the eschatological sign of continence when writing about those who choose virginity or celibacy:

> This way of existing as a human being (male and female) points out the eschatological "virginity" of the risen man, in which, I would say, the absolute and eternal spousal meaning of the glorified body will be revealed in union with God himself, by seeing him "face to face," glorified moreover through the union of a perfect intersubjectivity that will unite all the "sharers in the other world," men and women, in the mystery of the communion of saints. Earthly continence "for the kingdom of God" is without doubt a sign that *indicates* this truth and this reality. It is a sign that the body, whose end is not death, tends toward glorification; already by this very fact it is, I would say, a testimony among men that anticipates the future resurrection.[169]

John Paul II calls to mind that in the biblical history of redemption the ideal of continence for the kingdom of heaven had important realizations. Above all, every choice for continence for the kingdom consists in following Christ (*imitatio Christi*), who himself remained unmarried. Moreover, the fundamental characteristic of continence for the kingdom is spousal love, for the supernatural purpose of this vocation, as indicated by Christ's use of the term "for the kingdom" (διὰ τὴν βασιλείαν), is a "*particular response to the love* of the Divine Bridegroom," and acquires "*the meaning of an act of spousal love,* that is, of a spousal gift of self with the end of answering in a particular way the Redeemer's spousal love."[170]

---

169. Ibid., 419.

170. Ibid., 436. Moving testimonies of such a spousal self-gift to Christ can often be found in the writings of the saints. Saint Faustina Kowalska writes thus about her spousal love: "I came to know how very much God loves me. Eternal is His love for me. It was at vespers. In simple words, which flowed from the heart, I made to God a vow of perpetual chastity. From that moment I felt a greater intimacy with God, my Spouse" (Faustina Kowalska, *Divine Mercy in my Soul: The Diary of Sr. M. Faustina Kowalska* [Stockbridge, Mass.: Marian Press, 1987], 9). In another passage of her diary we can find a clear refer-

The virginal marriage of Mary and Joseph is the second supernatural example of continence for Christians. John Paul II writes thus about the birth of Christ and of his relationship to his earthly parents:

> Although he is born from her like every man, as a son from his mother, although this coming into the world was accompanied also by the presence of a man who was Mary's betrothed and [then], before the law and men, her husband, still Mary's motherhood was virginal; and to this virginal motherhood corresponded the virginal mystery of Joseph, who, following the voice from above, did not hesitate to "take Mary ... because what is begotten in her comes from the Holy Spirit" (Mt 1:20).[171]

The pope emphasizes that the virginal marriage of Mary and Joseph—in a manner characteristic of every choice of continence for the kingdom—became the witness of "a fruitfulness different from that of the flesh, that is, of a fruitfulness of the Spirit" as well as the witness of "the perfect communion of persons, of Man and Woman in the conjugal covenant."[172]

Sacramentality of the Body

In the part of Wednesday catecheses entitled "Sacrament," John Paul II takes on another theological attempt to overcome a dualistic anthropology by reflecting on the sacrament of marriage and the changes the understanding thereof has undergone throughout the centuries. The primary biblical text for his reflec-

---

ence to the Song of Songs: "I turned to the Blessed Sacrament and said to Jesus, 'Jesus, my Spouse, do You not see that my soul is dying because of its longing for You? How can You hide Yourself from a heart that loves You so sincerely? Forgive me, Jesus; may Your holy will be done in me. I will suffer silently like a dove, without complaining'" (ibid., 15; cf. Sg 1:15; 2:14; 3:1–4; 4:1; 5:2; 6:9).
171. *TB,* 420.
172. Ibid., 420–21. In his exhortation on St. Joseph, *Redemptoris custos,* John Paul II writes that Mary, united with Joseph by the bond of virginal and spousal love, reveals the mystery of the Church, virgin and bride (*RC,* 20).

tions on the sacrament is an excerpt from the fifth chapter of the Letter to the Ephesians. Despite its lengthiness, we will begin by quoting it:

> Be subject to one another out of reverence for Christ. Wives, be subject to your husbands as you are to the Lord. For the husband is the head of the wife just as Christ is the head of the church, the body of which he is the Savior. Just as the church is subject to Christ, so also wives ought to be, in everything, to their husbands. Husbands, love your wives, just as Christ loved the church and gave himself up for her in order to make her holy by cleansing her with the washing of water by the word, so as to present the church to himself in splendor, without a spot or wrinkle or anything of the kind—yes, so that she may be holy and without blemish. In the same way, husbands should love their wives as they do their own bodies. He who loves his wife loves himself. For no one ever hates his own body, but he nourishes and tenderly cares for it, just as Christ does for the church, because we are members of his body. *For this reason a man will leave his father and mother and be joined to his wife, and the two will become one flesh.* This is a great mystery, and I am applying it to Christ and the church. Each of you, however, should love his wife as himself, and a wife should respect her husband.[173]

According to John Paul II, the proper understanding of the first sentence of this passage from Ephesians is key to the proper interpretation of the entire text: "Be subject to one another out of reverence for Christ" (ἐν φόβῳ Χριστοῦ). The primary message of this exhortation is that the relationship of the spouses takes on its proper shape only as the fruit of the common reverence of wife and husband to Christ. This fundamental "reverence for Christ," notes the pope, is close in its meaning to the Old Testament notion of the fear of God, which in the tradition of the Church is called "piety" (Latin *pietas*), or, most simply, may be defined as "reverence for holiness."[174]

---

173. Eph 5:21–33.
174. *TB*, 472. See note 56 above.

John Paul II emphasizes that the common reverence of wife and husband for Christ leads to a mutual subjection of the spouses. This mutuality of subjection is the condition for a proper understanding of the following passage: "Wives, be subject to your husbands as you are to the Lord [ὡς τῷ κυρίῳ]." The pope rejects any interpretation of this text that would suggest an inferior status of the woman in respect to the man:

> When he expresses himself in this way, the author does not intend to say that the husband is the "master" of the wife and that the interpersonal covenant proper to marriage is a contract of domination by the husband over the wife.... Love excludes every kind of submission by which the wife would become a servant or slave of the husband, an object of one-sided submission. Love makes the *husband simultaneously subject* to the wife, and *subject* in this *to the Lord himself,* as the wife is to the husband. The community or unity that they should constitute because of marriage is realized through a reciprocal gift, which is also a mutual submission.[175]

The reciprocal self-giving in love of the husband and the wife thus creates a mutual submission, which is properly understood and acceptable only in the light of a loving and mutual self-gift.

A reflection on the vocation to marriage, seen in the light of the saving mystery of Christ, continues in a further part of the discussed passage:

> Wives, be subject to your husbands as you are to the Lord. For the husband is the head of the wife [κεφαλὴ τῆς γυναικὸς] just as Christ is the head of the church [κεφαλὴ τῆς ἐκκλησίας], the body of which he is the Savior [σωτὴρ τοῦ σώματος]. Just as the church is subject to Christ, so also wives ought to be, in everything, to their husbands. Husbands, love your wives, just as Christ loved the church and gave himself up for her.[176]

The relationship between the husband and the wife is compared by the author of the Letter to Ephesians to the relationship

---

175. *TB,* 473–74.
176. Eph 5:22–25.

between Christ and the Church. John Paul II calls attention to the double meaning of this analogy. On the one hand, the reality of marital love helps us to understand better the mystery of the eternal love of Christ for man and for the Church. On the other hand, this analogy reveals an important truth about Christian marriage: "Marriage corresponds to the vocation of Christians only when it mirrors the love that Christ, the Bridegroom, gives to the Church, his Bride, and which the Church (in likeness to the wife who is 'subject,' and thus completely given) seeks to give back to Christ in return."[177]

The analogy between human marital love and Christ's love for the Church is described in the Letter to the Ephesians with reference to a metaphor from human experience—the relationship between the head and the body. It should be clearly noted that in Pauline theology, the term "head of the Church" (κεφαλὴ τῆς ἐκκλησίας) has a Christological meaning. Christ is the head because he is the Savior of his mystical body (σωτὴρ τοῦ σώματος)—that is, the Church—which "receives from him everything by which she becomes and is his body, that is, the fullness of salvation as a gift of Christ, who 'gave himself for her' to the end."[178]

Calling the Church the Body of Christ also reveals the true nature of the Church: "The Church is herself in the degree to which she, as body, receives from Christ her head the whole gift of salvation as a fruit of Christ's love and of his giving for the Church: fruit of Christ's giving to the end."[179] The Christological and ecclesiological understanding of the metaphor of the head and the body allows us to comprehend the redemptive love of the Savior as spousal love: "Giving himself for the Church, with the same redeeming act, Christ united himself once and for all with her as the Bridegroom to the Bride, as husband with the wife."[180]

---

177. *TB*, 476.
178. Ibid., 478. For more on the concept of "the head" in the theology of St. Paul see Heinrich Schlier, "κεφαλη," in *TDNT*, 3:680–81.
179. *TB*, 478.   180. Ibid.

The merging of the redeeming and spousal dimensions of Christ's love for the Church becomes even more apparent in the next part of the passage from the Letter to the Ephesians: "Husbands, love your wives, just as Christ loved the church and gave himself up for her, in order to make her holy by cleansing her with the washing of water by the word, so as to present the church to himself in splendor, without a spot or wrinkle or anything of the kind—yes, so that she may be holy and without blemish."[181] The aim of Christ's redemptive love is the sanctification of the Church, and this happens through the cleansing of sinners in the sacrament of baptism: "cleansing her with the washing of water by the word."

John Paul II notes that calling the sacrament of baptism a "cleansing with water" clearly hearkens back to the ritual of ablution preceding a wedding in ancient cultures. Thus, Christ's intention "to present the church to himself in splendor, without a spot or wrinkle or anything of the kind, ... so that she may be holy and without blemish" seems to "indicate that moment of the wedding when the bride is led to the bridegroom already clothed in the wedding dress and adorned for the wedding."[182]

The Christological and ecclesiological metaphor of the head and the body in the Letter to the Ephesians points to the deep unity between husband and wife. This unity should resemble the unity between Christ and the Church; after all, both relationships are compared in the Letter to the Ephesians to the relationship between the head and the body. We read as follows in a later part of the fragment under consideration: "In the same way, husbands should love their wives as they do their own bodies. He who loves his wife loves himself. For no one ever hates his own body, but

---

181. Eph 5:25–27.
182. *TB*, 482. Margaret MacDonald interprets this verse from the Letter to the Ephesians in a very similar way: "The preparation of a Jewish woman for marriage by washing with water (Ez 16:9; cf. Ez 6:8–14) is juxtaposed with the ritual of baptism (cf. 1 Cor 6:11; Ti 3:5; Heb 10:22). In all likelihood the expression 'with the word' refers to the name of Christ spoken in the midst of baptism" (Margaret Y. MacDonald, *Colossians and Ephesians* [Collegeville, Minn.: Liturgical Press, 2000], 328).

he nourishes and tenderly cares for it, just as Christ does for the church."[183] John Paul II emphasizes that marital unity has a moral character and is attained through a supernatural love rooted in Christ: "Love not only unites the two subjects, but allows them to interpenetrate each other, belonging spiritually to one another, to the point that the author of the letter can affirm, 'The one who loves his wife loves himself' (Eph 5:28). The 'I' becomes in some way the 'you,' and the 'you' the 'I.'"[184]

The Letter to the Ephesians summarizes its reflection on marital unity with a quotation from the Yahwist account of creation: "Therefore a man leaves his father and his mother and clings to his wife, and they become one flesh."[185] John Paul II ascribes great weight to this Old Testament reference. In his view, St. Paul intends to connect the first covenant of the Creator, made with man through the act of creation, with the eschatological covenant made in Christ.[186] Moreover, indicating the fundamental role of marriage in revealing the essence of the covenant of God with man, the author of the Letter presents marriage as "the most ancient sacrament."[187]

The necessity of including the term "sacrament" in these reflections is to be found in the epistle itself, where the term is used. After describing marital unity by making a reference to the book of Genesis, St. Paul writes: "This is a great mystery [τὸ μυστήριον] and I am applying it to Christ and the church."[188] According to

---

183. Eph 5:28–29.   184. *TB*, 485.
185. Gn 2:24; Eph 5:30.
186. MacDonald makes a similar point: "The purpose of this quotation appears to be threefold. Most obviously it explains the origin of the union of man and woman in marriage and establishes that this union is from God but, as the following verse makes clear, the quotation is also being employed to shed light on the mysterious relationship between Christ and the church. Moreover, the quotation from Genesis—one of the few direct quotations from Scripture in the epistle—also serves to place marriage (both human marriage and the divine-human union) unquestionably within God's plan for salvation for the universe" (MacDonald, *Colossians and Ephesians*, 330).
187. *TB*, 491.   188. Eph 5:32.

common opinion among biblical scholars, the notion of mystery, central to the theology of the Letter to the Ephesians, and expressed in the text with the Greek word *mysterion,* signifies God's salvific plan, originally hidden in the thought of God, and then gradually revealed in the history of salvation.[189]

John Paul II points out that the fragment under consideration here from the Letter to the Ephesians is read primarily during the Church's liturgy of the sacrament of marriage. The pope agrees with the consensus among biblical scholars that when the author of Ephesians speaks of a "great mystery," it is not his direct intention to indicate that Christian marriage is a sacrament.[190] Nonetheless, the pope notes that the Greek word *mysterion* points to the foundations of the sacramentality of marriage and of the whole of the Christian life.

In order to elucidate the notion of marriage as "the most ancient sacrament," John Paul II turns to the theology of the Old Testament. Especially in the prophetic tradition, there exists a theological current in which the relationship between God and man is portrayed using the image of marriage, the love of the bridegroom and bride. The pope quotes a typical text of this genre from Isaiah:

Do not fear, for you will not be ashamed; do not be discouraged, for you will not suffer disgrace; for you will forget the shame of your youth, and the disgrace of your widowhood you will remember no more. For your Maker is your husband, the Lord of hosts is his name; the Holy One of Israel is your Redeemer, the God of the whole earth he is called. For the Lord has called you like a wife forsaken and grieved in spirit, like the wife of a man's youth when she is cast off, says your God.[191]

---

189. "Ephesians uses the term 'mystery' (τὸ μυστήριον, *mysterion*) here, as elsewhere, for the hidden purposes of God (v. 32; cf. 1:9; 3:3; 4:9; 6:19)" (Pheme Perkins, "The Letter to the Ephesians: Introduction, Commentary, and Reflections," in *NIB,* 11:451).

190. See: MacDonald, *Colossians and Ephesians* 201–2, 331; Perkins, "The Letter to the Ephesians," 451–52.

191. Is 54:4–6. Other similar texts are: Is 62:1–5; Ez 16; Hos 1–3.

In his reflections on the notion of sacrament, John Paul II delves into the most fundamental meaning of this word: the original semantic field, which has been defined by the Latin term *sacramentum* since the third century, was first indicated by the Greek word *mysterion* in the Old and the New Testament as well as in early patristic thought.[192] In Old Testament theology, *mysterion* means "God's creative plans and the end he assigns to the world, which are revealed only to those who are faithful confessors."[193] In New Testament theology, *mysterion* changes its meaning; it is "no longer merely God's eternal plan, but *the realization* of this plan on earth, revealed in Jesus Christ."[194]

New Testament theology of *mysterion* had a decisive influence on the early patristic understanding of this word. For St. Ignatius of Antioch and Sts. Justin and Meliton, *mysterion* means "the historical events that show God's will to save man."[195] Only since the third century, in the oldest Latin translations of the Bible, has the Greek term *mysterion* been translated as the Latin *mysterium* or *sacramentum*. The development of the theology of the sacrament, whose milestones are marked by the reflections of Tertullian, St. Augustine, St. Isidore of Seville, and St. Thomas Aquinas, established the understanding of a sacrament as "an effective sign of grace" (*signum efficax gratiae Christi*) and focused theological reflection on the seven sacraments of the Church.[196]

John Paul II notes that theological reflection in the twentieth century recovered the aspects of sacrament connected with the Greek term *mysterion*, especially its ecclesial and personalistic dimensions, the latter of which focuses on sacrament as a personal encounter between man and his Redeemer. The Second

---

192. Günther Bornkamm, "μυστήριον," in *TDNT*, 4:802–28.
193. *TB*, 489. 194. Ibid.
195. Ibid.
196. Irénée-Henri Dalmais describes the history of the concept of sacrament in a way very similar to the pope: "Sacraments," in *DS*, vol. 14, col. 45–51; also: Günther Wenz, "Sakramente: Kirchengeschichtlich," in *TRE*, 29:663–84.

Vatican Council "returns to the original meaning of '*sacramentum-mysterium*,' when it calls the Church 'the universal sacrament of salvation' (LG, 48), a sacrament, or 'a sign and instrument of intimate union with God and of the unity of all the human race' (LG, 1). In conformity with its original meaning, 'sacrament' is here understood as 'the realization of the eternal divine plan for the salvation of humanity.'"[197]

In his reflections on human marriage, John Paul II employs this most fundamental understanding of sacrament, which is connected with the Greek word *mysterion*. In this understanding, sacrament "presupposes the revelation of the mystery and presupposes that man also accepts it by faith. Still, it is at the same time something more than the proclamation of the mystery and the acceptance of the mystery by faith. The sacrament consists in '*manifesting*' that *mystery in a sign* that serves not only to proclaim the mystery, but also *to accomplish it* in man."[198] As discussed above, marriage fulfills all conditions spelled out in this definition of sacrament: it "proclaims the mystery" of God's love for man and also "accomplishes" it through grace in the marital relation of husband and wife. Due to the privileged nature of the irrevocable and indissoluble love of God for man, marriage is "the primordial sacrament."[199]

There is yet another reason why John Paul II calls marriage "the primordial sacrament." He points out that the definition of sacrament as "a visible and effective sign of grace" creates a theological basis for speaking about "the sacrament of creation." It was through creation that man was invited to a supernatural friendship with God and endowed with the gifts of grace. This supernatural endowing, which took place before original sin, is described by

---

197. *TB*, 490–91. The important influence of the Second Vatican Council on the thought of John Paul II is evident in the analyses of every chapter of this book.
198. *TB*, 489.
199. Ibid., 503.

classical theology as the grace of original innocence and of original justice. Also, the marital union, by which man and woman "become one flesh," is, in a sense, the crowning and central part of the sacrament of creation. Marriage, therefore, can be considered the primordial sacrament in this sense.

Original sin significantly disturbed the harmony of the sacrament of creation intended by the Creator. However, in agreement with the theological tradition of the Catholic Church, John Paul II emphasizes that the original order of creation was not completely destroyed by sin, and, therefore, marriage still remains "the platform for the realization of God's eternal plans."[200] In human history, the primordial sacrament becomes "the sacrament of redemption."[201]

Summarizing John Paul II's reflections on the sacramentality of marriage, as well as other reflections contained in this chapter, it is important to note the twofold reference of marriage to the sacramental order. First, marriage as the primordial sacrament is a figure of the whole sacramental order and the economy of salvation, because it proclaims the relationship of Christ and the Church to be one of spousal love. Second, marriage as one of the seven sacraments of the Church is an integral part of the new sacramental order. Certainly, Christ—the Head of the Church and the Savior of the body—unifies both approaches to the sacrament of marriage.

200. Ibid., 507.
201. Ibid.

Chapter Three

THE GIFT THAT CREATES COMMUNION

Both concepts mentioned in the title of this chapter, gift and communion, have an important philosophical and theological history. It is worthwhile, therefore, to begin our reflections with a short historical introduction. Many anthropologists and ethnologists convincingly prove that the giving and receiving of a gift is a fundamental element of every human culture, "one of the bases of social life."[1] In one of the first important modern publications on the cultural meaning of gift, *Essai sur le don,* Marcel Mauss writes that in archaic societies the ceremony of giving and receiving gifts had many essential social, economic, and religious functions.[2] In a gift-giving ceremony, bonds were established between members of a society, and their social position was defined: more prominent persons were given and gave greater gifts, while others were given and gave lesser gifts. A gift also played an important economic function. Gift giving was a form of redistribution of wealth in

---

1. Marcel Mauss, *The Gift: Forms and Functions of Exchange in Archaic Societies,* translated by Ian Cunnison (Glencoe, Ill.: Free Press, 1954), 2.
2. Ibid., 8–10.

societies, as well as the original means of making investments or loans: a gift should, after some time, be requited. Mauss emphasizes that the religious dimension was essential to the gift; that is, members of a society thrived on the conviction that every gift has a force proper to itself and that by joining in the rhythm of giving and receiving, they ensured their participation in this force.[3]

Gerardus van der Leeuw, a well-known philosopher of religion, who widely draws on the results of Mauss's research in his analysis of gift, calls attention to the personalistic dimension of gift. The gift is never merely a material thing whose value is measured by its usefulness. The gift always contains a part of the giver: "To offer somebody something, then, is to offer someone a part of oneself; similarly, to accept a thing from another person is to receive some portion of his spiritual being, of his soul."[4] Ralph Waldo Emerson writes about this in a moving way in his essay *Gifts:*

> The only gift is a portion of thyself. Thou must bleed for me. Therefore, the poet brings his poem, the shepherd, his lamb; the farmer, corn; the miner, a gem; the sailor, coral and shells; the painter, his picture; the girl, a handkerchief of her own sewing. This is right and pleasing, for it restores society in so far to the primary basis, when a man's biography is conveyed in his gift, and every man's wealth is an index of his merit.... The gift, to be true, must be the flowing of the giver unto me, correspondent to my flowing unto him.[5]

The concept of gift is currently an important theme of reflection for many philosophers from various traditions, for example,

---

3. Ibid., 29–31. Mauss's analyses are not only historical. The author of *Essai sur le don* argues that the ceremony of giving and receiving gifts, present in diverse forms, is an important element of life in every society (also, Charles J. White, "Gift Giving," in *The Encyclopedia of Religion*, edited by M. Eliade [New York: Macmillan Publishing Company, 1987], 5:552–57).

4. Gerardus van der Leeuw, *Religion in Essence and Manifestation: A Study in Phenomenology*, translated by J. E. Turner (New York: Harper and Row, 1963), vol. 2, 352.

5. Ralph Waldo Emerson, "Gifts," in Emerson, *Essays and Journals* (New York: Doubleday, 1968), 323–24.

Jacques Derrida, Jean-Luc Marion, Kenneth L. Schmitz, and Claude Bruaire.⁶ Marion's phenomenological attempt to describe the phenomenon of the gift as "what is given" (*donée, given, gegeben*) seems to be particularly philosophically promising, opening new avenues of thought.⁷ In the opinion of some of his readers, Marion's presentation of "what is given" as a fundamental element of perceived reality leads to finding a gift at the root of everything that exists and, ultimately, following the line of reasoning of *quinque viae* of St. Thomas Aquinas, points to the Giver.⁸ Marion himself warns against such an interpretation of his reflections and limits his intentions to a faithful, phenomenological description of *donée*.⁹

The concept of gift (Latin *donum*) traditionally played a very important role in Christian theology, especially in Trinitarian theology. Biblical revelation leaves no doubt as to the fact that God, in his essence, is gift. Jacques Guillet writes about this thus:

If the Father and the Son are united in the Spirit, they are not united in order to rejoice in the possession of one another but in the giving; their union is a giving and produces a giving. But if the Spirit who is the

---

6. Claude Bruaire, *L'être et l'esprit* (Paris: PUF 1983); Claude Bruaire, *La force et l'esprit* (Paris: Desclée de Brouwer, 1986); Jacques Derrida, *Given Time: I, Counterfeit Money* (Chicago: University of Chicago Press, 1992); idem, *The Gift of Death* (Chicago: University of Chicago Press, 1995); Jean-Luc Marion, *Being Given: Toward a Phenomenology of Givenness* (Stanford, Calif.: Stanford University Press, 2002); Jean-Luc Marion, *God without Being: hors-texte* (Chicago: University of Chicago Press, 1991); Kenneth L. Schmitz, *The Gift: Creation* (Milwaukee: Marquette University Press, 1982); Kenneth L. Schmitz, "The Given and the Gift: Two Different Readings of the World," in *The Human Person and Philosophy in the Contemporary World. Proceedings of the Meeting of the World Union of Catholic Philosophical Societies. Cracow 23–25 August 1978*, edited by Józef Życiński (Kraków: Wydawnictwo Papieskiej Akademii Teologicznej, 1980).

7. Marion, *Being Given*.

8. Jacques Derrida interprets the thought of Marion in this way ("On the Gift: A Discussion between Jacques Derrida and Jean-Luc Marion," in *God, the Gift and Postmodernism*, edited by John D. Caputo and Michael J. Scanlon [Bloomington: Indiana University Press, 1999], 66–67).

9. Ibid., 70–71.

gift thus seals the union of Father and Son, then they are essentially gifts themselves, their common essence is to give itself, to exist in the other and to give life to the other.[10]

Giving oneself belongs to the essence of God; therefore, in their nature each one of the three Persons of the Trinity is a gift. Simultaneously, gift (*donum*) is the proper name that Christian theology, on the basis of biblical revelation and following its great teachers, St. Augustine and St. Thomas Aquinas, attributed to the Holy Spirit.[11]

The concept of "communion" (Greek κοινωνία, Latin *communio*), similarly to the notion of gift, also has a rich philosophical and theological history. In ancient Greek, the term *koinonia* meant different forms of mutual relations: common participation in a given event, a joint undertaking, and, primarily, a close relationship.[12] In Greek philosophy, the term *koinonia* is used in a religious context; that is, it signifies a sacrificial feast that is an expression of communion (*koinonia*) between the people and the gods who participate in it.

In the New Testament, the concept *koinonia* underwent a radical reinterpretation; there, the term symbolized one of the fundamental elements of a new Christian identity. Jerome Hammer defines the New Testament *koinonia* as a specifically Christian way of life—a participation in Christ that undergirds the community between people: "The horizontal dimension in *koinonia* must thus be regarded as resulting from a vertical relationship, and can only be explained through this."[13] It is worthwhile to emphasize

---

10. Jacques Guillet, "God," in *Dictionary of Biblical Theology*, edited by Xavier Leon Dufour, SJ (New York: Desclee, 1967), 185.

11. St. Augustine, *The Trinity* XV, 19; St. Thomas Aquinas, *STh* I, 38, 2.

12. Friedrich Hauck, "καθαρός: Clean and Unclean in the NT," in *Theological Dictionary of the New Testament,* edited by Gerhard Kittel (Grand Rapids, Mich.: Eerdmans, 1965), 3:789.

13. Jerome Hammer OP, *The Church Is a Communion* (New York: Sheed & Ward, 1964), 162.

that, in the New Testament, *koinonia* does not signify a mere interior, subjective bond and closeness between those who believe in Christ, but also indicates the external unity of the visible Church. Cardinal Joseph Ratzinger states that "the word 'communion' has at this point its full Christian content, which includes the sacramental and spiritual dimension as well as the institutional and personal one."[14]

Another fundamental meaning of *koinonia* concerns the Eucharist. The primary text from the New Testament that points to this meaning is found in the First Letter to the Corinthians: "The cup of blessing that we bless, is it not a sharing in the blood of Christ? The bread that we break, is it not a sharing (κοινωνία) in the body of Christ? Because there is one bread, we who are many are one body, for we all partake of the one bread" (1 Cor 10:16–17). The Christological dimension of this text merges with its ecclesiological meaning: *koinonia* with Christ in the Eucharist always simultaneously means *koinonia* with the Church.[15] As a result, ecclesiology based on the term *communio* is often defined as Eucharistic ecclesiology.[16]

The Sources of Papal Thought

Before analyzing John Paul II's views on gift and communion, it is important to indicate some of the sources of his thought. We will begin this historical retrospective by discussing the place the concept of gift occupied in the philosophical anthropology and ethics of Karol Wojtyła before 1978. A key idea in this chapter is that the concept of "the communion of persons" (*communio personarum*) appeared in the thought of the archbishop of Kraków

---

14. Joseph Ratzinger, *Pilgrim Fellowship of Faith: The Church as Communion*, translated by Henry Taylor (San Francisco: Ignatius Press, 2005), 67.
15. Ibid., 77–88.
16. Ibid., 131.

only as a fruit of his participation in the Second Vatican Council. Therefore, we will briefly analyze four important meanings of the concept *communio* in the theology of the council: Trinitarian, ecclesiological, anthropological, and ethical. An important application of this understanding of *communio* is its usage by Cardinal Wojtyła himself in his reflections on marriage and family, which resulted in the articles he published on this theme in the 1970s. A short look at their content will complete our reflection on the sources of John Paul II's thought regarding gift and communion, and will make a more penetrating analysis of the theology of the Wednesday catecheses possible.

The Philosophical Anthropology of Karol Wojtyła

Prior to the Second Vatican Council, the concept of *communio personarum* is simply not present in Karol Wojtyła's philosophical and theological reflections. However, the philosophical analysis of human love in *Love and Responsibility* (1960) provided Wojtyła with some of the fundamental notions that he used after Vaticanum Secundum to describe the essence of the communion of persons. The most important of these notions are: gift, affirmation of the other person, spousal love, and unity in love. The concept of *communio personarum*, which can be found at the very center of Wojtyła's anthropological and ethical reflections in the 1970s, was fleshed out by the cardinal of Kraków with the content implied by the semantic field of each of the terms. Therefore, for a proper understanding of the notion "communion of persons," it is important to look first at Wojtyła's book *Love and Responsibility*, where all of these terms can be found.

Love and Responsibility consists of thorough metaphysical, psychological, and ethical analysis of love. Wojtyła begins with a metaphysical analysis, which is based on the classical Aristotelian-Thomistic distinction between the four types of love: attraction, desire, goodwill, and friendship.[17] Wojtyła adds to this list a fifth, the highest kind of love, that is, betrothed or spousal love.[18]

As presented in *Love and Responsibility,* spousal love is the most complete and radical form of love, because it consists in giving oneself to the beloved and making "one's inalienable and non-transferable 'I' someone else's property."[19] Spousal love thus understood, says Wojtyła, adds personal involvement and a self-giving to the beloved to benevolent love (*amor benevolentiae,* to want the good of the other person). Such an involvement and overcoming of a cold distance may be realized in many situations: in the mother's self-giving to the child, in the relation of the doctor to the patient, or in that of the teacher to the pupil. However, two relations in which the total gift of oneself is revealed as the essence of spousal love in the most complete way are man's gift of himself to God and the reciprocal self-giving of man and woman in marriage.

Wojtyła sees the spousal love of man for God in the context of the mystery of creation and redemption. We read in *Love and Responsibility:* "The rights of the Creator over the creature are very extensive: [creation] is in its entirety the property of the Creator."[20] The philosophical justification of this "property" of the Creator in relation to man consists in the concept of the inalien-

---

17. Wojtyła, *Love and Responsibility,* 73–95. There is no need to present here each of the four forms of love. Such a description, however, can be found in Rocco Buttiglione's book: *The Thought of the Man Who Became Pope John Paul II,* translated by Paolo Guietti and Francesca Murphy (Grand Rapids, Mich.: Eerdmans, 1997), 99–106; also another well-known contemporary reinterpretation of the discussed theory: Clive Staples Lewis, *Four Loves* (New York: Harcourt, Brace, 1960).

18. According to Aristotle and Aquinas, friendship (*amicitia*) is the highest and noblest form of love between persons. Wojtyła does not deny this in *Love and Responsibility,* but, rather, presents spousal love as the highest stage of the development of friendship. Due to his phenomenological method and usage of the concept of "gift," Wojtyła describes the phenomenon of human friendship using different language than is customary in the Aristotelian and Thomistic traditions.

19. Wojtyła, *Love and Responsibility,* 97.

20. Ibid., 249.

ability and uniqueness of every human person (*incommunicabilitas*): "The person as such is inalienable (*alteri incommunicabilis*), is *sui juris,* belongs to itself—and apart from itself belongs only to the Creator, in as much as it is a creature."[21] This uniqueness of every human person before God—another term used by Wojtyła here is the "virginity of the person"—allows man's self-giving to God that is a response to God's self-giving to man, seen in the light of the mystery of redemption. Wojtyła writes as follows: "The human soul, which is the betrothed of God, gives itself to Him alone."[22] The self-gift should be present at the very core of the relation of man to God.

The second privileged place of the realization of spousal love is the marital love of man and woman. As in the case of love between God and man, spousal love between man and woman is a reciprocal giving to one another and a mutual acceptance of this giving, which leads to a mutual belonging and union of persons. The sexual union is a sign and, simultaneously, a means to the union of persons in marriage. Wojtyła emphasizes that a necessary condition for the existence of true spousal love consists in the affirmation of the other person beyond his or her sexual value:

> The skill in giving and receiving which is typical of love is exhibited by the man whose attitude to a woman is informed by total affirmation of her value as a person, and equally by the woman whose attitude to a man is informed by affirmation of his value as a person. This skill creates the specific climate of betrothed love—the climate of surrender of the innermost self. Both man and woman need this genuine capacity for affirmation of the value of the person, if the gift of self is to be fully valid, and equally if acceptance of the gift is to be valid.[23]

Karol Wojtyła is certainly not the only thinker who gives a central place to the category of gift in a description of human love.

---

21. Ibid., 250–51.
22. Ibid., 251.
23. Ibid., 129.

In *Sens chrétien de l'homme* (1945), Jean Mouroux also analyzes love as a gift that creates the communion of persons.[24] A similar approach to love can be found in Alice and Dietrich von Hildebrand's *The Art of Living*, first published in 1965.[25] It is difficult to say who inspired Wojtyła's work on the philosophy of gift. In my estimation, his inspiration was rather of a theological nature, and most probably derived from the Trinitarian theology of St. Augustine and St. Thomas Aquinas, well known to Wojtyła, in which the concept of gift (Latin *donum*) plays a key role and always appears in the context of the description of love between the Persons of the Trinity as well as the sending of the Holy Spirit, the Gift.[26]

The Council's *Communio* Theology

Communio is one of the fundamental notions in the theology of the Second Vatican Council, especially in its ecclesiology, which is most fully laid out in the dogmatic constitution on the Church, *Lumen gentium*. Among the many commentaries and analyses of the council's theology of *communio*, of particular value for our reflections here is the book *Sources of Renewal* (1972),[27]

24. Jean Mouroux, *The Meaning of Man*, translated by A. H. G. Downes (New York: Sheed & Ward, 1948), 196–266.
25. Alice von Hildebrand and Dietrich von Hildebrand, *The Art of Living* (Manchester, N.H.: Sophia Institute Press 1994), 57–78.
26. I slightly disagree in this respect with Michael Waldstein, who sees the roots of Wojtyła's philosophical and theological theory of the gift in the mystical theology of St. John of the Cross (Waldstein, "Introduction," 23–34). One cannot deny the important influence of St. John on Wojtyła. However, Wojtyła's theory of the gift is presented in a comprehensive manner for the first time in Wojtyła's book *Love and Responsibility* (as it was summarized above) in a clearly Aristotelian-Thomistic context. Therefore, it seems to me that it is rather Augustinian-Thomistic theology of Trinitarian *donum* that foremost influenced Wojtyła.
27. Wojtyła, *Sources of Renewal*. Other commentaries on the council's *communio* theology: Otto Saier, *"Communio" in der Lehre des Zweiten Vatikanischen Konzils: Eine rechtsbegriffliche Untersuchung* (Munich: Hueber, 1973); Walter Kasper, "The Church as Communio," *Communio—International Catholic Review* 13, no. 2 (1986): 100–118; Heinrich Döring, "Die Communio-Ekklesiologie als Grundmodell und Chance der ökumienischen Theologie," in *Communio Sanctorum: Einheit der Christen—Einheit der*

written by Cardinal Karol Wojtyła in order to present the achievements of Vatican II to his local church, which was about to begin a synod at that time.[28] Wojtyła's reflections show how important the council's *communio* theology had become for him.

The concept *communio* appears primarily in the council's documents in reflections on ecclesiology, in the context of describing the unity existing in the Church. The dogmatic constitution *Lumen Gentium* clearly points to the supernatural and Trinitarian character of this unity: "The Church has been seen as 'a people made one with the unity of the Father, the Son and the Holy Spirit.'"[29] Wojtyła comments on this statement of the council in the following way:

> The reality of Christ's redemption continues in the Church, that is to say in men who "grow together" into a single people thanks to the effective inner working of the Holy Spirit. The union that forms this people is a union of men in spiritual community, but the content and principle of that community are of God: it proceeds from the divine choice, from Christ's redeeming act and the sanctification of the Spirit.[30]

Wojtyła notes that the word *communio* describes the nature of the Church better than the word "society" (*communitas*). *Communio*, therefore, signifies a unity that is only possible between persons; this unity can be created only through a mutual self-gift originating in supernatural love. Thus, *communio* points to the internal dynamism at work in the Christian community: the multitude and complexity of subjects forms a unity that simultaneously preserves the plurality and diversity of persons who love one another.[31]

Kirche, herausg. Josef Schreiner and Klaus Wittstadt (Würzburg: Echter, 1988), 439–70; Dennis M. Doyle, *Communion Ecclesiology: Visions and Versions* (Maryknoll, N.Y.: Orbis Books, 2000), 72–84.

28. Adam Kubiś, "Preface," in Karol Wojtyła, *Sources of Renewal*, 4.
29. *LG* 4.   30. Wojtyła, *Sources of Renewal*, 113.
31. Ibid., 120.

One of the fundamental meanings of *communio* therefore has an anthropological character: *communio personarum* signifies a unity that is possible only between persons who love one another and give themselves to one another. In the ecclesiological context, the concept *communio* owes its strength and depth to its theological reference to the Trinity, to the *communio personarum Sanctae Trinitatis*. The council's constitution *Lumen gentium* presents the community of believers, the *communio personarum* in the Church, as the work of the Trinity, which allows believers to participate in God's Trinitarian life: "It follows that though there are many nations there is but one people of God, which takes its citizens from every race, making them citizens of a kingdom which is of a heavenly rather than of an earthly nature. All the faithful, scattered though they be throughout the world, are in communion with each other in the Holy Spirit."[32]

In interpreting the teaching of the council, Wojtyła emphasizes that the baptized are called to participate in the life of the Trinity not only as individuals, but also as a community.[33] It is exactly *communio* that describes the character of this participation in the life of the triune God; consequently, the council teaches that there is "some similarity (*similitudo*) between the unity of the Divine Persons, and the unity of God's sons united in truth and love."[34]

The council, notes Wojtyła, also uses the term *communio* in two other ecclesiological meanings when it speaks of *communio munerum* and *communio ecclesiarum*. Since the Church is first of all a communion of love, every ministry, function and vocation in the Church should be seen as a sharing in this one exchange of love and service (*diakonia*). In the dogmatic constitution on the mystery of the Church, *Lumen gentium,* we read: "For the mem-

32. LG 13.
33. Wojtyła, *Sources of Renewal*, 139–40.
34. *GS* 24. Similarities between the *communio* of the Trinity and the *communio* of believers are discussed in detail in the next chapter of this work.

bers of the people of God are called to share these goods in common, and of each of the Churches the words of the Apostle hold good: 'According to the gift that each has received, administer it to one another as good stewards of the manifold grace of God' (1 P 4:10)."[35]

Cardinal Wojtyła comments on this passage from *Lumen gentium* in the following way:

If the concept of "estate" or "office" in the Church has a content, which indirectly expresses a personalistic reciprocal relationship between person and community, this is precisely because of the reality of *communio* as the union which constitutes the community of the Church as People of God. The *communio* thus indicates the proper place in that community not only of particular estates or social groups like the hierarchy, the laity and the religious orders, but also of individuals in the Church.[36]

Cardinal Wojtyła emphasizes that this method of interpretation concerns all ministries (*munus*) in the Church, which allows an understanding of the Church as *communio munerum*. The Second Vatican Council considers the Church to be a pluralistic unity, which is composed of the rich traditions of local churches: "Within the Church (*in ecclesiastica communione*) particular Churches hold a rightful place; these Churches retain their own traditions, without in any way opposing the primacy of the Chair of Peter, which presides over the whole assembly of charity."[37] Therefore, the primacy of the Holy See in the Church should be seen in the context of the collegiality of the bishops—pastors of the local churches. In explaining this truth, Cardinal Wojtyła appeals to the concept of *communio:* "The people of God is the Church, and the Church is also a communion of the churches—*communio Ecclesiarum*—constituted by the communion of bishops—pastors."[38]

In his commentary on the theology of the Second Vatican

35. LG 13.
36. Wojtyła, *Sources of Renewal,* 139.
37. LG 13.
38. Wojtyła, *Sources of Renewal,* 151.

Council, written for his local church, Cardinal Wojtyła differentiates four deeply interconnected meanings of the concept of *communio:* the human community of persons (*communio personarum*), the divine community of the Trinity (*communio Sanctissime Trinitatis*), the community of ministries in the Church (*communio munerum*), and the community of local churches (*communio ecclesiarum*).[39] We may therefore speak of the analogical character of the concept of *communio;* its content manifests itself in a different way on the four ontological levels touched on above: human community, the community of the Absolute Being, the community of the baptized, and the community of churches. In each of these dimensions, *communio* points to a specific and deep kind of unity and bond that may be obtained only through supernatural Love.

Karol Wojtyła's Theology of Marriage and Family

Karol Wojtyła's participation in the work of the Second Vatican Council undoubtedly helped him to deepen his theological reflection on the reality of *communio personarum.* Proof thereof are three articles he published in 1970s: "O znaczeniu miłości oblubieńczej" (On the meaning of spousal love), "Rodzina jako *communio personarum*" ("The Family as a Community of Persons") and "Rodzicielstwo a *communio personarum*" ("Parenthood as a Community of Persons"). A careful analysis of these publications shows the direction in which Wojtyła's reflection developed.

First, however, it is important to review Wojtyła's philosophical deepening of the concept of gift that took place in his publications from 1968 to 1978. It seems that there are two currents in evidence in these reflections: the first concerns the structure of human self-determination, and the second consists in Wojtyła's theory of participation in the humanity of other persons. Both of

---

39. Ibid., 138–39. Joachim Drumm similarly differentiates four meanings of *communio* in the theology of *Vaticanum Secundum* (Joachim Drumm, "*Communio,*" in *LTK,* vol. 2, col. 1281–82).

these currents of thought are presented first and foremost in Karol Wojtyła's magnum opus, *The Acting Person* (1969).

In *The Acting Person*, Wojtyła emphasizes that the key to a realistic description of human freedom consists in the truth that the human will is revealed not only by its intentionality in the choosing of different goods, but also in making decisions about oneself, or, in other words, in a self-determination that engages the whole person.[40] Simultaneously, because "only the things that are man's actual possessions can be determined by him,"[41] the phenomenon of self-determination presupposes the structures of self-possession and self-governance in man. Wojtyła argues in *The Acting Person* that "on the one hand, the person is understood as the one who governs himself, yet, on the other hand, as the one who is governed by himself."[42]

The human dynamic of self-possession and self-governance is essential for the possibility of a self-gift, because "only if one possesses oneself can one give oneself and do this in a disinterested way. And only if one governs oneself can one make a gift of oneself, and this again a disinterested gift."[43] In the language of his philosophical anthropology, Wojtyła justifies thus the well-known and important truth that the personal maturity of the subject is a necessary condition for his or her ability to enter into friendship and to love.

The second philosophical issue, essential for Wojtyła's reflec-

40. Wojtyła, *The Acting Person*, 105; also, Karol Wojtyła, "Transcendencja osoby w czynie a autoteleologia człowieka," in Wojtyła, *Osoba i czyn oraz inne studia antropologiczne* (Lublin: Wydawnictwo Naukowe Katolickiego Uniwersytetu Lubelskiego, 1994), 483–84.

41. Wojtyła, *The Acting Person*, 106.

42. Ibid. A theological interpretation of human self-governance, which is constructed in reference to the idea of the participation of Christians in Christ's royal dignity, was developed by Cardinal Wojtyła in his Vatican Lent retreat in 1976 (Wojtyła, *Sign of Contradiction* [New York: Seabury Press, 1979], 137–45).

43. Wojtyła, "The Personal Structure of Self-Determination," in Wojtyła, *Person and Community*, 194.

tion on gift, concerns the phenomenon of participation. This phenomenon is described in *The Acting Person* in its two dimensions. First, the participation that forms the basis of creating a true human community is such a way of being and acting with others that man realizes and fulfills himself. Such a participation is possible in situations when "man chooses what others choose and indeed often because others choose it, but even then he thus chooses it as his own good and as the end of his own striving."[44]

The second dimension of participation is even more fundamental than the first and concerns relations to other persons. Here, participation means "participating in the humanness of others."[45] In his article "Participation or Alienation?" (1975), Cardinal Wojtyła describes this sharing in the humanity of the other person as the consciousness that "the other is another I."[46] We read in this article:

> Thus the reality of the other does not result principally from categorical knowledge, from humanity as the conceptualized essence "human being," but from an even richer lived experience, one in which I as though transfer what is given to me as my own I beyond myself to one of the others, who, as a result, appears primarily as a different I, another I, my neighbor. Another person is a neighbor to me not just because we share a like humanity, but chiefly because the other is another I.[47]

According to Cardinal Wojtyła, participation thus understood is a necessary condition for a mature self-gift that builds a true *communio personarum*.[48]

We now return to Cardinal Wojtyła's theological reflection on *communio personarum* from the 1970s, which developed under

---

44. Wojtyła, *The Acting Person*, 280.
45. Ibid., 294.
46. Wojtyła, "Participation or Alienation?" in Wojtyła, *Person and Community*, 200.
47. Ibid., 200–201.
48. Wojtyła, "The Person: Subject and Community," in Wojtyła, *Person and Community*, 245–46.

the influence of Vatican II. Wojtyła's reflections in the article "O znaczeniu miłości oblubieńczej" (1974) resume the deliberations from his book *Love and Responsibility*. In the article, Wojtyła uses the Augustinian term *retractatio*, which indicates that he intends to revisit, on a theological level, issues from *Love and Responsibility*.[49] However, the influence of the Second Vatican Council is clearly evident in the article's description of spousal love, and the fundamental theological reference for Wojtyła's thought comes from the celebrated passage of the pastoral constitution *Gaudium et spes:* "Man, who is the only creature on earth which God willed for itself, cannot fully find himself except through a sincere gift of himself."[50]

Making reference to *Gaudium et spes* 24, Wojtyła uses the term "the law of the gift" for the first time in this article. This term summarizes his previous philosophical deliberations on giving and receiving as the essence of spousal love: "A consequence of who man is as a person, or a being who possesses himself and governs himself, is that he may 'give himself,' or may make himself a gift for others, without thereby violating his ontological status. 'The law of gift' is inscribed, so to speak, in the very being of the person."[51]

---

49. Wojtyła, "O znaczeniu miłości oblubieńczej," *Roczniki Filozoficzne* 22 (1974) 2, 162.

50. *GS* 24.

51. Wojtyła, "O znaczeniu miłości oblubieńczej," 166. Wojtyła emphasizes that giving, serving, and sacrificing is present in any love, yet "among different forms of love there is a difference as to the level of 'completeness' of this giving" (ibid., 168). Spousal love indicates a complete gift that may be discussed in its intensive meaning, when we are dealing with a single act of heroic love, or its extensive meaning, when the decision to give oneself to the other person is understood as a choice of vocation for the whole of one's life. Similarly, Zygmunt Bauman notes that "the idea of the 'gift' is a common name for a wide range of acts that differ in their purity. 'Pure' gift is, as it were, a liminal concept—a sort of benchmark against which all practical cases are measured. Such practical cases depart from the ideal in various degrees. In the purest of forms, the gift would be totally disinterested and offered without regard to the quality of the recipient. Disinterestedness means a lack of remuneration in any shape or form. Judged by ordinary standards of ownership and exchange, the pure gift is a pure loss. After all, it is a gain solely in moral terms and this is a basis for action that its logic cannot recognize"

Similarly to his philosophical analyses in *Love and Responsibility*, Wojtyła writes that spousal love leads to a union of persons. However, referring to the Second Vatican Council's constitution *Gaudium et spes*, he calls the marital communion of man and woman a *communio personarum* for the first time: "'The law of gift' which God as the Creator inscribed in the being of the human person, man and woman, and whose meaning He confirmed and deepened in the consciousness of every man as the Redeemer, constitutes the proper basis of *'communio personarum.'*"[52]

In his article "The Family as a Community of Persons" (1974), Wojtyła emphasizes that the starting point of a Christian theological anthropology consists in the truth about the similarity of man to God, which should be considered in its two dimensions: individual and social.[53] On the one hand, every human person is an image of God in his rationality and freedom. On the other hand—and Wojtyła makes reference here to *Gaudium et spes*—there exists "a certain likeness between the union of the Divine Persons, and the unity of God's sons in truth and charity."[54]

Wojtyła summarizes the truth about man's twofold likeness to God in the following way: "Human beings are like unto God not only by reason of their spiritual nature, which accounts for their existence as persons, but also by reason of their capacity for community with other persons."[55] According to Wojtyła, this "capa-

---

(Zygmunt Bauman and Tim May, *Thinking Sociologically* [Oxford: Blackwell Publishers, 2001], 80). The ambition to provide a complete description of the phenomenon of gift is the source of Pascal Ide's book *Eh bien, dites: don. Petit éloge du don* (Paris: ed. de l'Emmanuel, 1997).

52. Wojtyła, "O znaczeniu miłości oblubieńczej," 170. The segment of *Gaudium et spes* that Wojtyła references reads as follows: "But God did not create man as a solitary, for from the beginning 'male and female he created them' (Gn 1:27). Their companionship produces the primary form of interpersonal communion" (*GS* 12).

53. Wojtyła, "The Family as a Community of Persons," in Wojtyła, *Person and Community*, 316–20.

54. *GS* 24.

55. Wojtyła, "The Family as a Community of Persons," 318.

bility of community with other persons" cannot be understood merely as the human capacity for social life, but must be understood as something much deeper, as the capability to create *communio personarum*.

Wojtyła stresses again that in order to create a communion of persons, one must make a sincere gift of oneself. The theological source for this statement is, once again, the passage from *Gaudium et spes:* "Man cannot fully find himself except through a sincere gift of himself."[56] In his analysis of self-gift, Wojtyła emphasizes its sincere, nonutilitarian character, which is the condition for the fulfillment of oneself, which is promised by *Gaudium et spes:*

> In the communal relationship that occurs between persons, this self-fulfillment is realized through the mutual gift of self, a gift that has a disinterested character. As I mentioned earlier, the person is capable of such a gift because of the property of self-possession: only a being that possesses itself can give itself. At the same time, this gift has a disinterested character, which is why it fully deserves the name gift. If it were to serve some "interest" on one side or the other, it would no longer be a gift. It might perhaps be beneficial and even useful, but it would no longer be gratuitous.[57]

In his article "Parenthood as a Community of Persons" (1975) Wojtyła notes that, when a man becomes a father and a woman becomes a mother, a new form of a communion of persons is created: "Because this union and fulfillment through parenthood occurs in man thanks to the woman and in the woman thanks to the man, the entire structure of their *communio personarum* takes on a whole new shape, a whole new dimension."[58] This new parental *communio* is characterized by a new dynamic of mutual "giving and receiving": the husband has to accept the motherhood of his

---

56. *GS* 24.
57. Wojtyła, "The Family as a Community of Persons," 322.
58. Wojtyła, "Parenthood as a Community of Persons," in Wojtyła, *Person and Community*, 329.

wife, and the wife the fatherhood of her husband. According to Wojtyła, this mutual acceptance of one another has fundamental ethical importance for every marriage: for the husband it means first of all the acceptance of the fertility and maternal vocation of the wife, which is connected with being open to new life.[59]

When new life is conceived, because of the spousal love of the husband and wife, the marriage is transformed into a family. Wojtyła describes how the appearance of a child enriches the marital *communio personarum:*

> It is significant that the child—although deprived for a long time of the personal fullness of activity—nevertheless enters at once into the community as a person, as someone capable not only of receiving but also of giving. From the very beginning, the tiny new member of the family makes a gift of its humanity to its parents, and also, if it is not the first child to its siblings as well. It extends the circle of giving that existed before its birth and brings to this circle a new and wholly unique content.[60]

Cardinal Wojtyła presents an interesting philosophical description of the process of raising a child. This process, which is linked to the development of marital and familial *communio,* is described by Wojtyła as "making a gift of mature humanity to this little person, this gradually developing human being."[61] The child, therefore, appears in marriage as a person and a gift, which becomes a task for the parents in the process of education. The educational process is described by Wojtyła in the context of spousal love: "the family as a *communio personarum,* and parenthood as a particular element of it, requires the gift of the whole human being, a gift that is in some sense indivisible."[62] In this context, we can understand Wojtyła's conclusion about the necessary relationship between education in the family and self-education, as par-

---

59. Ibid., 330–32. Wojtyła's application of the notion of self-gift to an interpretation of Catholic sexual ethics is discussed in the fifth chapter of this work.
60. Ibid., 330–32.   61. Ibid., 334.
62. Ibid., 324.

ents educating their children also "constantly educate themselves through their children."[63] In Wojtyła's analysis the family holds a unique place not only in regard to procreation, but, first and foremost, in regard to the growth of all of its members in order to create a true and authentic Christian *communio personarum*.

The Created and Uncreated Gift

Without a doubt, it is the anthropological and ethical significance of the notions of gift and *communio personarum* that is fundamental for our reflections in this book. One has to be aware, however, that both concepts—gift and *communio*—are also used by John Paul II in many other theological contexts. It is worthwhile to point them out, since only in this way can we appreciate the profundity of the papal reflections in the Wednesday catecheses.

The concept of the gift refers primarily to the theology of creation. The pope calls the act of creation "a fundamental and 'radical' gift," because it means the calling of man and the world into existence from nothingness: "man appears in creation as the one who has received the world as a gift, and vice versa, one can also say that the world has received man as a gift."[64] The pope develops this thought in the encyclical *Dominum et vivificantem:* "To create means to call into existence from nothing: therefore, to create means to give existence. And if the visible world is created for man, the world is given to man. And at the same time that same man in his own humanity receives as a gift a special 'image and likeness' to God."[65]

According to John Paul II, redemption is also a giving:

Already the "giving" of the Son, the gift of the Son, expresses the most profound essence of God who, as Love, is the inexhaustible source of the

63. Ibid.
64. *TB*, 180–81.
65. *DV* 34.

giving of gifts. The gift made by the Son completes the revelation and giving of the eternal love: the Holy Spirit, who in the inscrutable depths of the divinity is a Person-Gift, through the work of the Son, that is to say by means of the Paschal Mystery, is given to the Apostles and to the Church in a new way, and through them is given to humanity and the whole world.[66]

In the encyclical *Redemptoris mater,* John Paul II writes that in Mary's hymn of thanksgiving, the *Magnificat,* there "shines a ray of the mystery of God, the glory of his ineffable holiness, the eternal love which, as an irrevocable gift, enters into human history."[67] In this document the pope also reminds us that the word "grace," in its biblical meaning, indicates a gift:

In the language of the Bible "grace" means a special gift, which according to the New Testament has its source precisely in the Trinitarian life of God himself, God who is love (cf. 1 Jn 4:8). The fruit of this love is "the election" of which the Letter to the Ephesians speaks. On the part of God, this election is the eternal desire to save man through a sharing in his own life (cf. 2 Pt. 1:4) in Christ: it is salvation through a sharing in supernatural life. The effect of this eternal gift, of this grace of man's election by God, is like a seed of holiness, or a spring which rises in the soul as a gift from God himself, who through grace gives life and holiness to those who are chosen.[68]

According to John Paul II, the action of the Holy Spirit in the Church may also be described using the notion of gift. It is precisely in this way that the pope interprets Christ's words that the Holy Spirit "will prove the world wrong about sin:"[69]

In this way "convincing concerning sin" becomes at the same time a convincing concerning the remission of sins, in the power of the Holy Spirit.... Conversion requires convincing of sin; it includes the interior judgment of the conscience, and this, being a proof of the action of the Spirit

---

66. Ibid., 23.
67. *RM* 36.
68. Ibid., 8.
69. Jn 16:8.

of truth in man's inmost being, becomes at the same time a new beginning of the bestowal of grace and love: "Receive the Holy Spirit." Thus in this "convincing concerning sin" we discover a double gift: the gift of the truth of conscience and the gift of the certainty of redemption.[70]

John Paul II emphasizes that only the Holy Spirit can convince a man about sin in his conscience, because "he who is the love of the Father and of the Son, he is gift, whereas the sin of the human beginning consists in untruthfulness and in the rejection of the gift and the love which determine the beginning of the world and of man."[71]

This brief overview shows that in John Paul II's theology, the most fundamental understanding of the concept of the gift has a Trinitarian character, and refers to the reality of the triune God, and particularly to the person of the Holy Spirit.[72] One of the fundamental texts concerning the Trinitarian meaning of the gift deserving of deeper reflection can be found in the encyclical *Dominum et vivificantem:*

In his intimate life, God "is love," the essential love shared by the three Divine Persons: personal love is the Holy Spirit as the Spirit of the Father and the Son. Therefore he "searches even the depths of God," as uncreated Love-Gift. It can be said that in the Holy Spirit the intimate life of the Triune God becomes totally gift, an exchange of mutual love between the Divine Persons and that through the Holy Spirit God exists in the mode of gift. It is the Holy Spirit who is the personal expression of this self-giving, of this being-love. He is Person- Love. He is Person-Gift.[73]

Traditionally, Christian Trinitarian theology differentiates clearly between God's nature, common to the three divine Persons of the Trinity, and the specific character of each of the divine Per-

---

70. *DV* 31.   71. Ibid., 35.

72. A good discussion of John Paul II's Trinitarian theology can be found in Antoine E. Nachef, *The Mystery of the Trinity in the Theological Thought of Pope John Paul II* (New York: Peter Lang, 1999).

73. *DV* 10.

sons.⁷⁴ Therefore, in the text cited above, John Paul II points out that one can speak in two different ways about love and gift in the Holy Trinity. First, God, in his essence, is love and the term "love" refers here to the nature of every one of the three divine Persons: it is "essential love." Similarly, the term "gift" refers to the nature of God and to the nature of every one of the Divine Persons. However, considering what is individual and unique to each of the three divine Persons of the Trinity, John Paul II emphasizes that the terms "love" and "gift" refer in a most fitting way to the Holy Spirit who is "Person-Love" and "Person-Gift."⁷⁵

Defining the person of the Holy Spirit with the term "gift" (Latin *donum*) has a long and rich theological tradition rooted in the biblical revelation of the New Testament. John Paul II, in his catechesis on the Holy Spirit from 21 November 1990, quoted the most important texts of the New Testament that indicate the possibility of such a definition,⁷⁶ and then summarized his reflections with the statement that "the conception of the Holy Spirit as Gift coming from the Father is a part of Jesus' Revelation." In the same catechesis, making a reference to the thought of St. Augustine and St. Thomas Aquinas, the pope outlined a theological link between the two names of the Holy Spirit—Love and Gift:

St. Augustine writes that, "just as for the Son, to be the being which is born, means that he is from the Father, so for the Holy Spirit, to be the being which is Gift means that he proceeds from the Father and the Son."⁷⁷ In the Holy Spirit there is an equality between being Love and

---

74. Theologians use the technical term "appropriation" in this context (Walter Kasper, *The God of Jesus Christ*, translated by Matthew J. O'Connell [New York: Crossroad, 1984], 282–84; Jean-Pierre Torrell, OP, *Saint Thomas Aquinas*, translated by Robert Royal [Washington, D.C.: The Catholic University of America Press, 2003], 2:157–61).

75. Yves Congar, OP, *I Believe in the Holy Spirit*, translated by David Smith (New York: Seabury Press, 1983), 1:85–92.

76. Mt 7:11; Lk 11:13, 24:49; Jn 3:35, 4:10, 7:38–39, 14:16 (John Paul II, "The Spirit as Gift: General Audience from 21 November 1990," http://www.vatican.va.

77. St. Augustine, *The Trinity* IV, 20, 188 (*CCSL* 50, 199).

being Gift. Saint Thomas explains it well: "Love is the reason for a free gift which is given to a person out of love. The first gift, therefore, is love (*amor habet rationem primi doni*).... Thus, if the Holy Spirit proceeds as Love, he proceeds also as First Gift."[78] All the other gifts are distributed among Christ's Body through the Gift which is the Holy Spirit, the Angelic Doctor concludes in harmony with St. Augustine.[79]

Gift and Communion in the Theology of the Catecheses

Having analyzed the philosophical and theological sources of John Paul II's understanding of gift and communion, and outlining the theological context in which John Paul II uses these concepts, we turn back to the Wednesday catecheses on the theology of the body. As was already emphasized in chapter 2, John Paul II analyzes gift and communion in light of the three theological ages of human history: original innocence, the fall permeated with God's initiative of salvation, and the time of the Resurrection. In each of these theological ages, gift and communion are realized in a different way and also describe the reality of being human, man and woman, differently.

Adam's original solitude is the first anthropological phenomenon, as analyzed in the catecheses, that illuminates the meaning of gift.[80] Biblical Adam is endowed with the gift of creation, but he notices in this gift a certain incompleteness that reveals itself in his experience of solitude. The biblical text laconically points to this experience, which follows Adam's naming of the animals: "But for the man there was not found a helper as his partner."[81]

78. St. Thomas Aquinas, *STh* I 38, 2.
79. John Paul II, "The Spirit as Gift"; St. Thomas Aquinas, *STh* I 38, 2; St. Augustine, *The Trinity* XV, 19, 504 (*CCSL* 50a, 510).
80. Original solitude was discussed in the second chapter of this work in the context of human subjectivity as revealed through the body. To avoid unnecessary repetition, we will draw on the conclusions from previous analyses in this chapter.
81. Gn 2:20.

Adam's solitude does not allow him fully to be a part of the gift of creation, because he does not find anyone for whom he himself could become a gift.[82]

The creation of Eve is a turning point for Adam, for it is then that "creative giving, which springs from Love, has reached man's original consciousness by becoming an experience of reciprocal gift, as one can already see in the archaic text."[83] Endowed with the gift of creation and especially with the gift of another, the woman, Adam may respond in full to this creative giving, and, moreover, may participate in it by himself becoming a gift.

Therefore, according to the pope, the gift reveals "a particular characteristic of personal existence," since to realize one's existence completely means to exist "with someone" and, even more, to exist "for someone." As he did prior to 1978 in his original and innovative theological anthropology, John Paul II speaks in the catecheses of the communion of persons by making reference to the concept of gift: "Communion of persons means living in a reciprocal 'for,' in a relationship of reciprocal gift."[84] Thanks to the creation of Eve, Adam too may become a gift and, in this way, create the first *communio personarum* together with Eve. Thus, the gift of creation is, so to speak, brought to completion.[85]

---

82. John Paul II notes that the first man is described by the biblical author as man (*is*) only after the creation of the woman (Hebrew *issa*). As a result, the Yahwist description of original solitude sheds light on the existential situation of every human person, both man and woman (*TB*, 146–47; also, Edmond Jacob, *Theology of the Old Testament* [New York: Harper & Row, 1958], 156–57).

83. *TB*, 184.

84. Ibid., 182.

85. That the human vocation consists primarily in being a gift is seen in the catecheses in the more fundamental and holistic—one could say "cosmic"—context of the creation of the world. Indicating love as the fundamental motive of the Creator, John Paul II describes creation *ex nihilo* as "a fundamental and 'radical' gift" (ibid., 180). Reflecting on the beings in the world, which were all created from nothingness, we may find in them a twofold trace of this creative giving. On the one hand, everything that exists "bears within itself the sign of the original and fundamental gift" (ibid). On the other hand, the gift of creation has meaning only with regard to man, because only man "*is able to understand the very meaning of the gift* in the call from nothingness to existence" and only he is "able to

John Paul II calls attention to the fact that the body plays a fundamental role in creating the *communio personarum* of Adam and Eve since "they become one flesh."[86] Therefore, the pope speaks of an "incarnated communion of persons," wherein, because of the diversity and complementary character of the sexes, "femininity in some way finds itself before masculinity, while masculinity confirms itself through femininity." According to the pope, due to the significance of the body for who man and woman are, we may speak of the "function of sex [that is, being male or female]" as being "constitutive for the person."[87]

John Paul II's theology of the body clearly warns us not to stop "on the surface of human sexuality" and not to describe the body and sex "outside the full dimension of man and of the 'communion of persons.'" The pope's anthropology rejects contemporary anthropological reductionism and emphasizes that sex is "something more than the mysterious power of human bodiliness, which acts, as it were, by virtue of instinct."[88] The biblical becoming "one flesh" should always be seen as a return to the mystery of creation and a confirmation of the gift as a fundamental dimension of reality.

In discussing the biblical description of the encounter of Adam and Eve, John Paul II pays special attention to the following statement from Genesis: "And the man and his wife were both naked, and were not ashamed."[89] The pope notes that the nakedness of Adam and Eve, which is accompanied by a lack of shame, reveals an important truth about the mutual experience of the body, feminine and masculine, in the state of original innocence.[90] This ex-

---

respond to the Creator with the language of this understanding" (ibid., 180). Only in this context does the creation of the woman acquire its full significance, since only her appearance allowed the man to begin to live as a gift.

86. Gn 2:24.   87. *TB*, 166.
88. Ibid., 167.   89. Gn 2:25.
90. John Paul II reminds us that one of the basic biblical meanings of nakedness consists in complete knowledge. For instance, the Letter to the Hebrews indicates that creation

perience of the body is characterized by the completeness and integrity of the knowledge of the other person. At the heart of this knowledge is a mutual and ethical affirmation of the person:

"They did not feel shame" can only signify... an original depth in affirming what is inherent in the person, that is, what is "visibly" feminine and masculine, through which the "personal intimacy" of reciprocal communication is constituted in all its radical simplicity and purity. To this fullness of *"exterior" perception,* expressed by physical nakedness, *corresponds the "interior" fullness of the vision of man in God, that is, according to the measure of the "image of God"* (see Gn 1:27).[91]

Before original sin, mutual nakedness did not hinder Adam and Eve from seeing one another as persons. This ethical depth in seeing is precisely what John Paul II calls the "affirmation of personal value." Because of the innocence of the first woman and man, their gaze does not stop at the sexual value of the naked body. Nakedness is "transparent"; through it one can see the person, whose main characteristics are: first, his or her resistance to being treated and used as an object, and second, the calling to become a gift. Adam and Eve's external, physical nakedness and their internal lack of shame indicate "the whole simplicity and fullness of this vision, which shows the 'pure' value of man as male and female, the 'pure' value of the body and of [its] sex."[92]

The most fundamental characteristic of a mutual gift is the freedom of the persons engaged in self-giving. Thus, Adam and Eve, aware of the procreative power of their own bodies and of their own sex, were interiorly free from the constraint of their own bodies and their own sex; free from the constraint of sexual instinct,

---

is naked before its Creator: "And before him no creature is hidden, but all are naked and laid bare to the eyes of the one to whom we must render an account" (Heb 4:13). Similarly in *DBI:* "Being unclothed becomes a metaphor for being exposed to the judgment of God" ("Naked, Nakedness," in *DBI*, 582).
91. *TB,* 176–77.
92. Ibid., 177.

Adam and Eve were "free with the very freedom of the gift."[93] John Paul II's understanding of the notion of human freedom as it is used here clearly echoes his philosophical analysis of human transcendence from *The Acting Person*. He uses philosophical concepts such as self-determination, self-possession, and self-governance in order to interpret *Gaudium et spes* 24: "Here we mean freedom above all as *self-mastery* (self-dominion). Under this aspect, self-mastery is indispensable *in order for man to be able to 'give himself,'* in order for him to become a gift, in order for him (referring to the words of the Council) to be able 'find himself fully' through 'a sincere gift of self.'"[94]

The "freedom of the gift" of Adam and Eve had been possible before original sin thanks to their being endowed with the grace of original innocence. In other words, it was the acceptance of a gift that made a gift possible: the acceptance of God's gift of divine grace enabled existence in a mutual relation of self-gift.

The text of the constitution *Gaudium et spes* 24, is a key source of inspiration for John Paul II's theology of the body. Therefore, it is worthy of more detailed analysis:

> Indeed, the Lord Jesus, when He prayed to the Father, "that all may be one ... as we are one" (Jn 17:21–22) opened up vistas closed to human reason, for He implied a certain likeness between the union of the Divine Persons, and the unity of God's sons in truth and charity. This likeness reveals that man, who is the only creature on earth which God willed for itself, cannot fully find himself except through a sincere gift of himself.

The first sentence of this passage speaks of the similarities between the community of the Divine Persons and the Christian community.[95] The second sentence is especially important for our

---

93. Ibid., 185.
94. Ibid., 186.
95. A detailed analysis of this notion can be found in the next chapter of this book.

present reflections; for if, as the pope notes, man is "the only creature in the world that the Creator willed 'for its own sake,'" then it is precisely the mutual self-gift that "allows both the man and the woman *to find each other reciprocally,* inasmuch as the Creator willed each of them *'for his own sake.'*"[96] Every true gift given to another person, and especially the gift of oneself, concentrates on the value of the other person, and confirms the other as "willed for their own sake."[97] John Paul II goes on:

In the first beatifying encounter, the man thus finds the woman, and she finds him. In this way he welcomes her within himself (and she welcomes him within herself), welcomes her as she is willed "for her own sake" by the Creator, as she is constituted in the mystery of the image of God through her femininity; and reciprocally, she welcomes him, in the same way, as he is willed "for his own sake" by the Creator, and constituted by him through his masculinity.[98]

The mutual exchange of self-gift, then, leads to gaining a deep knowledge of oneself and of the other, and to a mutual discovery of the truth about man and woman. Also, the consciousness of the fact that the other person is willed by the Creator "for his own sake"—which makes him unique and inalienable (*alteri incommunicabilis*)—forms the deepest theological justification for the dignity of the other person.[99]

---

96. *TB,* 187.

97. In his phenomenological analysis of love in *The Acting Person,* Karol Wojtyła discovers an essential element of the experience of true love: the recognition that the "you" is another "I" (Wojtyła, *The Acting Person,* 295–300). Seeing the "you" not only as an object of one's own perception and reflection, but as a subject and a legitimate center of knowing and experiencing the world seems to be analogical to the truth that the other person is "willed for his own sake." In Robert Spaemann's philosophy, the beginning of seeing "you" as another "I" is defined as "awakening" (Robert Spaemann, *Happiness and Benevolence,* translated by Jeremiah Alberg, SJ [Notre Dame, Ind.: University of Notre Dame Press, 2000], 92–96).

98. *TB,* 187–88.

99. The idea of treating another person "for their own sake" has a long tradition in the history of Christian philosophy and theology. As an example of this we may point

In his efforts to describe the first human *communio personarum*, which is constituted by mutual self-gift, John Paul II notes that the biblical description of the giving and receiving of the gift of self is different in the case of Adam, a man, and Eve, a woman, because of the sexual difference. The pope emphasizes that in the Yahwist account of creation the woman is presented first as a gift for the man, and the man as the one who receives the gift and who is endowed with the gift of the woman by the Creator: "the woman has 'from the beginning' been entrusted to his eyes, to his consciousness, to his sensibility, to his 'heart.'"[100]

In the experience of giving herself to the man and of being accepted by him as a gift, the woman finds her identity, primarily because she is accepted by the man in the same way as the Creator accepts her existence, "for her own sake," in the complete uniqueness and inalienability of her person (*incommunicabilitas*).[101] The woman, having found her identity and vocation in being a gift, becomes capable of an ever more complete giving of herself: "This *finding of oneself in one's own gift becomes the source of a new gift of self* that grows by the power of the inner disposition to the exchange of the gift and in the measure in which it encounters the same and even deeper acceptance and welcome as the fruit of an ever more intense consciousness of the gift itself."[102]

---

to some classic formulations used by St. Thomas Aquinas in *Summa contra gentiles*. In the third part of this work, Aquinas makes a teleological distinction between rational (*creatura rationalis*) and irrational (*aliae creaturae*) creatures: "God is the ultimate end of the whole of things; that an intellectual nature alone attains to Him in Himself, that is, by knowing and loving Him.... Therefore, the intellectual nature is the only one that is required in the universe, for its own sake [*propter se*], while all others are for its sake" (*SCG* III, cap. 112, 3 [2858]).

100. *TB*, 197.

101. Some representatives of relational anthropology have analyzed in detail the phenomenon of receptivity, or the ability to accept and receive a gift. They call attention to the fact that receptivity thus understood does not mean a pure passivity on the part of the subject, but rather an active, spiritual capability that can serve as the true measure of human maturity and the ability to love.

102. *TB*, 197.

According to John Paul II, the Yahwist account of creation indicates that the woman is, first and foremost, a gift, and the man the one who accepts the gift. The pope avoids, however, a perspective that would lead to simplistic understanding of the phenomenon of love, in which the active element would be attributed exclusively to the man, and the passive one to the woman. At the moment when Adam accepts the gift of Eve, he simultaneously gives himself to her. In doing so, also he finds himself, his identity and vocation:

> The man's act of self-donation, in answer to that of the woman, is for him himself an enrichment; in fact, it is here that *the specific essence, as it were, of his masculinity is manifested, which, through the reality of the body and of its sex, reaches the innermost depth of "self-possession,"* thanks to which he is able both to give himself and to receive the gift of the other.[103]

Man accepts the self-gift of the woman, but his self-gift is accepted by the woman at the same time. This exchange of gift "is reciprocal, and the mutual effects of the 'sincere gift' and of 'finding oneself' reveal themselves and grow in that exchange (GS 24)."[104]

Moreover, the mutual exchange of self-gift between male and female is of a sexual nature. The Yahwist author points to this dimension when he states that man and woman "become one flesh."[105] In this becoming "one flesh," the spousal meaning of the human body is revealed also as its parental sense, and the mutual self-gift leads to the creation of a new life. John Paul II writes that in the birth of a child, the full truth about femininity is revealed in motherhood, and the full truth about masculinity in fatherhood:

> This "knowledge" [obtained by mutual self-donation] includes also the consummation of marriage, the specific *consummatum;* in this way one obtains the grasp of the "objectivity" of the body, hidden in the somatic powers of man and woman, and at the same time the grasp of the objec-

---

103. Ibid.
104. Ibid.
105. Gn 2:24.

tivity of man, who "is" this body. Through the body, the human person is "husband" and "wife"; at the same time, in this particular act of "knowledge" mediated by personal masculinity and femininity, one seems to reach also the discovery of the "pure" subjectivity of the gift: that is, mutual self-realization in the gift.[106]

The pope calls attention to the fact parents get to know themselves because of the birth of their child. They discover not only a likeness to themselves in the child, as is evident in familiar facial features, but their very identity.

As already stated above, the ability to become a spontaneous and mutual self-gift for each other is characteristic for man and woman before original sin. We do not find a detailed analysis of original sin in the Wednesday catecheses on the theology of the body. John Paul II points only to the treacherous dynamic of temptation, in which the image of God-Love, who endows man with the gift of creation, was replaced with the false image of a jealous rival who carefully guards his privileges: "God knows in fact that the day you eat it your eyes will be opened and you will be like gods, knowing good from evil" (Gn 3:5). As a result, original sin is primarily a questioning of the gift and of the love "from which creation takes its origin as gift."[107]

The sinful turning away from the loving God radically changes the relationship of Adam and Eve, which is indicated in the Yahwist account by the appearance of sexual shame: "Then the eyes of both were opened, and they knew that they were naked; and they sewed fig leaves together and made loincloths for themselves."[108] According to John Paul II, sexual shame, which points to a profound change in looking at the naked body of the other person after original sin, signifies a radical transformation of the man-woman relation, a breakdown in the original spontaneity of mutual com-

---

106. *TB*, 211.
107. Ibid., 237.
108. Gn 3:7.

munication and exchange of self-gift: "Almost unexpectedly, an insurmountable threshold appeared in their consciousness that limited the original 'self-donation' to the other with full trust in all that constituted one's own identity and at the same time diversity, female on the one side, male on the other. The diversity, or the difference between the male and female sexes, was abruptly sensed and understood as an element of mutual opposition of persons."[109]

John Paul II writes that after original sin, the naked bodies of woman and man ceased to be "transparent" to the value of the whole person. Also, original sin threatened the spousal and unifying meaning of the body. The appearance of sexual shame "attests to the loss of the original certainty that through its masculinity and femininity the human body is precisely the 'substratum' of the communion of persons, a substratum that simply expresses this communion and serves to realize it (and thus also to complete 'the image of God' in the visible world).... Sexuality became an 'obstacle' in man's personal relationship with woman."[110]

In the biblical account, original sin also gives rise to fear, which is attested to by sexual shame. Man and woman both fear that the gaze of the other person will stop at the visible, objective dimension of the naked body and will not go deeper, to the subjective value of the person, as was the case in the age of original innocence. It is precisely this fear that explains the need to hide after original sin; Adam hides from God among the trees of the garden, and both Adam and Eve cover their intimate parts from one another.

In his description of man after original sin, John Paul II speaks of the "man of threefold concupiscence" referring to the first Letter of John: "for all that is in the world—the desire of the flesh, the desire of the eyes, the pride in riches—comes not from the Father

109. *TB*, 247–48.
110. Ibid., 248–49.

but from the world."¹¹¹ The pope emphasizes that each of these three sinful desires, but especially the desire of the flesh, disturbs the relation of self-donation between male and female: "By violating the dimension of the mutual gift of the man and the woman, concupiscence also casts doubt on the fact that each of them is willed by the Creator 'for himself.' The subjectivity of the person gives way in some sense to the objectivity of the body. Because of the body, man becomes an object for man: the female for the male and vice versa."¹¹²

John Paul II notes that concupiscence also threatens the freedom of mutual self-giving that characterized the state of original innocence: "*Concupiscence,* which manifests itself as a '*constraint "sui generis" of the body,*' limits and restricts self-mastery from within, and thereby *in some sense makes the interior freedom of the gift impossible.* At the same time, also the beauty that the human body possesses in its male and female appearance, as an expression of the spirit, is obscured."¹¹³

In place of mutual self-donation and union, concupiscence introduces the dynamic of treating the other person as an object: "The body is left as an object of concupiscence and, thus as a 'terrain of appropriation' of the other human being. Concupiscence as such is not able to promote union as a communion of persons. By itself, it does not unite, but appropriates to itself. *The relationship of the gift changes into a relationship of appropriation.*"¹¹⁴

According to John Paul II, the biblical description of the effects of original sin points to such an appropriation. Thus, Yahweh describes the new relationship between Adam and Eve in terms of domination, that is, "he shall rule over you."¹¹⁵

---

111. 1 Jn 2:16.
112. *TB,* 259.
113. *TB,* 260.
114. Ibid.
115. Gn 3:16. Thus, the biblical author seems to state prophetically that the woman will be the main victim of the "man of threefold concupiscence" in human history. A similar prophecy appears in the encyclical *Humanae vitae* (1968), written many centuries

It is important to remember that John Paul II's theological anthropology looks at the human person in the supernatural light of Christ's words. The words of the Redeemer, chosen by the pope for a thorough analysis in the catecheses, also refer the pope to other passages of the Old and New Testament, as well as to the whole tradition of Christian theology. However, the very fact that John Paul II begins his reflection in the catecheses with Christ's words suggests that the whole theology of the body should be read in the light of Christ's redemptive act, in the light of "the ethos of the redemption of the body."[116]

The choice of the word "ethos" to describe New Testament ethics indicates that, for a Christian, a transformation of the heart is far more important than a mere change in external behavior: "The new dimension of ethos is always linked with the revelation of the depth that is called 'heart' and with the liberation of the heart from 'concupiscence' *so that man can shine more fully in this heart:* male and female in all the inner truth of the reciprocal 'for.'"[117] The ethos of the redemption of the body does not see evil in the material dimension itself, nor in the erotic attractiveness of the human body, but, rather, in the human heart, which, when possessed by threefold concupiscence, cannot perceive the whole truth about the human body and its vocation to be a gift for another and to form a communion of persons.

John Paul II indicates that the following passage from the First Letter to the Thessalonians is fundamental to a reflection on

---

later, where Paul VI warns that women will become the first victims of the modern popularization of contraception (*HV* 17). Janet Smith is one of many commentators who, writing many years after the publication of *Humanae vitae,* points out sadly that Paul VI's prophecy has come true (Janet E. Smith, "Paul VI as Prophet," in *Why Humanae Vitae Was Right: A Reader,* edited by Janet E. Smith [San Francisco: Ignatius Press, 1993], 519–31).

116. *TB,* 322. For the philosophical and theological sources of the expression "ethos of the redemption of the body" see the second chapter of this book.

117. *TB,* 300.

the ethos of the redemption of the body: "For God did not call us to impurity but in holiness. Therefore whoever rejects this rejects not human authority but God, who also gives his Holy Spirit to you."[118] The pope notes that the concept of purity, which is of key importance for the ethos of the redemption of the body, can be understood in this text in two ways: first, as a moral virtue, or, second, as a gift of the Holy Spirit.[119]

Thanks to purity, a Christian "has received himself and his own body anew, as it were, from God."[120] This "receiving of oneself" and "receiving of one's own body" seem to point to a new integrity and maturity, received alongside the grace of Christ, for the Christian, or—to use the philosophical language of *The Acting Person*—to self-possession and self-governance, which are conditions of a mature and free gift of self that leads to the communion of persons.

Christ speaks of the eschatological future of the anthropological realities of gift and of the communion of persons in his dispute concerning the levirate law with the Sadducees.[121] In the Gospel according to St. Luke we read as follows: "Those who belong to this age marry and are given in marriage; but those who are considered worthy of a place in that age and in the resurrection from the dead neither marry nor are given in marriage. Indeed they cannot die anymore, because they are like angels and are children of God, being children of the resurrection."[122]

Listening to these words of the Teacher, John Paul II notes that "marriage and procreation do not constitute man's eschatological future. In the resurrection they lose, so to speak, their *raison d'être*."[123] Human marriage, in its procreative dimension, ac-

---

118. 1 Thes 4:7–8.
119. The papal reflection on purity, which frees the human heart from threefold concupiscence, was presented in the second chapter of this book.
120. *TB*, 350.
121. Mt 22:24–30; Mk 12:18–27; Lk 20:27–40.
122. Lk 20:34–36.   123. *TB*, 387.

tualizes the spousal meaning of the body only in history. In the Resurrection, the law of gift and of the communion of persons will be realized in a different way than in human history.

Reflecting on Christ's words that in the resurrection men and women are "like angels" and are "children of God," John Paul II, in line with traditional Christian teaching, calls this new eschatological state of man a "new spiritualization" and "divinization."[124] The first term, "new spiritualization," is defined by the pope as "another 'system of powers' within man" and "a new submission of the body to the spirit,"[125] in which an internal harmony will be reached within man thanks to infused grace. The self-possession and self-governance that are necessary preconditions for human maturity and the capacity to become a gift will not be a result of man's own effort, as it is now, but, rather, a fruit of receiving the grace of the resurrection.

The other term used by John Paul II, "divinization," indicates a "participation in the divine nature, participation in the inner life of God himself, penetration and permeation of what is essentially human by what is essentially divine."[126] The pope describes the reality of eschatological divinization using the categories of gift and communion: "that divinization should be understood ... as a new formation of man's entire personal subjectivity according to the measure of union with God in his trinitarian mystery and of intimacy with him in the perfect communion of persons."[127] Man's union with God, therefore, will be a loving participation in the internal, Trinitarian life of God himself: "The eschatological communion (*communio*) of man with God, which is constituted thanks to the love of a perfect union, will be nourished by the vision 'face to face,' by the *contemplation* of the most perfect communion—because it is purely divine—which is, namely, the *trini*-

---

124. Ibid., 389–94.
126. Ibid., 392.
125. Ibid., 389.
127. Ibid., 392–93.

tarian communion of the divine Persons in the unity of the same divinity."[128]

In the Resurrection, then, man's self-giving to God will be the response to God's self-giving to man in the richness of God's Trinitarian communion of Persons. The pope points to two fundamental consequences of this human self-giving to God that leads to "perfect communion with the living God."[129] First, man's participation in the reality of the Resurrection will reveal the virginity of the body as "the eschatological fulfillment of the 'spousal' meaning of the body, as the specific sign and authentic expression of personal subjectivity as a whole."[130] This eschatological virginity of the body indicates that man's loving concentration on God will fulfill all the potentialities and needs of every human person: "as a consequence of the vision of God 'face to face,' *a love of such depth and power of concentration on God himself* will be born in the person that it *completely absorbs the person's whole psychosomatic subjectivity.*"[131]

The second consequence of man's participation in God's Trinitarian life is that every man and woman will rediscover in God his or her communal relationships with other people. John Paul II speaks thus of this mystery, referred to as the communion of saints (*communio sanctorum*) in Catholic tradition, in his reflections: "The concentration of knowledge and love on God himself in the trinitarian communion of Persons can find a beatifying response in those who will become sharers in the 'other world' only *through realizing reciprocal communion commensurate with created persons.*"[132]

To summarize, participation in the future world will mean a rediscovery of a perfect subjectivity for every person and, simultaneously, of a perfect intersubjectivity, a community of all who are saved through a loving concentration on God. This eschatological

---

128. Ibid., 394.
130. Ibid., 395.
132. Ibid., 396.
129. Ibid.
131. Ibid.

THE GIFT THAT CREATES COMMUNION 131

state will mean "the perfect realization of the 'trinitarian order' in the created world of persons"[133] and, simultaneously, the highest fulfillment and realization of the law of the gift and the communion of persons.

Perspectives for Further Research

To summarize the reflections in this chapter, let us first dwell on the question why the theory of gift and communion seems to be of such significance for contemporary Christian philosophers and theologians. First, it should be emphasized that currently, in a time when Christian theology is suffering the effects of being divided into many specializations and detailed fields of expertise that relate to one another only with great difficulty, John Paul II is proposing that the theological concepts of gift and communion be treated as a bond between many different fields of theology: Trinitarian theology, theology of creation and redemption, ecclesiology, theology of grace, anthropology, theology of marriage and family as well as ethics.[134] Rooted in biblical theology, the papal theology of gift consists of two structurally connected parts: one dogmatic and the other moral. The former analyzes the concept of gift in reference to the triune God, who gives himself to man through creation and redemption. The latter concerns the concept of gift in the context of Christian anthropology and ethics, and especially the ethics of marital life.

The concepts of gift and communion turn out to be useful tools for anthropological reflection since they make an adequate description of human love possible. The phenomenon of self-gift

---

133. Ibid.
134. An excellent description of the disintegration of modern theology can be found in Servais Pinckaers OP, *The Sources of Christian Ethics,* translated by Mary Thomas Noble, OP (Washington, D.C.: The Catholic University of America Press, 1995), 240–323. Though Pinckaers's reflections refer primarily to moral theology, his analyses can also be applied to other branches of theology.

sheds light on the nonutilitarian character of human love. Therefore, with reference to *Gaudium et spes* 24, John Paul II frequently speaks about a "sincere gift" or a "disinterested gift." In the light of the theology of gift, love consists not in realizing one's own private desires or plans, but in an ecstatic concentration on the "I" of the other person, which—paradoxically—leads to the self-fulfillment and happiness of the one who loves.

The theology of the body presents a very realistic picture of human love. John Paul II emphasizes that only the person who has reached some necessary level of maturity and internal integrity, described as self-possession and self-governance, is able to become a self-gift for another. This fundamental dimension of ethical self-governance becomes especially important in relation to one's own sexuality. A harmonious integration of sensuality, emotions, reason, and will turns out to be a necessary condition for undertaking the effort to affirm the other person, that is, to treat the other person not as an object, but as a subject. The gift of Christ's redemptive grace is indispensable for bringing about interior order, which enables one, in turn, to love and to undertake the spiritual battle with the desire of the flesh that has its roots in original sin.

The emphasis on subjective preconditions that enable one to make a gift of oneself possible guards the papal theology of gift from "slipping" toward the quietistic conception of *l'amour pur*, which is characterized by its tendency to highlight primarily the disinterested nature of love.[135] It is the theological grounding of the theory of gift in the Christian teaching on creation also protects its realism; this teaching recalls that it is the responsibility of every created man and woman to be aware of his or her own needs and to remember to fulfill them rationally and according to nature.[136]

---

135. Jacques Le Brun and Eulogio Pacho, "Quiétisme," in *DS*, vol. 12-2, col. 2756-2842; Josef Pieper, *About Love*, translated by Richard and Clara Winston (Chicago: Franciscan Herald Press, 1974), 57–91.

136. This realism, deriving from the Christian teaching on creation, brings John Paul II's reflections on love in line with those of Josef Pieper (*About Love*, 67–77).

In John Paul II's theology of gift, only the person who accepts Christ's gift of redeeming grace, which alone is capable of healing the desire of the flesh, is able to become a gift of love for others. In the dynamic of the mutual gift, therefore, equally as important as the personal ability to become a gift is the ability to accept and receive a gift, which some thinkers describe as "receptivity."[137] A well-known Thomist scholar, Norris Clarke, writes:

> Here [in the order of creation] the absolutely primary status of our being, of our substantial *esse* itself, is receptivity: it is a gift received from another, i.e., from God our Creator. This status as gift generates in us an absolutely primordial relation of receptivity and dependence, inscribed inseparably in the very depths of our being, prior to any action or initiative of our own. Thus in us as created beings the divine order is reversed: first comes receptivity and the primordial relation flowing from it; then our taking possession of this gift so that we stand in ourselves as self-governing masters of the gift we have received; then we pour over in active self-communication of the gift we have received, generating as we go the relations flowing from action. Relationality is indeed a dimension of our being equally primordial with our substantiality, but the most primordial aspect of it is the foundational relation of receptivity in our very being as a whole from Another, from God.[138]

Certainly, John Paul II's theology of gift reserves a privileged place for the category of relation in the concept of the person, thus initiating dialogue with modern currents in anthropology that consider human relationality not as accidental but as a constitutive part of the *persona humana*.[139]

---

137. Shivanandan, *Crossing the Threshold of Love*, 161–62.

138. Norris Clarke, "Response to David Schindler's Comments," *Communio* 20, no. 3 (1993): 595; also, David L. Schindler, "Norris Clarke on Person, Being and St. Thomas," ibid., 580–92; Kenneth L. Schmitz, "Created Receptivity and the Philosophy of the Concrete," *Thomist* 61, no. 3 (1997): 339–71.

139. F. LeRon Shults, *Reforming Theological Anthropology: After the Philosophical Turn to Relationality* (Grand Rapids, Mich.: Eerdmans, 2003); also: Norris Clarke, "Person, Being and St. Thomas," *Communio* 19, no. 3 (1992): 601–18; Joseph Ratzinger, "Concerning the Notion of Person in Theology," *Communio* 13 (1990): 438–54.

In these summarizing remarks, it is worthwhile to mention an important statement made by the Church on the theme of *communio: Letter to Bishops of the Catholic Church on Some Aspects of the Catholic Church Understood as Communion* (1992), signed by Cardinal Joseph Ratzinger of the Congregation for the Doctrine of the Faith.[140] The *Letter* mainly addresses ecclesiological problems concerning the relation of local churches to the universal Church, as well as some false interpretations of "Eucharistic ecclesiology." However, this document also contains some statements essential for our reflections.

First, the *Letter* emphasizes that the concept of *communio* "is very suitable for expressing the core of the Mystery of the Church and can certainly be a key for the renewal of Catholic ecclesiology."[141] The term *communio* as used in the *Letter* parallels John Paul II's Trinitarian and anthropological understanding thereof: "The concept of communion lies 'at the heart of the Church's self-understanding,' insofar as it is the Mystery of the personal union of each human being with the divine Trinity and with the rest of mankind.... It is essential to the Christian understanding of communion that it be recognized above all as a gift from God, as a fruit of God's initiative carried out in the paschal mystery."[142] In its anthropological dimension, the theological concept of communion indicates therefore that the horizontal unity between people is the fruit of a vertical unity with God.[143] *Agape* must first of all be accepted as an undeserved gift, before it is able to be returned.

---

140. The document can be found on the official site of the Congregation for the Doctrine of the Faith: *Letter to Bishops of the Catholic Church on Some Aspects of the Catholic Church Understood as Communion,* Congregation for the Doctrine of the Faith, 1992, http://www.vatican.va/roman_curia/congregations/cfaith/documents.

141. *Letter* 1.

142. Ibid. 3.

143. In its classic definition, supernatural love (*caritas, agape*) is defined as love for others for the sake of God (*propter Deum,* see Thomas Aquinas, *STh* II-II 23, 1). In their attempt to find an analogy between human and divine *communio,* some commentators go as far as to describe the spiritual union between people with the term *perichoresis,*

Finally, we would like to emphasize the ecumenical character of *communio* theology. In the recent years, among many important publications devoted to this subject,[144] special attention should be paid to the work of John Zizioulas, professor at universities in Athens, Thessaloniki, Geneva, and Rome, and currently the Orthodox patriarch of Pergamon. Through his historical studies on the theology of the Cappadocian fathers, Zizioulas came to the conviction that it was the Cappadocians' experience of the Church's *communio,* that is, a communion living in unity that flows from grace, that enabled them to use the concept of person to describe the reality of the Holy Trinity. According to Zizioulas, the present renaissance of the relational concept of the person may help in overcoming modern individualism, which is also at the root of serious problems for Trinitarian theology, instantiated in the shift toward a tritheistic interpretation.[145] Patricia A. Fox writes: "While Zizioulas's Trinitarian theology of persons in communion is unambiguously the center point or source of his whole theological system, it incorporates within it, as essential elements, not only anthropology, Christology, and pneumatology, ... but

---

which was traditionally used in Trinitarian theology to describe the union, the permeating of the Persons of the Trinity (Mary Timothy Prokes, *Mutuality: The Human Image of Trinitarian Love* [New York: Paulist Press 1993], 28–32).

144. Michael Downey, *Altogether Gift: A Trinitarian Spirituality* (Maryknoll, N.Y.: Orbis Books, 2000); Stanley J. Grenz, *The Social God and the Relational Theology of the Imago Dei,* (Louisville, Ky.: Westminster Press, 2001); Mark Medley, *Imago Trinitatis. Toward a Relational Understanding of Becoming Human* (Lanham, Md.: University Press of America, 2002); Alvin F. Kimel, ed., *Speaking the Christian God: The Holy Trinity and the Challenge of Feminism* (Grand Rapids, Mich.: Eerdmans, 1992); Alvin F. Kimel, ed., *This Is My Name Forever: The Trinity and Gender Language for God* (Downers Grove, Ill.: InterVarsity, 2001); Miroslav Volf, *After Our Likeness: The Church as the Image of the Trinity* (Grand Rapids, Mich.: Eerdmans, 1998).

145. Some contemporary theologians, Karl Barth and Karl Rahner among them, called attention to the fact that the modern understanding of the person as an autonomous center of consciousness and freedom may lead to a false tritheism in the understanding of the Trinity (Patricia A. Fox, *God as Communion: John Zizioulas, Elizabeth Johnson, and the Retrieval of the Symbol of the Triune God* [Collegeville, Minn.: Liturgical Press, 2001], 25–32).

also an ecclesiology and cosmology."[146] The thought of the Orthodox patriarch, currently garnering great interest, may serve as the ecumenical inspiration for further development of the theology of gift and communion, as well as for creating theological connections to similar reflections in the thought of Catholic theologians, especially John Paul II.

146. Ibid., 52.

Chapter Four

MAN AS THE IMAGE AND LIKENESS OF GOD

The understanding of man as the image and likeness of God, fundamental for the development of Christian thought, is rooted in the first chapter of the Bible: "God said, 'Let us make humankind in our image, according to our likeness; and let them have dominion over the fish of the sea, and over the birds of the air, and over the cattle, and over all the wild animals of the earth, and over every creeping thing that creeps upon the earth.'"[1] These words that complete the process of creation should be understood in the context of Yahweh's absolute transcendence, which was safeguarded by the Old Testament ban on making graven images of God, as only man is the true image of Yahweh.[2] The following chapters of Genesis shed light on the meaning of man having been made in the image of God. The Old Testament scholar Paul Lamarche calls attention especially to the fact of human dominion over creation and the human ability to procreate, to give life to beings who are also made in the image of God.[3]

1. Gn 1:26.
2. Gerhard von Rad, "εἰκών: The Divine Likeness in the OT," in *TDNT*, 2:390. Other texts of the Old Testament that point to man's likeness to God: Ps 8:5 and Sir 17:3.
3. Paul Lamarche, "Image et ressemblance: Ecriture sainte," in *DS*, vol. 7-2, col.

In the New Testament, the term "the image of God" refers primarily to Christ.⁴ The Second Letter to the Corinthians explains why some listeners reject the Gospel: "the god of this world [ὁ θεὸς τοῦ αἰῶνος] has blinded the minds of the unbelievers, to keep them from seeing the light of the gospel of the glory of Christ [τὸν φωτισμὸν τοῦ εὐαγγελίου τῆς δόξης τοῦ Χριστοῦ], who is the image of God [εἰκὼν τοῦ θεοῦ]."⁵ The concept εἰκὼν has an ontological meaning here, since in Christ the essence of God and his glory (ἡ δόξα) has been revealed.⁶ In the Letter to the Colossians, the Christological expression "He is the image [εἰκὼν] of the invisible God" begins the hymn, whose main theme is Christ's divinity and his role as the only mediator in the work of creation and redemption.⁷

The ethical meaning of εἰκὼν derives from its Christological meaning. The Letter to the Romans states that in God's plan of salvation, believers are "to be conformed to the image of his Son [τῆς εἰκόνος τοῦ υἱοῦ], in order that he might be the first born within a large family."⁸ In its ethical meaning, εἰκὼν has a relational character, since it speaks of the special bond between believers and the Savior. The Letter to the Colossians makes men-

---

1401–5. Lamarche argues that when the author of Genesis speaks of the birth of Adam's son, "he became the father of a son in his likeness, according to his image" (Gn 5:3), he intends to say that even after original sin, Adam's offspring retained the dignity of God's image (*TB*, 212; Maxwell Miller, "In the 'Image and Likeness' of God," *Journal of Biblical Literature* 91 [1972]: 289–304—this article contains a thorough bibliography on the theology of *imago Dei* in the Old Testament).

4. Gerhard Kittel emphasizes that the New Testament way of using the Greek word εἰκὼν indicates that the original is always present in the image. For instance: "Since the law has only a shadow of the good things to come and not the true form [τὴν εἰκόνα] of these realities" (Heb 10:1; see Gerhard Kittel, "εἰκὼν: The Metaphorical Use of Image in the NT," in *TDNT*, 2:395).

5. 2 Cor 4:4.

6. Schnelle, *The Human Condition*, 98–102.

7. Col 1:15–20; see Jacob Jerwell, "Bild Gottes: biblische, frühjüdische und gnostische Auffassungen," in *TRE*, 6:494–98.

8. Rom 8:29. See also 2 Cor 3:18: "And all of us, with unveiled faces, seeing the glory of the Lord as though reflected in a mirror, are being transformed into the same image [τὴν αὐτὴν εἰκόνα] from one degree of glory to another."

tion of this bond, referring to the creation account in the Book of Genesis: "Do not lie to one another, seeing that you have stripped off the old self with its practices and have clothed yourselves with the new self, which is being renewed in knowledge according to the image of its creator [κατ' εἰκόνα τοῦ κτίσαντος αὐτόν]."[9] The spiritual transformation of the Christian that happens as a result of following Christ (*imitatio Christi*) is a renewal of the image of God that was "inscribed" in every man in the act of creation and later deformed by the reality of sin.[10]

The biblical truth about man's creation in the image of God became an important theme of reflection for the Fathers of the Church, both Greek and Latin, and reached its most complete formulation in the theology of St. Augustine.[11] *Imago Dei* also formed an important part of theological reflection for scholastic theology, for the Cistercian, Franciscan, and Dominican schools among others.[12] In the theology of the Rhineland and Carmelite mystics the Christological and soteriological understanding of *imago Dei* was

9. Col 3:9–10.

10. Paul's metaphor of the "old" and "new man" is analogical to another soteriological image of "the first Adam" and "the last Adam": "The first man was from the earth, a man of dust; the second man is from heaven. As was the man of dust, so are those who are of the dust; and as is the man of heaven, so are those who are of heaven. Just as we have borne the image of the man of dust [τὴν εἰκόνα τοῦ χοϊκοῦ], we will also bear the image of the man of heaven [τὴν εἰκόνα τοῦ ἐπουρανίου]" (1 Cor 15:47–49). The spiritual growth of every Christian consists in overcoming the sinful likeness to "the first Adam" in oneself in order to make oneself more similar to "the last Adam," Christ. The context of this passage from the First Letter to the Corinthians suggests that a Christian's perfect likeness to the image of Christ will be realized fully in the eschatological reality of the future life (Schnelle, *The Human Condition*, 100).

11. Peter Schwanz, *Imago Dei als christologisch-anthropologisches Problem in der Geschichte der Alten Kirche von Paulus bis Clemens von Alexandrien* (Halle: Niemeyer, 1970); this book also includes a thorough bibliography on the Fathers of the Church. For Augustine's theology see:. John Edward Sullivan, *The Image of God: The Doctrine of St. Augustine and Its Influence* (Dubuque, Iowa: Priory Press, 1963).

12. Rik Van Nieuwenhove, "In the Image of God: The Trinitarian Anthropology of St. Bonaventure, St. Thomas Aquinas and the Blessed Jan Van Ruysbroec," *Irish Theological Quarterly* 66 (2001), 109–23 (part 1), 227–37 (part 2); Juvenal D. Merrill, *To the Image of the Trinity: A Study in the Development of Aquinas' Teaching* (Toronto: Pontifical Institute of Mediaeval Studies, 1990).

supplemented by an ascetic interpretation—similarity to Christ, who is the image of God, is possible only through the ascetic and spiritual purification of the soul from all other images.[13]

Leo Scheffczyk notes that the concept of *imago Dei* has lost its significance in those modern theological currents in which the relation with biblical thought has been seriously weakened.[14] In some currents of negative theology, for example in dialectic and existential theology, or in the theology of the death of God, the concept of *imago Dei* has been rejected as excessively anthropomorphic. Political theology, on the other hand, has rejected this concept because of its connection to anthropological individualism, which is not capable of a critique of unjust social, political, or economic structures.

We owe the contemporary renaissance of the concept of *imago Dei* in Catholic theology to the Second Vatican Council, where it finds its primary expression in the pastoral constitution *Gaudium et spes*. The history of this document is well known, and there is no need to review it here.[15] It is important to note, however, that the concept of *imago Dei* appeared in Schema XIII as a fruit of the efforts of its authors to root the constitution in biblical theology and to present a Christian anthropology in the text. This anthropology, which begins with an inductive or phenomenological description of the experience of modern man, was meant to provide Christian answers for urgent questions posed by contemporary society.[16]

The concept of *imago Dei* appears already in the first section of the first part of the constitution, which presents the foundation of Christian anthropology: "Sacred Scripture teaches that man was

13. Raphael-Louis Oechslin, "Image et ressemblance: Des mystiques rhénans au Carmel réformé," in *DS*, vol. 7-2, col. 1451–63.

14. Leo Scheffczyk, "Image et ressemblance: Dans la théologie et la spiritualité d'aujourd'hui," in *DS*, vol. 7-2, col. 1463.

15. Charles Moeller, "Pastoral Constitution on the Church in the Modern World: History of the Constitution," in *Commentary on the Documents of Vatican II* (New York: Herder and Herder, 1969), 5:1–76.

16. John F. Kobler, *Vatican II and Phenomenology: Reflections on the Life-World of the Church* (Dordrecht: M. Nijhoff, 1985).

MAN AS THE IMAGE AND LIKENESS OF GOD 141

created 'in the image of God,' is capable of knowing and loving his Creator, and was appointed by Him as master of all earthly creatures that he might subdue them and use them to God's glory."[17] The biblical truth about man being the image of God is presented as the ultimate foundation for the dignity of the human person, and, at the same time, human freedom is emphasized as a special sign of God's image in man.[18]

The first chapter of the constitution, devoted to the subject of human dignity, ends with a presentation of the Christological understanding of *imago Dei* in the New Testament:

> He who is "the image of the invisible God" (Col 1:15), is Himself the perfect man. To the sons of Adam He restores the divine likeness which had been disfigured from the first sin onward.... The Christian man, conformed to the likeness of that Son Who is the first born of many brothers, received "the first-fruits of the Spirit" (Rom 8:23) by which he becomes capable of discharging the new law of love.[19]

The renewal of God's image in man is a fruit of the action of the Holy Spirit who makes believers similar to Christ, the perfect image of the Father.

The theology of *imago Dei*, as present in the council's documents, also has a social dimension. This is evident in the previously quoted following passage of the constitution, which is very important for John Paul II's reflections:

> Indeed, the Lord Jesus, when He prayed to the Father, "that all may be one ... as we are one" (Jn 17:21–22) opened up vistas closed to human reason, for He implied a certain likeness between the union of the Divine Persons, and the unity of God's sons in truth and charity. This likeness reveals that man, who is the only creature on earth which God willed for himself, cannot fully find himself except through a sincere gift of himself.[20]

---

17. *GS* 12.
18. Ibid. 17.
19. Ibid. 22.
20. Ibid. 24. This passage from *Gaudium et spes* was analyzed in the previous chapter. That analysis will be deepened in a later part of this chapter.

The declaration on the relation of the Church to non-Christian religions, *Nostra aetate,* speaks of the ethical meaning of *imago Dei* theology: "We cannot truly call on God, the Father of all, if we refuse to treat in a brotherly way any man, created as he is in the image of God."[21]

Scheffczyk notes the fundamental role that the concept of *imago Dei* plays in the council's theology, although it does not appear frequently in Vatican II documents, and its content is not discussed in a systematic manner. Scheffczyk writes thus about the importance of the anthropological dimension of this concept: "Theology after the Council must undertake again this truth and present its richness; this task was not undertaken systematically by the Council. Therefore, a further reflection needs to be conducted in the direction indicated by the Council. The static and ontological view should be rejected for the dynamic view connected with the history of salvation, which enabled personalistic and Christological interpretation of this doctrine."[22] Anticipating further reflections in this chapter, we may say that in his catecheses on the theology of the body, John Paul II undertakes the Second Vatican Council's commitment to restoring the concept of *imago Dei* to its proper place in Christian anthropology and theology.

The "Philosophical Exegesis" of the Concept of *Imago Dei* in the Elohist and Yahwist Accounts of Creation

John Paul II roots his reflection on the creation of man in the image of God in the inspired text of Genesis: "God created humankind in his image, in the image of God he created them; male and female he created them."[23] The papal interpretation of this

---

21. *NA* 5.
22. Scheffczyk, "Image et ressemblance," col. 1465.
23. Gn 1:27. The term "philosophical exegesis" in the heading, describing the method

MAN AS THE IMAGE AND LIKENESS OF GOD   143

fundamental text is twofold. First, the text needs to be interpreted in the context of the priestly account of creation,[24] and, second, this interpretation ought to be supplemented through a reflection on the theology of the older, Yahwist account of creation.[25]

John Paul II emphasizes that in the priestly account, the creation of man is presented as the most important moment, the crowning, of the whole process of creation. This truth is evident in the language of the biblical text itself: "speaking about matter not endowed with life, the biblical author uses different predicates, such as 'separated,' 'called,' 'made,' 'put.' Speaking about beings that have the gift of life, by contrast, he uses the terms 'created' and 'blessed.'"[26] The account of the creation of man clearly differs from the account of God's previous works; the creation of man, for instance, is preceded by a solemn introduction "as if it were a case of God deliberating before this important act."[27] Thus, the priestly account of the creation of man in the image of God points to the exceptional dignity and value of every human person in the eyes of God.[28]

The priestly account of creation places emphasis on the inclusion of man in the whole of the visible cosmos. The creation of man is a part of the rhythm of the seven days of creation: "man is created on earth together with the visible world"[29] and is to subdue the earth.[30] In reference to man, however, the biblical narra-

---

of thought used in the catecheses, comes from Marian Grabowski and was analyzed in the first chapter of this book. This term indicates, on the one hand, the fundamental significance of inspired biblical texts as direct sources for John Paul II's theological anthropology. On the other hand, it indicates that in his theology of the body, John Paul II interprets biblical texts with notions from contemporary philosophical anthropology.

24. Gn 1:1–2,4.   25. Gn 2:4–25.
26. *TB*, 135.   27. Ibid.
28. Pinto de Oliveira notes that the theory of human rights, as developed by John Paul II, derives from the truth about the dignity of every man, expressed by the biblical term *imago Dei* (Pinto de Oliveira, "Image de Dieu et dignité humaine," *Freiburger Zeitschrift für Philosophie und Theologie* 27 [1980]: 401–36).
29. *TB*, 135.
30. Gn 1:28.

tive "does not speak of his likeness with the rest of creatures, but only with God."[31]

John Paul II observes that the fact that man is created in the image of God excludes the possibility of a cosmological definition of man: "Man can neither be understood nor explained in his full depth with the categories taken from the 'world,' that is, from the visible totality of bodies."[32] In the priestly account of creation, the essence of man can be defined only in relation to God, and "it includes at the same time an affirmation of the absolute impossibility of reducing man to the 'world.'"[33] The pope emphasizes that the fundamental truth that man is created in the image of God and cannot be adequately defined by a cosmological definition applies equally to man and woman; it refers to what is common to them both.

According to John Paul II, Adam's original solitude, as described in the second creation account, is helpful for understanding the truth that man was created in the image of God.[34] Adam's experience of original solitude, which comes to the fore in the process of naming the animals, starts with his discovery that he is different from all other animals: "but for the man there was not found a helper as his partner."[35] Alone in the created world, Adam

---

31. *TB*, 135. Paul Lamarche points out that "man, who is created by God, cannot be compared with nature or with the animals. Man, as the image of God, is 'on the side' of God" (Lamarche, "Image et ressemblance," col. 1402). Another commentary to the biblical account of creation states that "in the oriental world as a whole, nature was deified and the presence of gods and spirits in its midst induced men to make them harmless by devoting a cult to them. In Hebrew religion there is no bond between man and nature. Thus salvation for man will not consist in the adoration of nature but in dominion over it" (Jacob, *Theology of the Old Testament*, 153). Certainly, according to the Old Testament human dominion over nature was not absolute, because it was to unfold, as all human activity, within obedience to God's law.

32. *TB*, 135.

33. Ibid.

34. The phenomenon of Adam's original solitude was already the subject of a more detailed analysis in the previous two chapters of this work.

35. Gn 2:20.

experiences his uniqueness and superiority. To use a term from the first creation account, in the whole visible cosmos only Adam is created "in the image of God."

In the Yahwist account—as in the priestly one—Adam's original solitude reveals the relational character of human existence: "*Man is 'alone': this is to say that through his own humanity,* through what he is, he is at the same time set into a unique, *exclusive and unrepeatable relationship with God himself.*"[36] Man created as "the image of God" is not defined primarily in relation to the world, but in relation to God as a "subject of the covenant and 'partner of the Absolute.'"[37]

In his analysis of the Yahwist account of creation, John Paul II distinguishes several constitutive elements of Adam's original solitude: (1) consciousness, (2) the alternative of life and death, which reveals human freedom, and (3) dominion over creation, which is connected with the experience of the meaning of the human body.[38] According to the pope, the fundamental meaning of man's original solitude has to do with his uniqueness in the whole of creation, which is rooted in his special relationship with God, and with his superiority over all other creatures. As a result, each of the three elements of Adam's original solitude—consciousness, freedom, and dominion—reveals the truth about his uniqueness and superiority, and indirectly the truth about the image of God in man.

Another fundamental term that John Paul II uses to clarify the biblical truth about the creation of man in the image of God is the concept of *communio personarum*.[39] The pope observes that the reality defined by this concept is present in both creation accounts, though differently in each. The author of the first creation

36. *TB*, 151.   37. Ibid.
38. Ibid., 146–56.
39. This concept was analyzed in the third chapter of this work. We refer back to notions explained earlier in order to clarify the notion of *communion personarum* in light of the theology of *imago Dei*.

account states immediately that man was created in the image of God as man and woman;[40] the Yahwist author precedes the account of the creation of woman by pointing to the experience of Adam's original solitude.[41] In both accounts, God's act of calling man into existence ends with the creation of the communion of persons, the communion of man and woman.

John Paul II emphasizes that the statement that man was created in the image of God in the priestly account refers not only to every person individually, but also to the communion of persons:

Man became the image of God not only through his own humanity, but also through the communion of persons, which man and woman form from the very beginning. The function of the image is that of mirroring the one who is the model, of reproducing its own prototype. Man becomes an image of God not so much in the moment of solitude as in the moment of communion. He is, in fact, "from the beginning" not only an image in which the solitude of one Person, who rules the world, mirrors itself, but also, and essentially the image of an inscrutable divine communion of Persons.[42]

As we have seen, the papal theology of *imago Dei*—which is a "philosophical exegesis" of the two creation accounts in Genesis—points to the fundamental elements of John Paul II's theological anthropology. The creation of man in the image of God reveals man's unique place in the cosmos, and points to the impossibility of understanding him "with the categories taken from the 'world.'"[43] Every human person is an *imago Dei*, and the *communio personarum* of man and woman created in love is the image of the community of the Trinity. These fundamental themes will be developed further in the next sections of this chapter, which will also contain other elements of the pope's theology of *imago Dei*: the theological concept of "gift," the sacramental meaning of the

40. Gn 1:27.
41. Gn 2:18–20.
42. *TB*, 163.
43. Ibid., 135.

human body, the negative role of sin in the transmission of the *imago Dei*, and the Christocentric and eschatological understanding of the *imago Dei*.

Gift Reveals the Human Likeness to God

The concept of gift plays an important role in the papal search for that dimension of man which makes him similar to God. In the economy of salvation, God endows man with many gifts through creation and redemption, and, primarily, the gift of himself. The creation of the world itself is "a fundamental and 'radical' gift."[44] Redemption, too, is a gift, though "not only the fruits of redemption are a gift, but above all Christ himself is a gift."[45]

John Paul II emphasizes that God is a "complete" and "radical" gift primarily in the uncreated Trinitarian communion of divine persons.[46] The pope writes as follows in the encyclical *Dominum et vivificantem*: "It can be said that in the Holy Spirit the intimate life of the Triune God becomes totally gift, an exchange of mutual love between the divine Persons and that through the Holy Spirit God exists in the mode of gift. It is the Holy Spirit who is the personal expression of this self-giving, of this being-love. He is Person-Love. He is Person-Gift."[47]

If creation is the work of God, who is gift in his essence, then "every creature bears within itself the sign of the original and fundamental gift."[48] Every gift, however, indicates first of all a personal relationship between the giver and the recipient. Therefore, this "sign of the gift" takes a completely different form in the case of nonrational creatures and in the case of man.

According to John Paul II, the unique meaning of the "sign of the gift" in man is based on the fact that only man is *"able to*

44. Ibid., 180.
46. Ibid., 501.
48. *TB*, 180.
45. Ibid., 493.
47. *DV* 10.

understand the very meaning of the gift in the call from nothing to existence. He is also able to respond to the Creator with the language of this understanding."⁴⁹ Only man is capable of comprehending that he is gratuitously endowed by the Creator and Redeemer; only man can consciously understand "the logic of gift," in which one responds to a gift with a gift.

Saint Thérèse of Lisieux presents a moving account of human experience, which may be defined, in line with the pope, as "an understanding of the meaning of gift":

> This grace, my Beloved, was only the prelude to the even greater graces which You willed to lavish on me; let me remind You of them now, and forgive me if it is foolish to want to tell You once again about my hopes and desires which border on the infinite; yes, forgive me and heal my soul by fulfilling all of them. To be Your Spouse, my Jesus; to be a Carmelite; to be, through my union with You, a mother of souls, surely this should be enough? Yet I feel the call of more vocations still; I want to be a warrior, a priest, an apostle, a doctor of the Church, a martyr—there is no heroic deed I do not wish to perform. I feel as daring a crusader, ready to die for the Church upon a battlefield.⁵⁰

The experiences described by St. Thérèse of Lisieux ought to be described as "classic": as fundamentally human, and at the same time very Christian: the experience of love leads to the desire to respond to love by love. Using the language of the catecheses, we may say that "an understanding of the meaning of gift" in creation and redemption ought to lead the recipient of the gift to answer the Creator with "the language of this understanding."⁵¹ This answer consists in becoming a gift.

Undoubtedly, "an understanding of the meaning of gift," which leads the recipient to answer with "the language of this under-

---

49. Ibid.
50. Thérèse of Lisieux, *The Story of a Soul: The Autobiography*, translated by Michael Day (Westminster, Md.: Newman Press, 1952), 186.
51. *TB,* 180.

standing," precisely describes the dynamic of love that creates human marriage and family. However, the law of the gift, which creates the communion of persons, concerns every person, including those who are unmarried. In the third part of the catecheses, John Paul II notes that a sincere self-gift also constitutes the essence of life in chastity: "when he chooses continence for the kingdom of heaven, man has the awareness that in this way he can realize himself 'differently,' and in some sense 'more' than in marriage, by becoming 'a sincere gift for others' (GS 24)."[52] In the exhortation *Vita consecrata* on the consecrated life (1996), the pope writes that the man who lives according to the three evangelical counsels reflects the dynamic of gift that exists within the Holy Trinity and also builds up the *communio personarum* in monastic communities and in the Church.[53] In the thought of John Paul II, therefore, gift is revealed as the destiny of every person, male and female, and, at the same time, as a trace of God's creative and redeeming activity, *imago Dei*.

The Communal Dimension of *Imago Dei*

In the theology of John Paul II,[54] mutual self-gift, understood as the existence of a person "for" another,[55] creates the communion of persons. The communion of persons, therefore, is indicative of a unity of persons that is created by mutual love. *Com-*

---

52. Ibid., 427.
53. *VC* 21.
54. In discussing the similarity between the human community and the divine Trinity, theologians often use the term "social image of the Trinity" or "social dimension of *imago Dei*" (John L. Gresham Jr, "The Social Model of the Trinity and Its Critics," *Scottish Journal of Theology* 46, no. 3 [1993]: 325–43). John Paul II does not use these expressions even once in the catecheses, preferring the terms "communal image of the Trinity" or "communal dimension of *imago Dei*" (*TB*, 426). Undoubtedly, this linguistic and theological choice made by the author points to the importance of the concept *communio personarum* in the theology of *imago Dei*.
55. *TB*, 163.

munio personarum, thus understood, is the basis for an analogy between the human community and the divine community of the Holy Trinity.[56] In the catecheses we read that "the value in question is that of the body's spousal meaning, the value of a transparent sign by which the Creator—together with the perennial reciprocal attraction of man and woman through masculinity and femininity—has written into the heart of both the gift of communion, that is, the mysterious reality of his image and likeness."[57]

The constitution *Gaudium et spes*, frequently cited in the catecheses, is an important source for John Paul II's reflection on the communal dimension of the *imago Dei*:

> Indeed, the Lord Jesus, when He prayed to the Father, "that all may be one ... as we are one" (Jn 17:21–22) opened up vistas closed to human reason, for He implied a certain likeness between the union of the Divine Persons, and the unity of God's sons in truth and charity. This likeness reveals that man, who is the only creature on earth which God willed for himself, cannot fully find himself except through a sincere gift of himself.[58]

The constitution speaks of a "certain likeness" (*aliqua similitudo*) between the unity of the human community and the divine community of the Holy Trinity. *Gaudium et spes* 24, much like

---

56. It is important to remember that when John Paul II introduces the term *communio personarum* for the first time in his theology of the body, he is referring to the understanding thereof as presented in the documents of the Second Vatican Council (*TB*, 162). As a result of the analyses already conducted in the third chapter of this book, we know that the term *communio* was used by the council in four different, deeply interrelated theological meanings: community of the Persons of the Trinity (*communio Sanctissime Trinitatis*), community of local churches (*communio ecclesiarum*), community of ministries in the Church (*communio munerum*), and the human communion of persons (*communio personarum*). Each of these four analogical terms refers to the others. The semantic relationship between the first and the last term is of particular importance for our present analyses. This relationship indicates that the term *communio personarum* intrinsically refers us to *communio Sanctissime Trinitatis*, and that there is a "certain likeness" between the human community and the divine communion of the Holy Trinity.

57. *TB*, 324.

58. *GS* 24; see also *TB*, 98.

the writings of John Paul II, presents the theory that the unity of persons, which is the basis of this "certain likeness," is created "through a sincere gift of oneself." "Living in a reciprocal 'for,' in a relationship of reciprocal gift,"[59] therefore, means imitating God in a twofold manner. First, it is a reflection of the interior structure of the Holy Trinity, where three Persons are a gift for one another. Second, man's self-donation to another person reflects God's relationship to every living person—it enables man to recognize the other person as "the only creature in the world which God willed for his or her own sake." Being a gift for another, by which one creates the communion of persons, is therefore a way of being that is nonutilitarian and that affirms that the other was made "for their own sake."

In his theology of the body, John Paul II clearly draws the limits of the analogy between the divine Trinity and the human community. The first boundary is ontological and protects the monotheistic teaching on the Trinity against tritheistic interpretations: uncreated Divine Persons, sharing one nature, exist completely in relation to one another in a way that is impossible for human existence. This theological truth of the Christian *credo* is accepted a priori in the catecheses, which are themselves based on the teaching on creation *ex nihilo*, and is not itself a theme for reflection.

For every human person living in history, that is for every "historical man" or "man of threefold concupiscence," to use John Paul II's terminology, the second fundamental limitation to the communion analogy of *imago Dei* is sin. Every sin, and particularly original sin, means "casting doubt in his [man's] heart on the deepest meaning of the gift, that is, on love as the specific motive of creation."[60] The pope illustrates this thesis by showing how this "casting doubt" radically changed the original communion of Adam and Eve: "Almost unexpectedly, an insurmountable thresh-

59. *TB*, 182.   60. Ibid., 237.

old appeared in their consciousness that limited the original 'self-donation' to the other with full trust in all that constituted one's own identity and at the same time diversity, female on the one side, male on the other."[61] Sin caused human sexuality to become "an 'obstacle' in man's personal relationship with woman," which in turn led to the destruction of "the original relationship 'of communion.'"[62] Treating the other person, especially in the dimension of his or her sexuality, as an object introduced shame and fear to the mutual relationship of man and woman. Appropriation replaced mutual belonging.[63]

The Body as a Sign of *Imago Dei*

John Paul II, inspired by biblical categories of thought, considers the human body as the only possible way that man can exist in the world; man is simply a "body among bodies."[64] Therefore, the creation of man in the image of God also concerns the creation of the human body: "Man, whom God created 'male and female,' bears the divine image impressed in the body 'from the beginning'; man and woman constitute, so to speak, two diverse ways of 'being a body' that are proper to human nature in the unity of this image."[65] This unity of the image of God, therefore, concerns what is common to man and woman—human nature, which always exists in the form of a specific sex, male or female. Thus the image of God refers to "humanity itself in all the truth of its male and female duality."[66]

John Paul II writes that created man was "endowed with a

---

61. Ibid., 247.
62. Ibid., 248–49.
63. Ibid., 261–62. The way in which threefold concupiscence (1 Jn 2:15–16) limits the spousal meaning of the body and the human ability to create *communio personarum* was analyzed in the two previous chapters of this work.
64. *TB*, 152.   65. Ibid., 179.
66. Ibid., 237.

MAN AS THE IMAGE AND LIKENESS OF GOD   153

deep unity" of what is male and female.[67] Human masculinity and femininity, as expressed in the body, are "two 'incarnations' of the same metaphysical solitude before God and the world— *two reciprocally completing ways of 'being a body' and at the same time of being human*—as two complementary dimensions of self-knowledge and self-determination and, at the same time, *two complementary ways of being conscious of the meaning of the body* ... femininity in some way finds itself before masculinity, while masculinity confirms itself through femininity."[68] John Paul II calls attention to the constitutive role of the human body in creating the *communio personarum* of man and woman. Certainly, the communion of man and woman exceeds the physical dimension and concerns every part of human existence. However, at the same time, the body is "the constitutive element"[69] of the marital union of man and woman, when two become "one flesh."[70] In this way, the human body participates in the dignity of the image of God in the communion of persons:

> The human body was from the beginning a faithful witness and a perceptible verification of man's original "solitude" in the world, while becoming at the same time, through masculinity and femininity, a transparent component of reciprocal giving in the communion of persons. Thus, in the mystery of creation, the human body carried within itself an unquestionable sign of the "image of God" and also constituted the specific source of certainty about this image, present in the whole human being.[71]

The place of the human body in the theology of *imago Dei* was a subject of various controversies in the history of Christian thought. For the Elohist author of the first creation account in the Book of Genesis, the question whether the image of God is present in the human soul or in the human body would be incompre-

67. Ibid., 164.
69. Ibid., 168.
71. *TB*, 241.
68. Ibid., 166.
70. Gn 2:24.

hensible, because according to Hebrew thought man is a unity of the spiritual and the corporeal. Gerhard von Rad notes, however, that if we had to choose one alternative, while remaining simultaneously in the Hebrew sphere of thought, then the *imago Dei* would concern physical likeness.[72]

Among the Fathers of the Church, two lines of interpretation in regard to the place of the body in the theology of *imago Dei* can be detected. Syrian exegetes (Ireneus, Theodore of Mopsuestia, Pseudo-Clemens) emphasize that the image of God is present both in the body and in the soul of man. This understanding frequently accompanies the Christological interpretation of *imago Dei* that presents the human person as created *ad imaginem* of God's incarnate Son.[73] On the other hand, representatives of the Alexandrian school (Clemens of Alexandria, Origen) teach that the image of God is realized primarily in the spiritual sphere of man. Man is the living image of God to the extent that he participates in the life of the spirit. The Fathers then point to the spiritual characteristics that make the soul similar to God: immateriality, indestructibility, freedom, *apatheia*.[74]

The Alexandrian understanding of the place of the body in the theology of *imago Dei* was accepted by the Cappadocian fathers, and also by the most outstanding theologian of Christian antiquity, St. Augustine. Indeed, the idea that the spiritual part of man is the place where the image of God is realized has dominated the development of Christian theology throughout the ages.[75] At

---

72. Von Rad, "εἰκών," 391. Edmond Jacob similarly states: "Man is representative by his entire being, for Israelite thought always views man in his totality, by his physical being as well as by his spiritual functions, and if choice had to be made between the two we would say that the external appearance is perhaps even more important than spiritual resemblance. The Old Testament teaches in fact that in man's exterior aspect there is a beauty and dignity found in no other living being" (Jacob, *Theology of the Old Testament*, 168).

73. Frederick G. McLeod SJ, *Image of God in the Antiochene Tradition* (Washington, D.C.: The Catholic University of America Press, 1999).

74. Jean Kirchmeyer, "Grecque (Eglise)," in *DS*, vol. 6, col. 818–19.

75. Thomas Aquinas states that "Man is said to be to God's image [*ad imaginem*

times, under the influence of Neoplatonism or radical spiritualistic currents, this perception that the image of God is limited to the soul has led to some extreme interpretations, in which the image of God did not refer to the body at all. For instance, Origen writes as follows:

> We do not understand, however, this man indeed whom Scripture says was made "according to the image of God" to be corporeal. For the form of the body does not contain the image of God, nor is the corporeal man said to be "made," but "formed," as is written in the words which follow. For the text says: "And God formed man," that is fashioned "from the slime of the earth." But it is our inner man, invisible, incorporeal, incorruptible, and immortal which is made "according to the image of God." For it is in such qualities as these that the image of God is more correctly understood. But if anyone suppose that this man who is made "according to the image and likeness of God" is made of flesh, he will appear to represent God himself as made of flesh and in human form. It is most clearly impious to think this about God.[76]

A contemporary author argues that nowadays the reflection about man is practiced "in the shadow of the body."[77] Certainly, this insight refers also to the attempts made by contemporary theological anthropology to once again find a place for the human body in the theology of the image of God. It seems that John Paul II's reflections, as presented above, should be interpreted in this way.

Dei] not because he has a body [*non secundum corpus*], but because of his superiority to other animals [*secundum id quod homo excellit alia animalia*].... This superiority man owes to reason and intellect [*quantum ad rationem et intellectum*]. So that man is to God's image because of his intellect and reason [*secundum intellectum et rationem*], which are not bodily characteristics [*incorporea*]" (*STh* I, 3, 1).

76. Origen, "Homilies about Genesis," I, 13 in Origen, *Homilies on Genesis and Exodus*, translated by Ronald E. Heine (Washington, D.C.: The Catholic University of America Press, 1981), 63.

77. Marcin Brocki, *Język ciała w ujęciu antropologicznym* (Wrocław: Astrum, 2001), 124.

The Influence of Sin on the Image of God in Man

The influence of original sin on the image of God in man has been the subject of long and numerous controversies in the history of Christian theology and has always been tied up with the way that the *imago Dei* is understood. The traditional interpretation, most common among theologians until the Reformation, linked the presence of God's image in man with human nature itself. According to this interpretation, original sin did not cause the loss of *imago Dei* by man,[78] because even after he sinned man retained his rational nature.

The traditional theology did not hold, however, that original sin and individual sins have no influence on the image of God in man. Generally, theologians accepted the existence of grades of perfection of the *imago*. Saint Ireneus, for instance, distinguishes the theological meaning of the two words used in the Elohist account of creation: image (εἰκών) and likeness (ὁμοίωσις).[79] According to St. Ireneus, in the act of creation man received the image and likeness of God, but while the image is connected with rational human nature, which is what differentiates man from the animals, likeness is connected with the grace of original innocence (*iustitia originalis*). Therefore, man retained the image of God after original sin, but lost the likeness that may be regained only through becoming similar to Christ, the perfect image of God.

---

78. Gn 5:3.

79. Gn 1:26. It was not the intention of the ancient author of the Elohist account of creation that the distinction between image (*selem*) and likeness (*demut*) have significant theological meaning. In the Septuagint translation of the Old Testament, these two Hebrew words were translated into Greek as εἰκών and ὁμοίωσις. According to the old Platonic school, *eikon* was understood as a copy, or pattern, which always differed from the original; *homoiosis*, on the other hand, was understood as a perfect spiritual similarity to the divinity, toward which man should strive. It is impossible to know the intentions of the translator of the Septuagint, however, for he uses the terms εἰκών and ὁμοίωσις interchangeably. It was the Fathers of the Church who added a theological interpretation to the semantic difference between the two terms (Lamarche, "Image et ressemblance," col. 1403).

This retrieval of human likeness to God (ὁμοίωσις) is possible only through Christ's grace of redemption.[80] Reformation theologians broke with the ontological interpretation of *imago Dei* and introduced a relational and existential understanding of God's image and likeness. For the Reformers, image and likeness are to be understood as an actual bond with God that can exist only in Christians living in grace and friendship with God. Martin Luther argues that "the likeness and the image of God consist in the true and perfect knowledge of God, supreme delight in God, eternal life, eternal righteousness, and eternal freedom from care."[81] Such an understanding of the *imago Dei* led Reformation theologians to the conviction that original sin destroyed both the image and likeness of God in man.[82]

In his theology of the body, John Paul II emphasizes that every living descendent of Adam is created in the image of God:

> According to the text of Genesis 1:26, the call to existence is at the same time a transmission of the divine image and likeness. Man must proceed to transmitting this image, thus continuing God's work. The account of the generation of Seth underlines this aspect. "When Adam was two hundred and thirty years old, he begot a son in his image, in his likeness" (Gn 5:3). Given that Adam and Eve were an image of God, Seth inherits this likeness from his parents to pass it on to others.[83]

Original sin did not, therefore, completely destroy God's image in man. Moreover, after original sin, not only the individual but also the communal dimension of *imago Dei* were preserved, and the marital *communio personarum* remains a sign of the mystery of the Trinity.[84]

---

80. St. Ireneus, *Adversus Haereses* 5.16.2 (*SC* 153, 217).

81. Quoted in Wolfhart Pannenberg, *Anthropology in Theological Perspective* (Philadelphia: Westminster Press, 1985), 49.

82. Scheffczyk notices that modern Protestant theologians depart from this original position of the Reformation, admitting that the *imago Dei* was not completely destroyed in man after sin (Scheffczyk, "Image et ressemblance," col. 1466).

83. *TB*, 212.

84. Ibid., 507–8; also, 213–14.

However, John Paul II indicates that original sin has led to a certain blurring of God's image in man: "This man ... was deprived of the supernatural and preternatural gifts that were part of his 'endowment' before sin; in addition, he suffered damage in what belongs to nature itself, to humanity in the original fullness 'of the image of God.' The threefold concupiscence does not correspond to the fullness of that image, but rather to the damage, to the deficiencies, to the limitations that appeared with sin.[85] In his theology of the body, John Paul II provides a theological interpretation of the "damage, the deficiencies, and the limitations that appeared with sin" in the human *imago Dei* through a reflection on the change in the meaning of original nakedness after the first sin of Adam and Eve.

According to the Book of Genesis, Adam and Eve notice their nakedness only after original sin. Only then does nakedness cease to be something that is matter of course, but becomes a problem and must be hidden with loincloths.[86] John Paul II explains the change in the meaning of nakedness after sin:

> in the mystery of creation, the human body carried within itself an unquestionable sign of the "image of God" and also constituted the specific source of certainty about this image, present in the whole human being.... The words, "I was afraid, because I am naked, and I hid myself" (Gn 3:10), attest to a radical change in this relationship. *Man in some way loses the original certainty of the "image of God" expressed in his body.*[87]

The radical change in the meaning of original nakedness after sin is linked with the appearance of shame in Genesis.[88] John Paul II stresses that it is a question of not only sexual shame, but also "immanent shame," which is "the shame produced in human-

---

85. Ibid., 239–40.
86. The phenomenon of original nakedness and the change in its meaning after original sin were already discussed in the previous two chapters of this work.
87. *TB*, 241.
88. Gn 3:7.

MAN AS THE IMAGE AND LIKENESS OF GOD 159

ity itself, that is, caused by the innermost disorder in that through which man, in the mystery of creation, was 'the image of God,' in his personal 'I' as much as in interpersonal relationship, namely, through the primordial communion of persons constituted by man and woman together."[89] The man who experiences "immanent shame" no longer identifies himself with his body. One could say that anthropological dualism expresses and systematizes this consciousness of man after original sin in a particular way.

The appearance of immanent shame reveals "a certain constitutive fracture in the human person's interior, *a breakup, as it were, of man's original spiritual and somatic unity.*"[90] Consequently, man experiences difficulty in identifying with his own body and "he realizes for the first time that his body has ceased drawing on the power of the spirit, which raised him to the level of the image of God."[91] As a result of original sin, the human body is constantly in danger of being given over to the determinism of sexual instinct, and, therefore, instead of being similar to God in the reality of mutual self-donation, man becomes similar to the animals, "which like man have received the blessing of fruitfulness."[92]

The Christocentric Character of *Imago Dei*

It is important to remember that John Paul II's Wednesday catecheses on the theology of the body have *in genere* a Christocentric structure. The main part of the catecheses is based on the three statements Christ makes in regard to the three states of human existence: original innocence;[93] the fall that is permeated by the ethos of redemption;[94] and eschatological fulfillment.[95] John Paul II provides a "philosophical exegesis" of these three fundamental state-

89. *TB*, 243.
91. Ibid., 244.
93. Mt 19:3–8; Mk 10:2–9.
95. Mt 22:24–30; Mk 12:18–27; Lk 20:27–40.
90. Ibid., 243–44.
92. Ibid., 257.
94. Mt 5:27–29.

ments of Christ, and it is precisely in the light of Christ's words that a theological anthropology is developed. The text of the Second Vatican Council's constitution *Gaudium est spes,* often cited by the pope, describes the Christocentric structure of the catecheses well: "The truth is that only in the mystery of the incarnate Word does the mystery of man take on light. For Adam, the first man, was a figure of Him Who was to come, namely Christ the Lord. Christ, the final Adam, by the revelation of the mystery of the Father and His love, fully reveals man to man himself and makes his supreme calling clear."[96] Getting to know Christ and his teaching leads to a greater understanding of the mystery of man.

The first part of the catecheses is based on an analysis of Christ's answer to the Pharisees' question about the indissolubility of marriage.[97] In his statement, Christ refers to "the beginning" in order to root the truth about the indissolubility of marriage in the mystery of creation, despite later historical distortions and compromises. John Paul II notes, however, that Christ's reference to "the beginning" already includes the perspective of redemption. Christ's listeners are burdened with the legacy of original sin and the weight of their own sins, but in the meeting with the Messiah they are invited to accept the gift of redemption. Only Christ's grace can enable them to undertake anew the task of realizing the destiny and plans given to man by the Creator in the mystery of creation.

The Christocentric character of the Wednesday catecheses means, above all, that the Redeemer who renews the image of God in created, sinful, and redeemed man is placed at the very center. Christ's gift of redemption helps man to rediscover that his life is a gift from the Creator and Savior, and to respond to this giving by becoming a gift himself. Christ's grace, which allows man to participate in the divine *communio personarum,* also renews man's ability to create the human communion of persons. For redemp-

---

96. *GS* 22.   97. Mt 19:3–8; Mk 10:2–9.

MAN AS THE IMAGE AND LIKENESS OF GOD 161

tion is a calling to overcome the sinful desires of the flesh and to live by the ethos of redemption of the body, which transforms human *eros*.[98] Through moderation, purity of heart, and the gift of piety (*pietas*) every Christian who lives by the ethos of redemption may rediscover the spousal meaning of the body, which allows the building up of the *communio personarum*.[99]

John Paul II's interpretation of the passage from the First Letter to the Corinthians, in which St. Paul reflects on the mystery of the resurrection, reveals the Christocentric character of his theology of *imago Dei:*

> What is sown is perishable, what is raised is imperishable. It is sown in dishonor, it is raised in glory. It is sown in weakness, it is raised in power. It is sown a physical body, it is raised a spiritual body. If there is a physical body, there is also a spiritual body. Thus it is written, "The first man, Adam, became a living being"; the last Adam became a life-giving spirit. But it is not the spiritual that is first, but the physical, and then the spiritual.[100]

Saint Paul's reflection is based on the opposition of "the first Adam" and "the last Adam." John Paul II emphasizes that every human person in history should be able to find himself in this opposition: "By contrasting Adam and (the risen) Christ—or the first Adam and the last Adam—the Apostle in fact shows in some way the two poles in the mystery of creation and redemption between which *man is situated* in the cosmos. One could even say that man is 'set in tension' between these two poles *in the perspective of eternal destiny* that concerns from the beginning to the end his same human nature."[101] The "tension" between Adam and

---

98. *TB*, 313–21.
99. Ibid., 340–58.
100. 1 Cor 15:42–46. The text of *Gaudium et spes* 22, quoted earlier in this chapter, which discusses the relation of Adam and Christ, is undoubtedly based on the theology of this passage from the First Letter to the Corinthians.
101. *TB*, 406.

Christ indicates that every human person experiences the mystery of creation and redemption in his or her life. Moreover, only thanks to Christ's grace of redemption is man able to fully understand and realize the "eternal destiny" contained in the mystery of creation in his life.

The key phrase for the theology of *imago Dei* as found in the excerpt from the First Letter to the Corinthians under consideration here reads as follows: "Just as we have borne the image of the man of dust [τὴν εἰκόνα τοῦ χοϊκοῦ], we will also bear the image of the man of heaven [τὴν εἰκόνα τοῦ ἐπουρανίου]."[102] The pope comments on this biblical sentence:

> This "heavenly man"—the man of the resurrection, whose prototype is the risen Christ—is not so much the antithesis and negation of the "man of earth" (whose prototype is the "first Adam") but above all his fulfillment and confirmation. He is the fulfillment and confirmation of what corresponds to the psychosomatic constitution of humanity in the realm of eternal destiny, that is, in the thought and plan of the one who created man from the beginning in his image and likeness. The humanity of the "first Adam," the "man of earth," carries within itself, I would say, *a particular potentiality* (which is capacity and readiness) *for receiving all that the "second Adam" became,* the heavenly Man, namely, Christ: what he became in his resurrection.[103]

It is worth noting that John Paul II chooses his words carefully so as not to suggest in any way that becoming similar to "the last Adam" (*imitatio Christi*) consists in a return to the mystery of creation. For the redemption of man in Christ is not a repetition, but a completely new and definitive stage in the history of salvation. On the other hand, however, redemption, however, does not mean breaking with the "eternal destiny" contained in the mystery of creation, but is its "confirmation" and "fulfillment."

The eschatological destiny of man therefore consists in becom-

102. 1 Cor 15:49.
103. *TB*, 407.

MAN AS THE IMAGE AND LIKENESS OF GOD 163

ing similar to the resurrected Christ. In becoming similar to Christ man becomes his icon (*eikon*), which simultaneously means the fulfillment of all possibilities and potentialities of human nature as inscribed in man by God in the act of creation. If similarity to "the first Adam" means that every man living in history carries within himself an image and likeness of God, which has been deformed by sin, then only the eschatological becoming similar to "the last Adam," who is "the image of the invisible God,"[104] will allow the human *imago Dei* to shine perfectly.

Eschatological Fulfillment

As is already made clear in the reflections of the previous section, John Paul II's theology of *imago Dei* is characterized by an eschatological dynamism. Christ's grace of redemption causes the recovery of the *imago Dei*, blurred by sin in man, and this action of sanctifying grace leads to the resurrection, when human beings "having regained their bodies in the fullness of the perfection proper to the image and likeness of God—having regained them in their masculinity and femininity—'will take neither wife nor husband.'"[105] As has already been discussed, Christ's words regarding the reality where they "do not marry"[106] indicate that "the resurrection ... means not only the recovery of bodiliness and the reestablishment of human life in its integrity, through the union of body and soul,"[107] but also the advent of a new meaning of the human body that will be different from its procreative meaning.[108]

Christ's statement that "those who are considered worthy of a place in that age and in the resurrection from the dead ... are like

---

104. Cor 1:15. 105. *TB*, 387.
106. Lk 20:35. 107. *TB*, 388.
108. John Paul II emphasizes that the human choice to live in celibacy or under vows of chastity—the biblical "continence for the kingdom of heaven" (Mt 19:12)—anticipates the eschatological fulfillment of *imago Dei*, in its both personal and communal dimensions, because of its character as an eschatological sign (*TB*, 426–29).

angels and are children of God" is crucial for John Paul II's reflection on the new state of the human body after the Resurrection.[109] The pope describes the eschatological reality of being "like angels" and being children of God with the aid of two notions: spiritualization and divinization. Each of them refers to the full restoration and perfection of God's image and likeness in man, deformed as it was by sin. Spiritualization indicates a new submission of the body to the spirit: "In the resurrection, the body will return to perfect unity and harmony with the spirit: man will no longer experience the opposition between what is spiritual and what is bodily in him. *'Spiritualization'* signifies not only that the spirit will master the body, but, I would say, that *it will also fully permeate the body and the powers of the spirit will permeate the energies of the body.*"[110]

According to John Paul II, eschatological divinization will consist in the unity of man with God and in human participation in God's Trinitarian life. Thanks to the loving gift of grace thus understood, eschatological man will obtain an authentic and mature personality that is "incomparably superior to what can be reached in earthly life."[111] This recovery of authentic subjectivity and identity will mean that the grace of divinization will embrace all of man, especially—given the context of the papal theology of the body—his attitude toward his own body and his relationships with others. The mysterious likeness between created man and the Creator will find its perfect fulfillment in *"God's most personal 'self-giving': in his very divinity to man."*[112]

John Paul II stresses that eschatological man's participation in God's Trinitarian life will not suspend or break interhuman relations. Rather, it will bring about the perfect realization and fulfillment of human *communiones personarum*. The truth about the

---

109. Lk 20:35–36.
110. *TB*, 391.
111. Ibid., 392.
112. Ibid., 393.

communion of the saints (*communio sanctorum*), as stated in the *credo*, points therefore to "the perfect realization of the 'trinitarian order' in the created world of persons."[113] One could say that if the human communion of persons is the image of the divine communion of the Holy Trinity in the order of creation and redemption, then the communal *imago Dei* thus understood will find its fulfillment and perfection in the reality of heaven: "The concentration of knowledge and love on God himself in the trinitarian communion of Persons can find a beatifying response in those who will become sharers in the 'other world' only *through realizing reciprocal communion commensurate with created persons.*"[114]

The Synthetic Character of John Paul II's Theology of *Imago Dei*

In his comprehensive treatise on the theology of *imago Dei*, Stanley Grenz distinguishes two ways of understanding the *imago Dei:* one structural and the other relational.[115] The structural understanding of *imago Dei*—the approach that clearly dominates the history of Christian theology—attempts to find and isolate that dimension of human nature which differentiates the human person from the animals and which makes him to be in the image of God. A classic example of such an understanding of *imago Dei* is St. Augustine's psychological analogy that finds the image of the Trinity inside the human mind.[116]

The relational interpretation of God's image in man emphasizes the living relationship and bond of love between God and man. Grenz finds examples of such an understanding of *imago Dei* in the theology of the Reformers: Martin Luther and John Calvin.[117]

113. Ibid., 396. 114. Ibid.
115. Grenz, *The Social God*, 141–82.
116. Augustine, *The Trinity* IX, 286–307 (*CCSL* 50, 292–310).
117. Grenz, *The Social God*, 162–70.

Paul Ramsey, one of the commentators cited by Grenz, summarizes Calvin's relational view of *imago Dei* in the following way:

> The image of God ... should be understood as internal relation, thanks to which an obedient man as the mirror reflects God's will in his life and actions.... The mirror in itself is not an image; the mirror reflects; the image of God is in the mirror. In this view, the image of God consists in man's attitude to God; or rather the image of God is reflected in man thanks to his attitude before him.[118]

The sharp distinction drawn by Grenz between the structural and relational understanding of the *imago Dei* leads to a deformation of the rich heritage of Christian theology, especially as it also surfaces elsewhere under different forms.[119] Both dimensions of *imago Dei* are present in the thought of the great masters of Christian theology. Saint Ireneus is merely one example here. The relational and Christocentric understanding of the difference between *imago* and *similitudo* as laid out in his works was discussed earlier in this chapter in the context of the influence of original sin on the *imago Dei*. The structural dimension of *imago Dei* is also present in the theology of St. Ireneus, who claims that God's image in man consists in man's rationality.[120]

Both the structural and relational dimensions of imago Dei are present in John Paul II's theology of the body. The structural understanding of *imago Dei* comes to the fore in the papal distinction between the cosmological and personalistic definitions of man: "Man can neither be understood nor explained in his full

---

118. Paul Ramsey, *Basic Christian Ethics* (New York: Scribner, 1950), 255.

119. Douglas John Hall, *Imaging God: Dominion as Stewardship* (Grand Rapids, Mich.: Eerdmans, 1986), 88–112.

120. St. Ireneus, *Adversus Haereses* 4.4.3 (*SC* 100, 425). The theologies of Augustine and Thomas Aquinas are quoted most frequently as examples of the structural view of *imago Dei*. For the account of the relational view of *imago Dei* in the thought of these two theologians see Bernard de Margerie, SJ, *The Christian Trinity in History* (Still River, Mass.: St. Bede's Publications, 1982), 297–305; Augustine DiNoia OP, "*Imago Dei—Imago Christi:* The Theological Foundations of Christian Humanism," *Nova et Vetera* (English Edition) 2, no. 2 (2004): 267–78.

depth with the categories taken from the 'world,' that is, from the visible totality of bodies."[121] It is precisely this dimension of the human person, to which he owes his transcendence over material creation and other creatures, that constitutes the trace of *imago Dei* in man. The biblical experience of original solitude, therefore, is what reveals the structural dimension of *imago Dei*, and, moreover, it can only be explained by means of aspects of human nature—such as consciousness, freedom, and self-governance—that are responsible for man's superiority over other creatures.

The relational dimension of *imago Dei* in the thought of John Paul II is indicated primarily by the theological category of gift, which serves in the papal analyses as a fundamental tool for explaining the meaning of supernatural love (*agape, caritas*) and of the communion of persons in man's vocation. Man, in similarity to the divine Trinity who is Gift, is called to become a gift himself. "An identification of the sense of gift" of God's creation and redemption leads a Christian to answer God with "the language of this understanding."[122] In practice, this answer is realized through creating the communion of persons in its vertical and horizontal dimensions.

The relational dimension of God's image in man, reminiscent of the theology of St. Ireneus, is present in the thought of John Paul II due to its Christocentric character, emphasized by the pope through his application of St. Paul's distinction between "the first Adam" and "the last Adam"—Christ, the perfect image of God.[123] Man, who is created in the image of God, can understand and realize his eternal destiny in life as communicated in the mystery of creation only by becoming similar to Christ—the Redeemer (*imitatio Christi*), which is possible only through the grace of redemp-

---

121. *TB*, 135.
122. *TB*, 180.
123. 1 Cor 15:46; Col 1:15. No theological distinction is made between *imago* and *similitudo* in the theology of the catecheses. John Paul II uses both terms interchangeably.

tion. Likeness to Christ will find its fulfillment in the eschatological mystery of the resurrection.

Noteworthy in the Wednesday catecheses is the importance that the pope assigns to the communal dimension of *imago Dei*. Man is the image of God not only as an individual, but also as a communion of persons, which is formed by grace and supernatural love, and which reflects the reality of the Trinity. The communal or social image of the Trinity, so important for John Paul II, has rarely appeared in the history of Christian theology. In a historical survey of the social understanding of *imago Dei* one generally finds references to the theology of the Cappadocian fathers, and of Richard of St. Victor who argued in the twelfth century that the perfect love of God requires the existence of three Persons.[124] However, in Western Christianity, the theology of *imago Dei* was mostly dominated by the psychological model of St. Augustine, which was then taken up and adapted by St. Thomas Aquinas.

Currently, historians of theology point to a renaissance of the social model of the Trinity that began in the twentieth century.[125] Claude Welch pinpoints the beginning of this renaissance among British Anglican theologians at the beginning of the twentieth century, and mentions among its later representatives the theologians of different Christian denominations such as Jürgen Moltmann, Wolfhart Pannenberg, Juan Segundo, Leonardo Boff, Joseph Bracken, and Kallistos Ware. In Catholic theology, it was the Second Vatican Council that was crucial for the present renaissance of the social image of the Trinity. The most important statement concerning this issue from *Gaudium et spes* was quoted earlier in this chapter.[126]

---

124. Nico Den Bok, *Communicating the Most High: A Systematic Study of Person and Trinity in the Theology of Richard of St. Victor* (Paris: Brepols, 1996), 303–7.

125. Claude Welch, *In This Name: The Doctrine of the Trinity in Contemporary Theology* (New York: Scribner, 1952), 29–43.

126. It should be emphasized that "carefully crafted" statements of the constitution

Communion and Stewardship: Human Persons Created in the Image of God, put out by the International Theological Commission in 2002,[127] sheds light on the stance the Church takes on the social dimension of *imago Dei:*

> When one speaks of the person, one refers both to the irreducible identity and interiority that constitutes the particular individual being, and to the fundamental relationship to other persons that is the basis for human community. In the Christian perspective, this personal identity that is at once an orientation to the other is founded essentially on the Trinity of Divine Persons. God is not a solitary being, but a communion of three Persons.[128]

Today, the concept of *imago Dei* arouses great interest among theologians and is often the main thrust for theological explorations, particularly in the area of theological anthropology. The communal dimension of *imago Dei* seems to be an especially promising theological subject in the context of intellectual efforts to overcome modern individualism as well as to find a place for female experience of and thought about God in theology.[129] Undoubtedly, in an era of increased interrelatedness and of an ever-greater dependency of people on one another, the development and deepening of the communal dimension of *imago Dei* theology remains an important task for Christian theologians.

---

on the social dimension of *imago Dei* are the result of a long debate and compromise between many earlier ways of describing the phenomenon. For the council's discussion on the social dimension of *imago Dei* during the process of preparing the constitution see: Jarosław Kupczak, OP, "Komunijny wymiar obrazu Bożego w człowieku w soborowej konstytucji *Gaudium et spes,*" *Studia Theologica Varsaviensia* 44, no. 1 (2006): 139–58.

127. This document can be found on the Theological Commission's website: www.vatican.va/roman_curia/congregations/cfaith/cti_index.htm.

128. Ibid. 41.

129. Grenz, *The Social God,* 267–303.

Chapter Five

THE LANGUAGE OF THE BODY

The concept of "the language of the body" occupies an important place in John Paul II's Wednesday catecheses on the theology of the body. Before analyzing this concept in papal thought, it is helpful to examine how it is understood in other fields of knowledge about man, for example in ethnology and psychology. In both of these disciplines, this concept signifies a nonverbal type of communication, which takes place, for example, through gestures, facial expressions, or signs.

The Philosophical and Psychological Understanding of the Language of the Body

In the history of philosophy there has always been an awareness of the significance of the human body, of the gestures and movements of the body for interpersonal communication, as for example, in the following discussion between Socrates and Hermogenes in Plato's dialogue "Cratylus":

THE LANGUAGE OF THE BODY 171

Socrates: Answer me this question: If we had no voice or tongue, and wished to make things clear to one another, should we not try, as dumb people actually do, to make signs with our hands and head and person generally?
Hermogenes: Yes. What other method is there, Socrates?
Socrates: If we wished to designate that which is above and is light, we should, I fancy, raise our hand towards heaven in imitation of the nature of the thing in question; but if the things to be designated were below or heavy, we should extend our hands towards the ground; and if we wished to mention a galloping horse or any other animal, we should, of course, make our bodily attitudes as much like theirs as possible.
Hermogenes: I think you are quite right; there is no other way.
Socrates: For the expression of anything, I fancy, would be accomplished by bodily imitation of that which was to be expressed.[1]

In the history of human culture, this knowledge of the meaning of different poses and gestures of the body has certainly influenced playwrights, directors, and actors in their development of different forms of stage performance, theater, and film. Visual art such as painting, especially that which is symbolical and allegorical, used the language of the body and, at the same time, deepened and enriched it. Various kinds of sign language within different ethnic cultures created a wealth of communication through the body.

Umberto Eco writes thus about the historical and cultural richness of the phenomena that come to mind when speaking about nonverbal communication accomplished with the aid of gesticulation and different movements of the body:

The mute language of gestures of contemplative monks, of the deaf mute, of Indian and Persian traders, gypsies, thieves, tobacco smugglers; the ritual hand movements of Buddhist and Hindu priests; the communi-

---
[1]. Plato, *Cratylus* 422e–23b; in *Plato in Twelve Volumes,* translated by H. N. Fowler (Cambridge, Mass.: Harvard University Press, 1970), 4:133–35.

cation of Afghan fishermen; oriental and Mediterranean kinesics, particularly the gesticulation of Neapolitans; ... stylized gestures of certain figures in Mayan painting, helpful in deciphering their written language and, similarly, the study of gesticulation in Greek vase paintings.... In like manner, kinesics studies ritualized gestures found in the theatre (in classical oriental theatres, in mime, in dance), styles of walking (which vary in different cultures and communicate different types of ethos), styles of standing.... Different kinds of laughter, smiles, crying, being elements of paralanguage, are at the same time elements of kinesics.[2]

The language of the body is undoubtedly a part of our daily, most basic interpersonal communication. Sixteenth-century Polish writer Mikołaj Rej, "the father of the Polish language," writes of this as follows:

From the posture, you will quickly recognize the matters and deeds of the excited mind. Because you will quickly recognize the quick-tempered, the kind-hearted, mean, wasteful, sad, cheerful, doughty, faint-hearted, and all others, whatever their state. You will quickly know the dull man from the timid one, for when he wants to say something serious he keeps moving his feet, bites his nails, picks at his beard, preens, lisps, and stammers every word thrice over. But, on the other hand, when the person is level-headed, with an honest mind, and thinks nothing of which he should be ashamed of, then his very gaze, words, and posture are as the eagle's who always looks at the sun.[3]

---

2. Umberto Eco, *La Struttura assente* (Milan: Tascabili Bompiani, 1989), 396. By kinesics Eco understands the study of nonverbal communication that is transmitted through human gesticulation and movements of the body (Mark L. Knapp, Judith A. Hall, *Nonverbal Communication in Human Interaction* [Fort Worth, Tex.: Harcourt, 1997], 21). Marcin Brocki emphasizes that because of the diversity of behavior that is defined as nonverbal communication, only interdisciplinary research can hope to understand this issue: "Contemporary research on gesticulation is conducted within several disciplines, especially within semiotics, general linguistics, psychology, ethnology, and cultural anthropology.... Linguistics, and especially sociolinguistics, presently provides conceptual instruments for ethnography and sociology in this respect ..." (Brocki, *Język ciała w ujęciu antropologicznym,* 39). Theology should undoubtedly be added to this list of disciplines conducting research in the area of the language of the body.

3. Mikołaj Rej, "Zwierciadło," quoted in Maria Bogucka, *Staropolskie obyczaje w XVI–XVII wieku* (Warsaw: Państwowy Instytut Wydawniczy, 1994), 82–83.

Erasmus of Rotterdam's conviction that a man's character can always be recognized by his outward posture, and that "outward bodily propriety proceeds from a well-composed mind" has always been one of the axioms of human communication.[4]

Since it is gesticulation that plays a key role in nonverbal communication, the first researchers in this field focused primarily on the study of the language of gestures. In 1832, Andrea de Jorio, a Neapolitan canon, in his work *La Mimica degli antichi investigata nel gestire Napoletano* "compared the gestures of Neapolitans with the gestures of the ancients as depicted on vases, in reliefs, paintings, sculpture, and in literature, in order to explain and understand contemporary gestures."[5] Many researchers compiled catalogues of gestures, especially in the United States, where such research resulted from the practical necessity of communicating with indigenous inhabitants. In 1881, Garrick Mallery published "Sign Language among North American Indians Compared with That among Other Peoples and Deafmutes," in which, as the title suggests, the sign language of North American Indians is compared with the sign systems used by Neapolitans, Sicilians, and the deaf.[6] Marcin Brocki—while noting the importance of these first attempts to systematize the language of gestures—points out that their weakness stemmed from the false assumption that the structure of gesticulation reflects the structure of oral language. Early researchers took on the impossible task of finding in the language of gestures some of the most fundamental structural and grammatical elements, and of preparing complete lexicons thereof.[7]

---

4. Erasmus from Rotterdam, *De civilitate morum puerilium*, quoted in Norbert Elias, *The Civilizing Process: History of Manners*, translated by Edmund Jephcott (New York: Urizen Books, 1978), 56.
5. Brocki, *Język ciała w ujęciu antropologicznym*, 54.
6. Garrick Mallery, "Sign Language among North American Indians Compared with That among Other Peoples and Deafmutes," *U.S. Bureau of Ethnology Report* 1 (1879–1880): 269–552.
7. Brocki, *Język ciała w ujęciu antropologicznym*, 56–58.

Mark Knapp states that "the scientific study of nonverbal communication is primarily a post–World War II activity."[8] Edward T. Hall, an American psychologist and anthropologist, pioneered in systematically analyzing this issue. According to Hall, all of human culture consists of communication, of which only a small part is communicated through words, or verbal communication: "Whenever people talk, they supply only part of the message. The rest is filled by the listener. Much of what is not said is taken for granted. However, cultures vary in what is left unsaid."[9] Hall claims that nonverbal communication belongs to the hidden world of culture, or "a hidden dimension" linked to ethnic cultural diversity, and thus fundamental for human communication.[10]

In his classic work *Psychology and Life*, Philip G. Zimbardo defines nonverbal expression as "any communication that does not rely solely on words or word symbols."[11] Besides proxemics, which was mentioned above, Zimbardo differentiates three other fields of research on nonverbal communication: (1) reflection on facial expression, (2) kinesics, which focuses on gestures, poses, and movements of the body, and (3) paralanguage research, "which

---

8. Knapp and Hall, *Nonverbal Communication in Human Interaction*, 20.
9. Edward T. Hall, *The Hidden Dimension* (Garden City: Doubleday, 1966), 96.
10. In his research, the American psychologist focused especially on interpersonal communication made by means of creating and shaping spatial structure, and thus originated a new field of research called proxemics. Hall defines proxemics as the "study of how man unconsciously structures microspace—the distance between men in the conduct of their daily transactions, the organization of space in his houses and buildings, and ultimately the layout of his towns" (Hall, "A System for the Notation of Proxemics Behavior," quoted in Joseph DeVito, *The Interpersonal Communication Book* [New York: Harper & Row, 1986], 216). A good illustration of communication through spatial structure is the theory of four distances, which according to Hall, correspond to the four types of interpersonal relations: intimate, personal, social and public (Hall, *The Hidden Dimension*, 107–22; DeVito, *The Interpersonal Communication Book*, 216–18). Basing his conclusions on empirical research, the American psychologist argues that through the distance we keep between persons, we communicate to the interlocutor and to our surroundings about the bond between us: i.e., whether it is intimate, friendly, formal, or official.
11. Philip Zimbardo, *Psychology and Life*, 9th ed. (Glenview, Ill.: Scott, Foresman and Company: 1977), 156.

covers aspects of communication that are vocal but not verbal—voice qualities, such as pitch, intensity, and rate of speech; hesitations, errors, and other speech nonfluencies; and non-language sounds, such as laughs and yawns."[12]

This work does not aim at a detailed presentation of the psychological understanding of the "language of the body."[13] Nonetheless, it is worthwhile to call attention to some of the most popular examples of nonverbal communication. Everyone knows from personal experience (objectivized by the modern philosophy of dialogue) that the human face creates many possibilities for communication. Zimbardo argues that

the eyes have long been held to be one of the most expressive parts of the body. People "make eyes" at those to whom they're attracted, while antagonists have "eyeball-to-eyeball" confrontations. Untrustworthy characters "won't look you straight in the eye," while people who are embarrassed, shy, or respectful will "avert their gaze." In general, it seems that eye contact helps establish the nature of relationship between people—positive or negative, intimate or distant. People tend to engage in mutual glances, if they like the person they are with, but they will try to avoid looking at a companion they dislike.[14]

Another issue worth mentioning—however briefly—is the nature of contradictory or inconsistent messages as well as lies in the language of the body.[15] DeVito notes that in daily interpersonal communication it is frequently impossible to clearly separate verbal and nonverbal behavior, as both generally occur together

---

12. Ibid., 157.

13. Michael Argyle, *The Psychology of Interpersonal Behaviour* (Baltimore: Penguin Books, 1972), 36–94; Argyle, *Social Interaction* (London: Methuen, 1969), 91–126; DeVito, *The Interpersonal Communication Book*, 187–237; Zimbardo, *Psychology and Life*, 156–61.

14. Ibid., 157.

15. DeVito, *The Interpersonal Communication Book*, 188–92; Knapp and Hall, *Nonverbal Communication in Human Interaction*, 17–19; Zimbardo, *Psychology and Life*, 160–61.

and complement each other. Also, the concept of nonverbal communication concerns the interpretation of the behavior of the whole human body, and not of individual and separated parts, for example, only the eyes or hands:

> All parts of the body generally work together to communicate a particular meaning. We do not express fear with our eyes while the rest of our body relaxes as if sleeping. Rather, the entire body expresses the emotion. We may, for purposes of analysis, focus primarily on the eyes, the facial muscles, or the hand movements, but in everyday communication, these do not occur in isolation from other nonverbal behaviours.[16]

DeVito refers to this holistic structure of human nonverbal communication as the structure of "nonverbal packages."[17]

Due to the holistic structure of nonverbal packages, in which the verbal and nonverbal messages affect each other, different messages sent at the same time may be inconsistent or even contradictory. We can imagine a situation, when during a marital quarrel the husband, accused of infidelity, replies to his wife, "Of course I love you," but at the same time he avoids eye contact, feels disconcerted, and wants to finish the conversation as quickly as possible, explaining that he is in a hurry for an important meeting. In a different situation, an employee, following a difficult discussion with his superior, explains to his colleagues that there is no reason to worry though his voice is shaking and his brow is covered with sweat. Psychologists emphasize that in the case of inconsistent or contradictory messages we generally tend to believe the channels of communication that the interlocutor controls to a lesser degree and that he is less capable of manipulating. This means that we tend to trust the nonverbal language of the body more than spoken words.[18]

16. DeVito, *The Interpersonal Communication Book*, 188.
17. Ibid.
18. Knapp and Hall, *Nonverbal Communication in Human Interaction*, 13–17.

The topic of truth and falsehood in the language of the body, very important for John Paul II's reflections, is linked to the concept of mask and masking oneself in the psychology of communication. Alfred Bierach defines a mask as "the tendency to hide true opinions and attitudes to other people in some arbitrarily accepted way."[19] Let us look at two examples of masking. In the first situation, a professor, proctoring his students' oral exams, tries to hide his boredom at the end of a long day in response to the rather banal answers of his student. The professor makes eye contact and seemingly listens carefully to the student, and even asks leading questions, but his badly suppressed yawning, and his involuntary glances at the clock, reveal that in his thoughts he is already at home. In another situation, at an informal meeting of people generally unfamiliar with one another, several members of the group begin to tell offensive racist jokes. One of the guests, whose family is in large part Nigerian, feels very uncomfortable in this situation, but because he is timid by nature and tends to avoid confrontation, he tries to laugh along with the others, though his nervous laughter seems to be so unnatural that a woman sitting nearby asks him whether he is feeling well.

In both situations, true emotions and thoughts are masked. In both situations, the masking is an attempt, not quite successful in

---

Knapp and Hall emphasize that there may be many reasons for inconsistent or contradictory messages. Sometimes, an inconsistent message has its source in the personality of its sender; for example, timidity causes one to simultaneously communicate openness and kindliness toward another person, but also distance and aversion. In the case of sarcasm and irony, when words say one thing, and the tone of voice and face something opposite, the intended incongruency of the message is an example of the richness and sophisticated character of human expression. Also, psychologists emphasize that there are exceptions in regard to the greater credibility of nonverbal messages in case of their inconsistency with verbal messages. For example, in patient-doctor or student-teacher interaction the combination of the positive content of a verbal message with a harsh tone of voice of the doctor or teacher may sometimes lead to higher satisfaction in the student or patient (ibid., 35–39).

19. Alfred J. Bierach, *Za maską człowiek: Czy można kłamać mową ciała w drodze do władzy, miłości, sukcesu?* (Wrocław: Astrum, 1997), 6.

either case, to control not only verbal behavior, but also nonverbal behavior, which communicates just as much. Moving from a psychological to an ethical perspective, proper to John Paul II's reflections on the language of the body, we may say that each of the two attempts at masking has a different moral value: the former is positive, and the latter—in its lack of assertiveness and courage to protest—is negative.

The examiner who tries to hide his weariness before the student in order to conduct the examination in a proper and appropriate way acts morally well. The man who is afraid to criticize his interlocutors for their insulting and racist jokes acts morally badly. Even this simple analysis indicates that the psychological situation of masking should be judged very carefully. The concept of a falsehood or a lie contains a negative moral judgment, whereas not every situation where masking takes place deserves such a judgment.

Sources of the Concept of "the Language of the Body" in the Philosophical Anthropology of Karol Wojtyła

The description and analysis of the human body have a prominent place in the pre-1978 philosophical anthropology of Karol Wojtyła. There are two main reasons for the importance of the philosophy of the body for Wojtyła. First, a considerable part of his reflections concerns the love between man and woman as well as issues of sexual and marital ethics. A proper understanding of the concept of the body plays a key role in both of these areas. Second, Wojtyła emphasizes the epistemological role of the body and of human sense perception in his polemics with idealism, characteristic of phenomenology, the philosophical movement in which John Paul II was rooted. We will briefly review these two philosophical contexts, important for the later development of John Paul II's theology of the language of the body.

The subject of love and marital ethics appeared very early on in Wojtyła's philosophical works.[20] In one of his first publications, the article "Tajemnica i człowiek" (Mystery and man) from 1951, the then thirty-one-year-old priest outlined some of the major topics in the philosophy of man, to which he would later frequently return. Referring to the thought of German twentieth-century philosopher Nicolas Hartmann, Wojtyła describes the human person as a microcosm, in which all levels of existence present in the macrocosm are present: "Man has in himself something of a stone and a star, something of a plant, and how much of an animal."[21] "The limit to man's similarity to the material world,"[22] however, consists in the human spirit, in which the likeness of man to the Creator is realized.

Wojtyła's first article on marital ethics, "Instynkt, miłość, małżeństwo" (Instinct, love, marriage), from 1952, discusses how the nature of human sexual desire, transformed by the virtue of purity, becomes one of the necessary components of long-lasting marital love. According to Wojtyła, it is precisely due to the virtue of purity that husband and wife do not merely fulfill their sexual drive and experience sexual pleasure, but build an interpersonal relationship of love, whose essence is mutual belonging.[23] In another article, "Wychowanie miłości" (The education of love) from 1960, Wojtyła stresses that authentic and deep marital love is the fruit of a long educational process. Love is often incorrectly identified with emotions and sensual experiences, which are short-lived and changeable. If the bond between man and woman is to be built on a long-lasting foundation, it must be based on the conscious decisions of two persons, undertaken with both their intellects and wills.[24]

20. Kupczak, *Destined for Liberty*, 41–47.
21. Wojtyła, "Tajemnica i człowiek," in Wojtyła, *Aby Chrystus się nami posługiwał*, 29.
22. Ibid.
23. Wojtyła, "Instynkt, miłość, małżeństwo," in Wojtyła, *Aby Chrystus się nami posługiwał*, 36–50.
24. Wojtyła, "Wychowanie miłości," in idem, *Aby Chrystus się nami posługiwał*, 88–93.

Wojtyła presents a more complete, systematic, and mature reflection on the body, sexuality, and marital love in his book *Love and Responsibility,* published for the first time in 1960. In the introduction to the book the author rejects modern attempts to limit sexuality to its bodily dimension and argues instead that "sexual morality is within the domain of the person."[25] At the same time, a philosophical description of the role of the body in the encounter of man and woman occupies an important place in the book as a whole. In the first part of *Love and Responsibility,* the author presents his views on the sexual urge, which is "a natural drive born in all human beings, a vector of aspiration"[26] toward representatives of the other sex. Wojtyła call attention to the uniquely human and ethical character of the sexual urge:

> The sexual urge in man functions differently from the urge in animals, where it is the source of instinctive actions governed by nature alone. In man it is naturally subordinate to the will, and *ipso facto* subject to the specific dynamics of that freedom which the will possesses. The sexual urge can transcend the determinism of the natural order by an act of love. For this very reason manifestations of the sexual urge in man must be evaluated on the plane of love, and any act which originates from it forms a link in the chain of responsibility, responsibility for love. All this is possible because, psychologically, the sexual urge does not fully determine human behavior but leaves room for the free exercise of the will.[27]

In his description of love between man and woman, Wojtyła pays special attention to sensual experience, which is the experience of the sexual value linked to the body of the person of the opposite sex: "Sensuality expresses itself mainly in an appetitive form: a person of the other sex is seen as an 'object of desire' specifically

---

25. Wojtyła, *Love and Responsibility,* 18.
26. Ibid., 46.
27. Ibid., 50. The reinterpretation of the concept of the sexual urge as carried out by Wojtyła within his methodological project of developing an adequate anthropology was discussed in the first chapter of this work.

because of the sexual value inherent in the body itself, for it is in the body that the senses discover that which determines sexual difference, sexual otherness."[28] The author emphasizes that sensuality is in a way "blind to the person" in its concentration on the sexual attractiveness of the human body.[29] The subject is informed about this attractiveness through sensory cognition: external senses, such as sight, hearing, touch, and internal senses, as for example imagination and memory.[30] By means of sensory knowledge one can make "contact with the body,"[31] with both that of a person in whose presence one is at a particular point in time and that of a physically absent person: someone seen on TV, read about in a book, or someone recalled in one's memory. As a result of sensual desire, which is rooted in the sexual drive, the body of the other person is thus experienced as a possible object of use and a source of erotic pleasure. Wojtyła notes that the nature of this stormy dynamic present in every man and woman ought to be well recognized, in order that it may be ordered by reason and become the raw material of a mature love. "Sensuality by itself," emphasizes the author, "is not love, and may very easily become its opposite."[32]

Emotions are another important element of the love between a man and a woman. While sensual experience orients one toward the body, emotional experience means rather "the susceptibility (which is different from sensual excitability) to the sexual value residing in 'a whole person of the other sex,'"[33] susceptibility to femininity and to masculinity. Wojtyła argues that emotions have no consumerist tendency, typical of human sensuality, which tends to the use of the other person. Emotions focus rather on the con-

28. Ibid., 107.
29. Ibid., 108.
30. In his differentiation between external and internal senses, Wojtyła clearly shows his dependence on Aristotelian and Thomistic epistemology.
31. Wojtyła, *Love and Responsibility*, 108.
32. Ibid.
33. Ibid., 110.

templation of the beauty, mystery, and charm of the other person: "In the male, affection is permeated with a strong feeling for and admiration of 'femininity,' and in the woman with a similar feeling and admiration for 'masculinity.'"[34] Wojtyła emphasizes that unlike sensual desire, which is characterized by a desire to use the other person, emotions concentrate on closeness, exclusivity, and intimacy, "alone" and at the same time "together": "Sentimental love keeps two people close together, binds them—even if they are physically far apart—to move in each other's orbit."[35]

Wojtyła argues that despite of the beauty of the feeling of love, which is the primary leitmotif of world poetry and literature, emotional experience does not constitute the essence of love. Human love must not take place "on the surface" of the subject, in his senses and emotions, but should engage the whole person, the mind and will of the one who loves: "Love is always an interior matter, a matter of the spirit. To the extent to which it ceases to be an interior matter and a matter of the spirit it also ceases to be love. What remains of it, in the senses and in the sexual vitality of the human body, does not constitute its essential nature."[36] According to Wojtyła, the essence of love consists in the affirmation of the other person for his or her own sake, and not because of his or her attributes: intelligence, appearance, or sex appeal: "Love is an affirmation of the person or else it is not love at all."[37] The pope states that the sexual value, to which the senses and emotions react first, should not be dismissed, but that "Our concern is simply to bind these values tightly to the value of the person, since love is directed not towards 'the body' alone, nor yet towards 'a human being of the other sex,' but precisely towards a person."[38]

Wojtyła's epistemological polemics with idealism is the second important philosophical context in which the topic of the

34. Ibid.
36. Ibid., 117.
38. Ibid.

35. Ibid.
37. Ibid., 123.

human body appears. It can be observed above all in his magnum opus, *The Acting Person* (1969). Instead of delving into the details of Wojtyła's complex philosophical argumentation, we intend here to concentrate on the main theses that concern the philosophical underpinnings of the concept of "the language of the body." While reflecting on human consciousness, Wojtyła comes to conclusions that set him apart from the phenomenological tradition. He argues that the basic role of consciousness consists not in intentional cognition of things, but in reflecting on things that are already known to the subject: "Consciousness as such is restricted to mirroring what has already been cognized. Consciousness is, so to speak, the understanding of what has been constituted and comprehended."[39]

Wojtyła's rejection of the intentional character of consciousness should be properly understood.[40] The father of phenomenology, Edmund Husserl, defined intentionality as "the own peculiarity of mental processes to be consciousness of something [*von etwas*]."[41] Wojtyła does not deny that consciousness is always "consciousness of something." In his view, however, consciousness does not play a cognitive role in the objectification of reality, because cognition—here Wojtyła is faithful to the epistemological tradition of Aristotelian-Thomistic realism—happens only through the body and sensory contact with reality.

An important element of Wojtyła's polemics with epistemological idealism is his break with the modern tradition of absolutizing consciousness. One of the elements of this break consists in an attempt to present the limits of what is conscious in man. Wojtyła notes that of the two fundamental dynamisms of the

39. Wojtyła, *The Acting Person*, 32.
40. Buttiglione, *The Thought of the Man*, 129–41; Kupczak, *Destined for Liberty*, 95–101.
41. Edmund Husserl, *Ideas Pertaining to a Pure Phenomenology and to a Phenomenological Philosophy*, translated by F. Kersten (Hague: Martinus Nijhoff Publishers, 1983), 1:200; quoted in Wojtyła, *The Acting Person*, 303–4.

human person, the psycho-emotive and the somatic-vegetative, only the former is clearly present in the reflecting consciousness. One reads in *The Acting Person* that

> it is not owing to consciousness that the dynamic unity of the man-subject is achieved at the vegetative level. The unity is attained apart from and in a way outside of consciousness, which in its reflecting function is not instrumental in this respect; for, as we saw, dynamic unity is antecedent and primary to consciousness in both its mirroring and reflexive functions. In the man-subject it consists—at least at the somatic level—primarily in the unity of life and only secondarily and, as it were, accidentally in the unity of experience.[42]

The philosophy of the human body as constructed by Wojtyła before 1978 is one of the key sources for the theological theory of the language of the body created by John Paul II. Though it anticipates some of the analyses to be carried out in the following pages, let us look at two dimensions of this causal relationship. First, John Paul II's understanding of the language of the body excludes any form of anthropological dualism in which the body would be considered as a secondary or less important part of the human person. It is worth noting that Wojtyła's philosophy of the body, developed in the polemics with modern idealism, creates the basis for John Paul II's theological position since it rejects the absolute character of consciousness and thus restores the body to its proper place in the *humanum*.

Second, according to *The Acting Person,* the human body plays a fundamental and irreplaceable role in the human cogni-

---

42. *The Acting Person,* 91. In his theory of integration, Wojtyła describes and analyzes the dynamisms of the human *soma* and *psyche,* which are not always present in human consciousness. The author of *The Acting Person* argues that every conscious human act (*actus humanus*), and especially an act of love, integrates the whole psychosomatic complexity of the human person, and creates "a whole and a unity emerging on the basis of some complexity" (ibid., 191).

tive process. Wojtyła seems to be inspired by St. Thomas Aquinas's axiom: *Nihil est in intellectu quod non sit prius in sensu* (There is nothing in the intellect that is not present earlier in the senses).[43] This axiom constitutes the *principium* of epistemological realism in the Aristotelian-Thomistic tradition. Since through his body man is a part of nature, and therein also similar to animals, Wojtyła defines the fundamental character of man's somatic dynamism as reactive, which means it is capable of reacting to different external stimuli. Therefore, the human body is—to a large extent beyond the consciousness of the subject—in a continual exchange of stimuli with the surrounding world. This reactive and often involuntary exchange is called by Wojtyła the "subjectivity of the body."[44] This subjectivity can be illustrated with a simple example: Let us imagine a tourist who becomes completely soaked through during a bicycle trip in autumn. On the way home, he stops at an unheated bar where, despite the best efforts of his will, he cannot control his shivering. The body becomes its own source of activity, which is quasi-independent of the will. The psychological theory of nonverbal communication, which interprets such behavior, as discussed in the previous section of this chapter, is thus linked to Wojtyła's philosophical thesis of the subjectivity of the body, as analyzed in *The Acting Person*.

The body speaks because it is a means of the conscious expression of the human subject. However, it also speaks because of its own subjectivity, rooted in sensory cognitive reactivity, which is not always present in the consciousness of the person. According to Wojtyła, the body speaks especially in the encounter of man and woman, when through its sensuality and emotionality, the body becomes a means of mutual cognition, fasci-

43. Thomas Aquinas, *Quaestiones disputatae de veritate*, q. 2, a. 3.
44. Wojtyła, *The Acting Person*, 210–13.

nation, communication, and union. We may therefore say that the human body speaks of love in a most complete and most moving way. This final conclusion of Wojtyła's philosophical account of the body directly leads us to John Paul II's theological understanding of the language of the body as presented in his Wednesday catecheses.

The Song of Songs: An Unsuccessful Attempt to Return to the Innocence of Creation

In the Wednesday catecheses on the theology of the body, John Paul II presents his theological theory of the language of the body by reflecting on two books of the Old Testament, in which the language of the body has a particularly prominent place: the Song of Songs and the Book of Tobit.[45] The papal reflections on the language of the body, as opposed to the psychological theory of nonverbal communication and Karol Wojtyła's philosophical theory of the body, consist in a theological interpretation of the divinely inspired Holy Scriptures. This interpretation, therefore, aims at revealing normative and objective truths about the meaning of the human body.

John Paul II notes that a person speaks by means of his or her body, but also that every kind of human speech is expressed in the body: "In the prophetic texts, the human body speaks a *'language'* of which it is not the author. *Its author is man,* as male or female, as bridegroom or bride: man with his perennial vocation to the communion of persons."[46] It is man who gives meaning to the activities and gestures of his body. The body can sometimes "speak"

---

45. John Paul II always demarcates the term "the language of the body" by quotation marks in order to emphasize its metaphorical character. When this concept is used in its psychological or philosophical meaning, as it was in the first two sections of this chapter, it is generally used without quotation marks.
46. *TB,* 537.

of unfaithfulness, anger, adultery; at other times the body can "speak" of faithfulness, tenderness, and love.

John Paul II emphasizes, however, that man cannot give meaning to his body in a completely arbitrary way. On the contrary, the language of the body, as used by every man, has to be interpreted through reference to objective and "perennial" meanings of the body.[47] Due to these references to the objective and perennial meanings of the human body, we may speak of truth and falsehood in the language of the body: "in the texts of the prophets, who see in marriage the analogy of Yahweh's covenant with Israel, *the body tells the truth* through faithfulness and conjugal love, and, when it commits 'adultery' it tells a lie, *it commits falsehood.*"[48]

John Paul II's understanding of a lie of the body differs significantly from the psychological interpretation of this mechanism, as described in the first part of this chapter. In communication psychology, we speak of a lie of the body in the case of an inconsistency or contradiction in the message sent by the subject. Such a situation suggests the subject's intention to wear a mask, or his wish to hide his true thoughts and aspirations from his surroundings. In the thought of John Paul II, the theological concept of a lie in the "language of the body" has a deeper meaning from the one accepted in social psychology. The pope interprets a lie to be a departure from the meaning of the body inscribed in human nature by the Creator.

The introduction of the criterion of objective truth into reflections on the language of the body points to the objective and eternal meanings of the human body, whose first author is the Creator. The most important task of every man and woman is to properly read these meanings and to understand and accept the spousal and parental meaning of one's own body. As opposed to the assumptions of dualistic anthropology, the proper reading of

47. Ibid., 540.   48. Ibid., 538.

the role and destiny of one's body also leads to the recognition of the vocation of the person, above all the vocation to love. At the same time, it should be noted that the reading of the meanings of the body, or the "language of the body," may occur on two levels: the natural (philosophical) or the theological, where the supernatural light of faith complements the capabilities of natural reason. The papal reflections in the catecheses are primarily of a theological nature, concerning the supernatural dimension of cognition.

In the Song of Songs, the very first verses of the text give an inkling as to the atmosphere in the poem in which "the bridegroom and the bride seem to move in the circle traced by the inner irradiation of love:"[49] "Let him kiss me with the kisses of his mouth! For your love is better than wine.... Draw me after you, let us make haste. The king has brought me into his chambers. We will exult and rejoice in you; we will extol your love."[50] John Paul II notes that this "internal irradiation of love," analogical to the first words of Adam upon seeing Eve in the Yahwist account of creation,[51] expresses fascination, astonishment, and admiration for the other sex. This fascination with the body of the other person and the experience of the beauty of the other sex is expressed in metaphors taken from the visible world:

How beautiful you are, my beloved, how beautiful you are! Your eyes are doves, behind your veil, your hair is like a flock of goats surging down Mount Gilead. Your teeth, a flock of sheep to be shorn when they come up from the washing. Each one has its twin, not one unpaired with another. Your lips are a scarlet thread and your words enchanting. Your cheeks, behind your veil, are halves of pomegranate. Your neck is the Tower of David built on layers, hung round with a thousand bucklers, and each the shield of a hero. Your two breasts are two fawns, twins of a gazelle, that feed among the lilies.[52]

49. Ibid., 552.
51. Gn 2:23.
50. Sg 1:2–4.
52. Sg 4:1–5.

A careful reading of the Song of Songs reveals that the mutual fascination with the body, male and female, is an expression of a fascination with the other person, another "I":

> The words of love spoken by both of them are therefore concentrated on the "body," not so much because in itself it constitutes the source of reciprocal fascination, but above all because the *attraction toward the other person*—toward the other "I," female or male, which in the inner impulse of the heart gives rise to love—lingers directly and immediately on it. In addition, *love unleashes a special experience of the beautiful,* which focuses on what is visible, although at the same time it involves the entire person. The experience of beauty gives rise to pleasure, which is reciprocal.[53]

To use John Paul II's term (which was already used in the same sense in his analysis of the role of corporeality in the biblical account of creation), it can be said that in the Song of Songs the human body is "transparent" to the dignity and spirituality of the person. Wojtyła's philosophical theory of human sexuality, already presented in this chapter, can be also useful in the interpretation of the Song of Songs: in an encounter with a person of the opposite sex, human sensuality and emotionality are transformed and sublimated in the affirmation of the whole person.

The enthusiastic tone of the Song of Songs originates in its depiction of a love that is ideal, unsullied by sin or any other human weakness. As John Paul II suggests, this ideal of love ought to be interpreted in reference to the first loving encounter of Adam and Eve, as presented in the biblical account of creation. Also, the ideal of love described in the Song of Songs is the expression of a natural human longing, which is the echo and trace of God's plan for creation reverberating in the depths of every man. Through

---

53. *TB*, 554. It seems that the term "attraction" was used intentionally by John Paul II. This term refers to a description of the loving fascination of man and woman in the classic metaphysical phrase "love of attraction" (*amor complacentiae*). A few pages further, in his analysis of the love of the bride and groom the pope analogously uses the term *amor amicitiae* (*TB*, 548–94).

its reference to the mystery of creation, the love described in the Song also establishes normative and ethical demands of every human love.

John Paul II notes that the fascination with the other "I," rooted in the fascination with the beauty of the opposite sex, is particularly clearly expressed in the words of the bridegroom, when he calls the bride "friend" and "sister": "You are altogether beautiful, my love.... You have ravished my heart, my sister, my bride."[54] The pope comments on this text in the following way: "*The term 'friend' indicates what is always essential for love, which puts the second 'I' beside one's own 'I.'* 'Friendship'—the love of friendship (*amor amicitiae*)—signifies in the Song a particular approach ... felt and experienced as an interiorly unifying power."[55]

The term "sister," used by the biblical author, strongly emphasizes the closeness of the two selves, the closeness of "I" and "you":

The expression "sister" speaks of union in humanity and at the same time of feminine diversity, of the originality of this humanity. This difference and originality exists not only with regard to sex, but to the very way of "being a person." If "being a person" means both "being a subject," but also "being in relation," the term "sister" seems to express in the simplest way *the subjectivity of the feminine "I"* in its personal relation, that is, *in its openness* toward others, toward the neighbor the particular addressee of this openness becomes *the man understood as "brother."*[56]

Undoubtedly, John Paul II's "philosophical exegesis" of the term "sister" goes much deeper than the usual biblical exegesis of this

---

54. Sg 4:7, 9. In the New Revised Standard Version of the Holy Scriptures, which is used throughout this book, the sentence from Sg 4:7 uses the word "my love" in reference to the bride. John Paul II uses a different translation of the Song of Songs which translates the same word as "friend." The former translation is present, e.g., in the New Jerusalem Bible ("my beloved") and the New American Standard Bible ("my darling"). The latter translation is used, e.g., in the Vulgate ("*amica mea*"), the Italian La Sacra Bibbia Nuova Riveduta ("*amica mia*"), the German Schlachter Version ("*meine Freundin*"), the Spanish Reina-Valera Revised ("*amiga mía*").

55. *TB*, 562. See also note 46 above.

56. *TB*, 562.

term, in which its meaning—as used often in ancient love poems—is an expression of feeling.[57]

The pope observes that maintaining a sisterly and brotherly bond in the relation of the bride and bridegroom excludes the danger of objectifying the other person, which is usually connected to the sexual urge. The sister and brother are linked by a feeling of intimacy rooted in the consciousness of a common past and memory. In the relationship of a brother and sister mutual closeness is socially accepted without suspicion and fear.[58]

Another way of looking at the bride, other than "sister" and "friend," is described in the next fragment of the Song of Songs: "A garden locked is my sister, my bride, a garden locked, a fountain sealed."[59] The word "garden" appears frequently in the Song and always refers to the woman.[60] Marvin Pope notes that etymologically this Hebrew word is close to such verbs as "to cover," "to shield," and "to defend." This meaning is strengthened by the term "a garden locked," which refers to closing the house (garden), or bolting it from within. Therefore, Marvin Pope notes that the expressions "a garden locked" and "a fountain sealed" point to sexuality and the virginity of the woman, and further, to the proper behavior of man and woman in their sexual relations.[61]

---

57. Roland E. Murphy, *The Song of Songs: A Commentary on the Book of Canticles or the Song of Songs* [Minneapolis: Fortress Press, 1990], 156). Another exegete, Arthur Herbert, claims that the term "sister" indicates the psychological closeness of the woman and man. Linking the relation of the bride and bridegroom from the Song of Songs with the Yahwist account of creation, Herbert adds that "they are already 'one flesh' in thought" (Arthur S. Herbert, "The Song of Solomon," in *Peake's Commentary on the Bible*, edited by Matthew Black [London: Thomas Nelson, 1962], 472). Certainly, this "being one flesh" (Gn 2:24) does not indicate only sexual intercourse, but symbolizes the whole truth about the integrity and depth of *communio personarum*, which existed before original sin. Herbert's reflection, which links the Song of Songs to the story of Adam and Eve, is reminiscent of the reflection of the catecheses in its methodological assumptions.

58. Also in the Book of Tobit is the newly wedded wife referred to as "sister" twice, as John Paul II argues, with a meaning very similar to the one presented in the Song of Songs (Tb 7:12; 8:7).

59. Sg 4:12.   60. Sg 4:15–16; 5:1; 6:2.11; 8:13.

61. Marvin H. Pope, *Song of Songs: A New Translation with Introduction and Commentary* (New York: Random House, 1977), 488–89.

This sensuous verse of the Song touches on the sexuality of the woman, toward which the man turns his desire, curiosity, and fascination. John Paul II's commentary on this verse of the Song delights by virtue of its discretion, dignity, and beauty of language. Therefore, despite its length, it is worth presenting in its entirety:

> From the "beginning," in fact, femininity determines the mystery about which Genesis speaks in relation to the man's "knowledge," that is, to "union" with the man. ("Adam united with Eve, his wife, who conceived and gave birth," Gn 4:1). Although the Song of Songs in its content as a whole does not directly speak about this "knowledge" or "union," nevertheless the metaphors just quoted remain in indirect, but at the same time very strict, relation with it. The bride appears to the eyes of the bridegroom as "a garden closed" and "a fountain sealed," or she speaks to him with what seems most profoundly hidden in the entire structure of her feminine "I," which also constitutes the strictly personal mystery of femininity. The bride presents herself to the eyes of the man as the master of her own mystery. One can say that both metaphors, "garden closed" and "fountain sealed," express the whole personal dignity of the sex, of that femininity which belongs to the personal structure of self-possession, and can consequently decide not only the metaphysical depth, but also the essential truth and authenticity of the personal giving. This gift of self has its dimension, when, in view of spousal love, that "knowledge" of which the Book of Genesis speaks must reveal itself.[62]

It is difficult to find a description of the sexual relation of woman and man in philosophical and theological literature that could be compared with this text in regard to its realism and dignity in treating corporeality and eroticism, but at the same time in regard to its depth in the description of the mystery of the person and his or her vocation. The love of man and woman is presented here simultaneously as sensual and spiritual. Mutual intimacy and be-

---

62. *TB*, 570–72. In his commentary on the biblical account of creation, John Paul II points out the personalistic understanding of sexual intercourse, linked to the biblical term of "knowing" the woman by the man (*TB*, 204–18). This has already been discussed in this book.

longing lead to the unveiling of the mystery of the two sexes, and at the same time reveal the truth about the internal inviolability and dignity of the person. Using philosophical language from *Love and Responsibility*, it can be said that the catecheses speak of how the sensuality and emotionality of the human body reveal the beauty and mystery of the other sex and also how mature love transcends the physical "language of the body" and moves toward the affirmation of and responsibility for the other person.

The papal commentary on the Song of Songs concludes with important comments on the weaknesses and limitations of human love. John Paul II observes that the rhythm of this love poem is marked by the lovers' continuous searching for each other, which results in a joyful meeting, and then changes into an anxious longing: "I opened to my beloved, but my beloved had turned and was gone. My soul failed me when he spoke. I sought him, but did not find him; I called him, but he gave no answer.... I adjure you, O daughters of Jerusalem, if you find my beloved, tell him this: I am faint with love."[63] The pope notes that the bride's words, "I am faint with love," point to the fragility of human love, which in its aspiration for the ideal of beauty, perfection, and fulfillment, exceeds the possibilities of real, historical man and woman.[64]

Another statement made by the bride contains a similar trace of truth about the limitations of human love: "for love is strong as death, jealousy is cruel as the grave."[65] Words that speak of love

---

63. Sg 5:6. 8.
64. Calling love a sickness is indicative of "the language of the body": somatic consequences of strong emotions feature frequently in the history of literature. In Shakespeare's comedy *The Two Gentlemen of Verona* the servant Speed explains to his master, Valentine, the external "illness-like" signs of his master's love: "You have learned, like Sir Proteus, to wreathe your arms, like a malcontent; to relish a love-song, like a robin-redbreast; to walk alone like one that had the pestilence; to sigh, like a schoolboy that had lost his ABC; to weep, like a young wench that had buried her grandma; too fast, like one that takes diet; to watch, like one that fears robbing; to speak puling, like a beggar at Hallowmas" (William Shakespeare, *The Two Gentlemen of Verona*, act II, scene I, in *The Complete Plays of William Shakespeare* [New York: Chatham River Press, 1984], 26).
65. Sg 8:6. The King James Bible is used here instead of the New Revised Standard

being strong as death seem to indicate the strength of human *eros*, but also the fact that this strength born of desire and fascination for the opposite sex has a natural end, and that is death. Analogically, the expression "jealousy is cruel as the grave" shows the positive face of love, its exclusivity and indivisibility, which are the sources of the indissolubility and monogamy of marriage. At the same time, however, these words indicate the limitation of sensual love, which cannot free itself from sinful jealousy. The story of the ideal love of the bride and bridegroom, outlined in the Song of Songs, ultimately shows the inability of a return to the purity of the reciprocal belonging of Adam and Eve before original sin. The love presented in the poem needs redemption.

Accordingly, the last papal comment on the Song of Songs concerns the necessity of the development of human erotic love toward greater maturity and depth in order to transcend itself, which will allow for an overcoming of the dark side of human meanness, weakness, and sin:

The truth of love expresses itself in the consciousness of reciprocal belonging, which is the fruit of the reciprocal aspiration and search, and at the same time this truth of love expresses itself in the necessity of the aspiration and search, which springs from the experience of reciprocal belonging. Love demands from both that they take a further step on the staircase of such belonging, always seeking a new and more mature form

---

Version. In the second part of this quotation, the New Revised Standard Version reads as follows: "passion fierce as the grave." John Paul II makes use of the translation that uses the word "jealousy" instead of the word "passion," and his commentary refers to both the negative and the positive dimensions of jealousy. On the one hand, jealousy is a positive feature of the great love of Yahweh for his people (Dt 32:16, 21; Ps 73:58). On the other hand, in contrast to God's love, human jealousy also shows the dark and unpredictable face of human love. Similarly to John Paul II's reflection, American Protestant theologian Renita J. Weems characterizes the warning of Sg 8:6 in the following way: "Beware, for 'human passion' (*gin'a*) sometimes manifests itself in a number of intense and indistinguishable shades. 'Jealousy', which is frequently the translation of the Hebrew word (*gin'a*), is the dark, dangerous side of love, as unrelenting as the grave itself and as vehement and intense as a blazing fire" (Renita J. Weems, "The Song of Songs: Introduction, Commentary, and Reflections," in *NIB*, 5:430).

of it. What becomes apparent in this inner necessity, in this dynamic of love, is *the impossibility*, as it were, *of one person being appropriated and mastered by the other*. The person is someone who stands above appropriation and domination, possession and satisfaction emerging from the same "language of the body."⁶⁶

Human *eros*, maturing by means of transcending itself, "seeks to integrate itself by means of a further truth of love"⁶⁷—a love that Christians call *agape*. It is a love whose source does not lie in human corporeality or sex, but in the triune God who created and redeemed us.

The Book of Tobit: Love Strong through Hope

The Book of Tobit is another book of the Old Testament where the topic of the language of the body plays an important role. The love of Sarah and Tobias described therein must face the danger of death. It turns out that this love is, using the words from the Song of Songs, "strong as death,"⁶⁸ and even, ultimately, stronger than death. The author of the Book of Tobit relates that Sarah married seven times, but each of her new husbands died on the wedding night because of an evil demon.⁶⁹

We read in the Book of Tobit that the angel Raphael comes to help Sarah and Tobias. The angel accompanies Tobias and advises him how to free himself from the evil demon.⁷⁰ It is Raphael who advises Tobias to turn together with Sarah to God in prayer on their wedding night. In the Book of Tobit we find the content of this prayer:

---

66. *TB*, 588.
67. Ibid., 590.
68. Sg 8:6.
69. Tb 7:11. For folk and literary sources on the Book of Tobit see Irene Nowell, O.S.B., "The Book of Tobit. Introduction, Commentary, and Reflections," in *The New Interpreter's Bible*, edited by L. E. Keck (Nashville: Abingdon Press, 1997), 3:975–88.
70. Tb 6:16–18.

You are blessed, O God of our fathers; blessed too is your name for ever and ever. Let the heavens bless you and all things you have made for evermore. You it was who created Adam, you who created Eve his wife to be his help and support; and from these two the human race was born. You it was who said "It is not right that the man should be alone; let us make him a helper like him." And so I take my sister not for any lustful motive, but I do it in singleness of heart. Be kind enough to have pity on her and on me and bring us to old age together.[71]

John Paul II emphasizes the richness of the biblical references found in the prayer of Sarah and Tobias; these are an indication of the fact that "their desire is to become a new link in the chain that goes back up to man's very beginnings."[72] Elements of both biblical accounts of creation—Elohist and Yahwist—are present in the newlyweds' prayer, and they constitute a specific conjugal *credo*. The Elohist account is present in Sarah and Tobias's prayer in the reference to the creation of man as male and female,[73] and to the gift of the blessing of fertility.[74] The theology of the Yahwist account is present above all through the reference to the original solitude of man: "It is not good that the man should be alone."[75]

John Paul II points out the significance of the fact that on their wedding night, before they become "one flesh," Sarah and Tobias attempt to reread the meaning of their union, of their "lan-

---

71. Tb 8:5–8. Christian exegetes acknowledge the existence of several different versions of the Book of Tobit. The prayer of Sarah and Tobias, quoted above, appears in the same form in several ancient codices (Christian J. Wagner, *Polyglotte Tobit—Synopse: Griechisch—Lateinisch—Syrisch—Hebräisch—Aramäisch* [Göttingen: Vandenhoeck & Ruprecht, 2002], 92–95).

72. *TB*, 606.   73. Gn 1:27.

74. Gn 1:28.

75. Gn 2:18. For references to the Elohist and Yahwist accounts of creation in the prayer of Sarah and Tobias see Joseph A. Fitzmyer, *Tobit* (Berlin: Walter de Gruyter, 2003), 244–46. Kenneth Stevenson argues in his historical work *Spousal Blessing: A Study of Christian Marriage Rites* (New York: Oxford University Press, 1982) that the prayer of Sarah and Tobias became the prototype of the blessing that was traditionally a part of the liturgy of the sacrament of marriage in the majority of Christian denominations. For the prayer of blessing in the Catholic liturgy of the sacrament of marriage after the Second Vatican Council see ibid., 182–89.

guage of the body," in the light of God's words. In this way the language of the body becomes the language of their marital liturgy:

> The "language of the body" becomes the language of the liturgy. Tobias and Sarah *speak the language of the ministers of the sacrament,* who are aware that in the conjugal covenant of man and woman—precisely through the "language of the body"—the mystery, which has its source in God himself, is expressed and brought into being. Their conjugal covenant is in fact the image—and the primordial sacrament of the covenant of God with man, with the human race—of the covenant that draws its origin from eternal Love.[76]

Thanks to their prayer together, Sarah and Tobias are able to consider their situation and the danger that they face in the light of faith in God, faith that gives hope.

For John Paul II, the prayer of Sarah and Tobias, rooted in the inspired words of the Bible, is a prototype and symbol of the marital liturgy in its two meanings. First, this prayer can be the inspiration for the common prayer of all spouses. Second, the pope observes that the liturgy of the sacrament of marriage draws inspiration from the Book of Tobit. During their prayer together, Tobias says: "I now am taking this kinswoman of mine, not because of lust, but with sincerity. Grant that she and I may find mercy and that we may grow old together."[77] In the liturgy of the Roman Catholic Church, newlyweds pronounce words with a very similar meaning: "I, N., take you, N., to be my wife. I promise to be true to you in good times and in bad, in sickness and in health. I will love you and honor you all the days of my life."[78]

As already noted in our discussion of the Song of Songs, the words of the marriage vows, which constitute the sacramental sign of the sacrament of marriage, are rooted in the truth of the language of the body of man and woman who have been united

---

76. *TB*, 606–8.
77. Tb 8:7–8.
78. Roman Missal.

by love. The words of the marriage vows that speak of "love, fidelity, and conjugal honesty" thus express the spousal and parental meanings of the human body, male and female. The truth of the marriage vows flows from the truth of the relation between man and woman. In other words, it is rooted in the integral experience of marital love.

Moreover, the Christian sacrament of marriage endows the newlyweds' love with dignity through the gift of supernatural grace:

> The sacraments infuse holiness into the terrain of man's humanity: they penetrate the soul and body, the femininity and masculinity of the personal subject, with the power of holiness. All of this is expressed in the language of the liturgy: there it is expressed, and there it is realized. *The liturgy,* liturgical language, *elevates the conjugal covenant* of man and woman, which is based on the "language of the body" reread in the truth, *to the dimensions of the "mystery,"* and at the same time enables that covenant to be realized in these dimensions through the "language of the body."[79]

The sacrament fills the life of the spouses, its *eros* and *ethos,* with content. In this sense, one could say that "liturgical language becomes the 'language of the body,'"[80] and the marital language of the body is a continuation of the liturgy.

Both the Song of Songs and the Book of Tobit speak about the love between man and woman. John Paul II, however, calls attention to the differences in the content and emotional temperature of these two texts. In the Song of Songs, the power of love is identified with passion and admiration for the opposite sex, whereas the Book of Tobit is more moderate in its description of love. The pope writes:

> The fact that Tobias loves Sarah "to the point of no longer being able to draw his heart away from her" (Tb 6:19) finds its expression above all *in his readiness to share in her lot* and to remain together "for better or

---

79. *TB*, 613.
80. Ibid., 614.

worse," whatever their lot. It is not eros that characterizes Tobias's love for Sarah, but from the beginning this love is confirmed and *validated by ethos,* that is, by the will and the choice of values. On the very threshold of marriage, the criterion of these values becomes the test of life-or-death that both must face already during their first night.[81]

Facing the danger of death, the love of Tobias and Sarah stands before a great trial. The language of their marital relation is defined not so much by passionate emotion as by faithfulness and courage in the face of evil, as well as by faith and trust in the help of the Almighty.

Ethical Consequences of the Language of the Body

The last part of John Paul II's Wednesday catecheses is devoted to a reflection on Paul VI's encyclical *Humanae vitae* (1968). It seems that the best way to present these reflections is to briefly summarize the major points of ethical argumentation made by Paul VI in the encyclical, and then to present the interpretation of this argumentation as found in the catecheses.

Humanae vitae: On Nature as a Reflection of the Plan of God

The fundamental aim of the encyclical *Humanae vitae* is to outline the moral principles that should guide spouses in the process of procreation in the current cultural climate—characterized as it is by demographic, economic, and social transformations. Paul VI rejects as morally evil all artificial methods (*artificiae viae*) of birth control and states that natural methods, in which the spouses use the woman's infertile period, are the only ethically acceptable way of responsible parenthood:

81. Ibid., 598–600.

The Church is coherent with herself when she considers recourse to the infecund periods to be licit, while at the same time condemning, as being always illicit, the use of means directly contrary to fecundation, even if such use is inspired by reasons which may appear honest and serious. In reality, there are essential differences between the two cases; in the former, the married couple makes legitimate use of a natural disposition; in the latter, they impede the development of natural processes.[82]

Paul VI's ethical argumentation proceeds on two levels: the first appeals to the universally binding natural law, whereas the second level takes into account the light of Christian revelation. The argumentation based on the natural law appeals to the concept of human nature: the moral goodness of human activity is determined by its agreement with human nature. Any activity directed against the true goods that perfect human nature is morally evil. Therefore, in order to define particular ethical norms that may be used to evaluate the ethical value of the conjugal act it is necessary to know the nature of this act.

It is especially important, according to Paul VI, to consider the two meanings present in the conjugal act, that is, unitive and procreative:

Indeed, by its intimate structure, the conjugal act, while most closely uniting husband and wife, capacitates them for the generation of new lives, according to laws inscribed in the very being of man and of woman. By safeguarding both these essential aspects, the unitive and the procreative, the conjugal act preserves in its fullness the sense of true mutual love and its ordination toward man's most high calling to parenthood.[83]

The indissoluble and natural relation of the two meanings of the conjugal act, the unitive and the procreative, cannot be ruptured by the spouses, because, inscribed as it is in the nature of the conjugal act, this relation agrees "with the design constitutive

---

82. *HV* 16.
83. Ibid., 12.

of marriage, and with the will of the Author of life."[84] Christian spouses, enlightened by the light of faith, can thus become "collaborators of God the Creator" through the life-giving conjugal act.[85]

The Ontological and Phenomenological Truth of the Language of the Body

In his commentary on the encyclical *Humanae vitae,* John Paul II points to two levels on which his predecessor Paul VI bases his ethical argumentation regarding the conjugal act. First of all, on the ontological level, which refers to the concept of human nature: "The encyclical leads one to look for the foundation for the norm determining the morality of the actions of man and woman in the conjugal act, in the nature of this act itself and more deeply still in the nature of the acting *subjects themselves.*"[86]

The second dimension in Paul VI's reasoning concerns the experience of the spouses. In this context, the encyclical *Humanae vitae* speaks of the meaning of the conjugal act. These two notions, fundamental for Paul VI's argumentation—the ontological understanding of the nature of the conjugal act and the experiential meaning of the conjugal act—are intrinsically linked:

> The *"innermost structure" (or nature)* of the conjugal act constitutes *the necessary basis for an adequate reading and discovery of the meanings* that must be carried over into the conscience and the decisions of the acting persons. It also constitutes the necessary basis for grasping the adequate relationship of these meanings, namely, their inseparability.... What is at stake here is the *truth,* first *in the ontological dimension* ("innermost structure") and then—as a consequence—in the *subjective and psychological dimension* ("meaning").... *"Meaning"* is born in consciousness *with the rereading of the (ontological) truth of the object.* Through this rereading, the (ontological) truth enters, so to speak, into the cognitive, that is, subjective and psychological dimension.[87]

84. Ibid., 13.
86. *TB,* 619.
85. Ibid., 1.
87. Ibid., 619–20.

John Paul II emphasizes that the ethical norms concerning the conjugal act and procreation, as presented in *Humanae vitae*, belong to the natural law. Therefore, an important aspect of Paul VI's argumentation consists in the justification of the magisterium's right to formulate norms of the natural law.[88] John Paul II's interpretation of Paul VI's thought, however, moves in another direction. It attempts to show the truth of *Humanae vitae* in light of the theology of the body, especially through reference to the theological depth contained in the notion of the "language of the body."

John Paul II reiterates his conviction, confirmed also by social psychology, that the language of the body plays an important role in interpersonal communication:

The human body is not only the field of reactions of a sexual character, but it is at the same time the means of the expression of man as an integral whole, of the person, which reveals itself through the "language of the body." This "language" has an important interpersonal meaning, especially in the area of the reciprocal relations between man and woman.[89]

However, the pope notes that the body does not only express man:

The subject of the natural law is man, not only in the "natural" aspect of his existence, but also in the integral truth of his personal subjectivity. He is shown to us in revelation as male and female in his full temporal and eschatological vocation. He is called by God to be a witness and interpreter of the eternal plan of love by becoming the minister of the sacrament, which has "from the beginning" been constituted in the sign of the "union of flesh."[90]

---

88. *HV* 4.
89. *TB*, 631.
90. Ibid., 631–32. See chapter 2 of this work under "The Sacramentality of the Body."

The language of the body, therefore, not only should express the wishes and intentions of its human subject, but is also meant to express "the eternal plan of love." As mentioned earlier, it is possible to judge ethically the language of human bodies in the reference to the objective criterion of truth, which points to the perennial meaning of the human body as presented by John Paul II in his biblical theology of the body. The language of the body re-read in truth becomes "an indispensable condition for *acting in the truth or for behaving in conformity with the value and the moral norm.*"[91] Thus, the language of the body informs us about the moral norm.[92]

In lieu of Paul VI's language that refers to the natural law, John Paul II, in his reinterpretation of *Humanae vitae*, makes an ethical argument that refers to the language of the body:

According to the criterion of this truth, which must be expressed in the "language of the body," the conjugal act "means" not only love, but also potential fruitfulness, and thus it cannot be deprived of its full and adequate meaning by means of artificial interventions. In the conjugal act, it is not licit to separate artificially the unitive meaning from the procreative meaning, because the one as well as the other belong to the innermost truth of the conjugal act.[93]

The effect of such an artificial separation of the two meanings of the conjugal act is that the corporeal marital union "does not correspond to the inner truth and dignity of personal communion, '*communio personarum.*' This communion demands, in fact, that the 'language of the body' be expressed reciprocally in

---

91. Ibid., 619.
92. The reader will not find a precise answer to the following meta-ethical question in John Paul II's catecheses: how does the truth about the meaning of the human body, or the truth of "the language of the body," become a particular moral norm? The pope indicates only the direction one should head to formulate an answer: the truth of "the language of the body" defines true human goods, in accord with human nature, which serve the fulfillment of the human subject.
93. *TB*, 632–33.

the integral truth of its meaning."⁹⁴ John Paul II summarizes his argumentation thus: "Such a violation of the inner order of conjugal communion, a communion that plunges its roots into the very order of the person, *constitutes the essential evil of the contraceptive act.*"⁹⁵

The pope argues, therefore, that contraception is a lie in the language of the body of man and woman. According to the logic of a loving gift, the corporeal union, in the marital language of the body, means a mutual and complete self-gift that originates in devotion and affirmation. Contraception clearly limits this affirmation, as man and woman say to each other: "I accept you, but not your fertility."

In the apostolic exhortation *Familiaris consortio* (1981), John Paul II discusses the falsehood of contraception in the context of opposing God's plan for marriage:

> When couples, by means of recourse to contraception, separate these two meanings that God the Creator has inscribed in the being of man and woman and in the dynamism of their sexual communion, they act as "arbiters" of the divine plan and they "manipulate" and degrade human sexuality—and with it themselves and their married partner—by altering its value of "total" self-giving. Thus the innate language that expresses the total reciprocal self-giving of husband and wife is overlaid, through contraception, by an objectively contradictory language, namely, that of not giving oneself totally to the other. This leads not only to a positive refusal to be open to life but also to a falsification of the inner truth of conjugal love, which is called upon to give itself in personal totality.⁹⁶

If using contraception is characteristic of the attitude of "arbiters" of the divine plan, then using natural methods of regulating fertility causes the spouses, according to John Paul II, to become "servants" in God's economy of salvation.

94. Ibid., 633.   95. Ibid.
96. *FC* 32.

A careful reader of the catecheses is struck by the theological depth of the concept of the language of the body. The semantic richness of this concept is built through reference to the mystery of creation, when the Author of the language of the body first began realizing his plan of Love in human history, as well as to the mystery of salvation that is realized in the sacramental mission of the Church. Having in mind this role that the couple holds in the history of salvation, John Paul II calls man and woman "ministers of a sacrament": "As ministers of a sacrament that is constituted through consent and perfected by conjugal union, man and woman are called *to express* the mysterious *'language' of their bodies in all the truth that properly belongs to it*.... In the language of the body, man and woman carry on the dialogue that—according to Genesis 2: 24–25—began on the day of creation."[97] John Paul II indicates that the celebration of the sacrament of marriage is a particularly important instance of rereading the language of the body in truth, especially when the bride and groom pronounce the words of the marriage vows: "I, N., take you, N., to be my wife. I promise to be true to you in good times and in bad, in sickness and in health. I will love you and honor you all the days of my life." It is precisely in the sacrament of marriage that man and woman reread the language of their bodies in the full truth, because thanks to the liturgy of the Church, both the mystery of creation and of Christ's salvation are once again realized in their love. We may therefore say that while ministering the sacrament of marriage to one another, the bride and groom carry out a prophetic act. Since a prophet is one who "expresses with human words the truth that comes from God,"[98] the ministers of the sacrament of marriage play a prophetic role, "proclaiming the 'language of the body' reread in the truth as the content and principle of their

---

97. *TB*, 632.
98. Ibid., 539.

new life in Christ and the Church."⁹⁹ The truth of the language of the body of man and woman, formulated in the marriage vows, later becomes the ethos and content of their daily marital and family life.

99. Ibid., 539.

FINAL REMARKS

George Lindbeck's book *The Nature of Doctrine* may well be regarded as one of the most important theological publications of the late twentieth century.[1] In the context of dialogue between religions, the Yale professor suggests a particular hermeneutics of sacred texts, that is, an intra-textual interpretation that is to enable dialogue among followers of different religions.[2] According to Lindbeck, a proper hermeneutics of religion should have a cultural and linguistic character so that truths of faith are interpreted not only cognitively, but also as a *regula fidei* for the whole of life of the community of believers.[3] More important for our reflections, however, is Lindbeck's distinction between Christian liberal and postliberal theology.

In his view, the method of liberal theology broadly used in different Christian denominations in the twentieth century consisted in translating the truths of faith into modern categories and concepts, which could be understood by a contemporary reader of the Gospels: "Liberals start with experience, with an account

---

1. George A. Lindbeck, *The Nature of Doctrine: Religion and Theology in a Postliberal Age* (Philadelphia: Westminster Press, 1984).
2. The summary of Lindbeck's argument can be found in Jeanrond, *Theological Hermeneutics*, 161–62.
3. Lindbeck, *The Nature of Doctrine*, 15–19.

of the present, and then adjust their vision of the kingdom of God accordingly, while postliberals are in principle committed to doing the reverse."[4] The method of postliberal theology, according to Lindbeck, consists first of all in a renaissance of the language of biblical revelation, with all the richness of its concepts, content, and historical connotations. Such a method ought to take care to avoid the dangers that are characteristic of modernity: reduction and adaptation of revelation to modern categories and notions.

Basing his theses on observations of American society (though they also seem to apply to other post-Christian Western cultures), Lindbeck notes the alarming disappearance of knowledge of the Bible, and even more, the disappearance of biblical culture. According to Lindbeck, this appalling process has serious consequences not only for Christian churches, but also for all of society, as it impoverishes the language of public discourse:

> Post-modern men and women do not easily survive in what for them is a cold and empty universe clothed only in the abstract jargon of sociological and psychological reason.... Furthermore, without the biblical shaping of the social mind and imagination, some societies, at least traditionally Christian ones, are likely to be even less just, less compassionate, less caring for the stranger then they would be if they had never been Christian. Nazism was not a reversion to Nordic barbarism, but far more savage. When Christian influence lapses, seven devils worse than the one originally expelled may rush into the swept and garnished emptiness.[5]

John Paul II's theology of the body, discussed in this book, fulfils George Lindbeck's requirements for a postliberal theology. The papal theology of the body, rooted in the biblical revelation of the Old and New Testaments, gives primacy to reflection on the Holy Scriptures. In his "philosophical exegesis," the pope tries

---

4. Ibid., 125–26.
5. George A. Lindbeck, "The Church's Mission to a Postmodern Culture," in *Postmodern Theology: Christian Faith in a Pluralist World,* edited by Frederic B. Burnham (San Francisco: Harper and Row, 1989), 53–54.

to make biblical texts understandable to modern man, in such a way, however, as not to reduce their meanings to contemporary human culture and to the expectations of contemporary man.

To paraphrase Paul Ricoeur's statements, as discussed in the first chapter of this work, we may say that the pope uses biblical symbols in such a way as not to invalidate them. Biblical images of original solitude, nakedness, lack and appearance of shame, the communion of persons, becoming one flesh, threefold concupiscence of the heart, and the language of the body are presented in such a way in the catecheses that a contemporary reader of the Bible is able to identify with them. Simultaneously, each of these images reveals some "surplus of meaning"—characteristic of God's Word—which the pope neither exhausts nor makes inaccessible to the reader.

Werner Jeanrond argues that the main dilemma of contemporary theological hermeneutics may be outlined as a conflict between the methods of Rudolf Bultmann and Karl Barth.[6] According to Bultmann, the biblical text, in order to be understood by the modern reader, must be demythologized; in other words, biblical truths must be translated into the language of contemporary culture. Bultmann explains why demythologization is necessary in the following way: "On the one hand, the mythical view of the world does not agree with the scientific view, which determines the way of thinking of contemporary man. On the other hand, there is the hermeneutical intention to make, thanks to existential interpretation, the kerygma of the New Testament understandable for man today."[7]

---

6. Jeanrond, *Theological Hermeneutics*, 127–48.

7. Rudolf Bultmann, *Foi et Comprehension: Eschatologie et demythologisation* (Paris: Editions du Seuil, 1969), 209. Jeanrond summarizes Bultmann's project of demythologization thus: "Biblical images such as 'kingdom of God,' 'begotten of the Holy Spirit,' 'born of a virgin,' etc. are mythological. That is not to say that they make no sense, but that these expressions produce sense in a way which needs explaining and translation for a modern reader of the biblical text" (Jeanrond, *Theological Hermeneutics*, 144).

Bultmann's method, thus summarized, was strongly criticized by Karl Barth, who feared that such demythologization of the Bible would impoverish the supernatural meaning of inspired texts. According to Barth, it is not the biblical text that is to be read in the light of the human experiences of the addressee of God's words, but, rather, human experiences that ought to be interpreted in the light of biblical revelation. To make this possible, the theological meaning of biblical texts must remain intact.[8]

The theological hermeneutics of John Paul II attempts to find a "compromise" or "a third way" between Bultmann and Barth. As presented in the first chapter of this work, the pope consistently uses interpretative tools provided by the historical-critical method in his reading of the Bible. This scientific exegesis leads to an integral reading of biblical texts and takes into account both the richness of their original meanings and their roots in ancient cultures.

Such interpretation, which is carried out with respect for the inspired texts and which does not invalidate biblical symbols and images, enables the contemporary reader to look at the texts as into a mirror. Simultaneously, John Paul II is consistent in his intention to "enlighten" biblical texts using notions taken from contemporary philosophy. As per Marian Grabowski, we called this interpretation "philosophical exegesis" and "translation of biblical images into philosophical concepts and of biblical narration into philosophical narration." Such biblical interpretation, described in the first chapter as "the hermeneutical circle," became possible due to John Paul II's concept of human experience and his conviction that the nature of the inspired biblical author and of the contemporary reader is the same. A presentation of John Paul II's methodological

---

8. In his famous essay on Bultmann's hermeneutics, Barth writes: "Thus, God's Word should never be presented and explained to man as something different than the truth and reality radically and always again alien, escaping man's capability to comprehend and given to him exactly provided that it does not belong to him" (Karl Barth, "Rudolf Bultmann, un essai pour le comprendre," in Karl Barth and others, *Comprendre Bultmann: Un dossier* [Paris: Editions du Seuil, 1970], 188).

principles, laid out in the first chapter, is followed by an exposition of the three historical dimensions of John Paul II's theological anthropology in the second chapter.

The predominant role of inspired biblical texts in the Wednesday catecheses points to the connection between the thought of John Paul II and the achievements of the Second Vatican Council. Undoubtedly, the whole Catholic Church—and particularly John Paul II's thought—is indebted to Vatican II for the renaissance of the interest in the Bible and for a renewed theological focus on the interpretation of biblical texts. In the third and fourth chapters of this book, which are devoted to the theological concepts of gift, communion, and *imago Dei*, the connection between John Paul II's reflections and the achievements of the council is presented as the interpretational key for understanding the papal theology of the body.

The relationship between John Paul II's pontificate and the Second Vatican Council is currently one of the most important debates in Catholic theology. In this discussion we may outline two fundamental positions. The first one is presented, among others, by George Weigel in his monumental book *Witness to Hope: The Biography of Pope John Paul II*. There, Weigel argues that the pontificate of John Paul II credibly interprets and implements both the theology and the decisions of the council. He also argues that after the first few years of confusion following the council, it was the teaching of John Paul II on different areas of Catholic life and doctrine that enabled us to perceive the authentic teaching of the council. Another position, supported by many theologians and journalists, clergy and laity alike, indicates differences between the achievements of the pontificate of John Paul II and the theology of Vatican II, which so optimistically assessed human history and emphasized the necessity of the Church's dialogue with the world.[9]

9. This thesis is present in the well-known work of Peter Hebblethwaite, *Paul VI: The First Modern Pope* (New York: Paulist Press, 1993), where Paul VI, representing the

Certainly, John Paul II's theology of the body presents an aspect of his theological work that supports Weigel's thesis about the deep link between Vatican II and John Paul II's pontificate. The papal theology of the body, as delivered during the Wednesday catecheses, presents many possibilities for its use in contemporary debates underway in the Church and the world. The concept of the language of the body, discussed in the fifth chapter of this work, seems to be an important tool for a new interpretation of Catholic marital ethics. It also goes without saying that the papal theology of the body could also serve as the inspiration for ethical debates on the meaning of sex in contemporary culture, on the role of women and the challenges created by feminism, as well as on the theology of marriage and family. It is my hope that this modest work will prove to be helpful in such important discussion.

---

spirit of Vatican II, is contrasted with John Paul II, who, according to Hebblethwaite, stopped the reforms initiated by the last council. Similarly, the Portuguese Jesuit Herminio Rico contrasts Vatican II and John Paul II's pontificate in the book *John Paul II and the Legacy of Dignitatis Humanae* (Washington, D.C.: The Catholic University of America Press, 2002). For a critique of Rico's book, see Kupczak, "John Paul II and the Legacy of *Dignitatis Humanae*," *Thomist* 67, no. 4 (2003): 662–65.

Bibliography

Acta Synodalia Sacrosancti Concilii Oecumenici Vaticani II. Città del Vaticano: Typis Polyglottis Vaticanis, 1970–1986.
Aquinas, Thomas [St.]. *Quaestiones disputatae de veritate*. www.corpus thomisticum.org.
———. *Summa contra gentiles*. www.corpusthomisticum.org.
———. *Summa theologiae*. www.corpusthomisticum.org.
Argyle, Michael. *Social Interaction*. London: Methuen, 1969.
———. *The Psychology of Interpersonal Behaviour*. Baltimore: Penguin Books, 1972.
Aristotle. *Categories*. www.classics.mit.edu/Aristotle.
———. *Metaphysics*. www.classics.mit.edu/Aristotle.
———. *On the Soul*. www.classics.mit.edu/Aristotle.
Ashley, Benedict, OP. *Theologies of the Body: Humanist and Christian*. Braintree: Pope John XXIII Medical-Moral Research and Education Center, 1985.
Augustine [St.]. *Confessions*. Translated by E. B. Pusey. Oxford: Parker, 1943.
———. *On Christian Doctrine*. www.ccel.org/a/augustine.
———. *On the Trinity*. www.ccel.org/a/augustine.
Augustine through the Ages: An Encyclopedia. General editor, Allan D. Fitzgerald, OSA. Grand Rapids, Mich.: Eerdmans, 1999.
Bacon, Francis. *The New Organon and Related Writings*. Indianapolis: Bobbs-Merrill, 1960.
Barth, Karl, and others. *Comprendre Bultmann: Un dossier*. Paris: Editions du Seuil, 1970.
Bauman, Zygmunt, and Tim May. *Thinking Sociologically*. Oxford: Blackwell, 2001.
Bierach, Alfred J. *Za maską człowiek: Czy można kłamać mową ciała w drodze do władzy, miłości, sukcesu?* Wrocław: Astrum, 1997.
Boethius. *Contra Eutychen et Nestorium*. www.gutenberg.org.
Bogucka, Maria. *Staropolskie obyczaje w XVI–XVII wieku*. Warsaw: Państwowy Instytut Wydawniczy, 1994.

Boniecki, Adam. *The Making of the Pope of the Millennium: Kalendarium of the Life of Karol Wojtyła*. Stockbridge, Mass.: Marian Press, 2000.

Bornkamm, Günther. "μυστήριον." In *Theological Dictionary of the New Testament*, edited by Gerhard Kittel, 4:802–28. Grand Rapids, Mich.: Eerdmans, 1967.

Brocki, Marcin. *Język ciała w ujęciu antropologicznym*. Wrocław: Astrum, 2001.

Bruaire, Claude. *L'être et l'esprit*. Paris: PUF 1983.

———. *La force et l'esprit*. Paris: Desclée de Brouwer, 1986.

Büchsel, Hermann M.-F. "θιμος, , ἡ ἐπιθυμία." In *Theological Dictionary of the New Testament*, edited by Gerhard Kittel, 3:168–69. Grand Rapids, Mich.: Eerdmans, 1967.

Bultmann, Rudolf. *Foi et Comprehension: Eschatologie et demythologisation*. Paris: Editions du Seuil, 1969.

Buttiglione, Rocco. *The Thought of the Man Who Became Pope John Paul II*. Translated by Paolo Guietti and Francesca Murphy. Grand Rapids, Mich.: Eerdmans, 1997.

Cassuto, Umberto. *A Commentary on the Book of Genesis*. Jerusalem: Magness Press, Hebrew University, 1989.

Catechism of the Catholic Church. Citta del Vaticano: Libreria Editrice Vaticana, 1993.

Clarke, Norris. "Person, Being and St. Thomas." *Communio* 19, no. 3 (1992): 601–18.

———. "Response to David Schindler's Comments." *Communio* 20, no. 3 (1993): 592–96.

Communion and Stewardship: Human Persons Created in the Image of God. International Theological Commission, 2002. www.vatican.va.

Congar, Yves, OP. *I Believe in the Holy Spirit*. Translated by David Smith. 3 vols. New York: Seabury Press, 1983.

Copleston, Frederick, SJ. *A History of Philosophy*. Westminster: Newman Press, 1959.

Cotter, David W. *Genesis*. Collegeville, Minn.: Liturgical Press, 2003.

Dalmais, Irénée-Henri. "Sacrements." In *Dictionnaire de spiritualité, ascétique et mystique, doctrine et histoire, fondé par M. Viller, continué par A. Derville*, vol. 14, col. 45–51. Paris: Letouzey et Ané, 1990.

De Lubac, Henri, SJ. *Augustianism and Modern Theology*. New York: Herder and Herder, 1968.

De Margerie, Bernard, SJ. *The Christian Trinity in History*. Still River, Mass.: St. Bede's Publications, 1982.

Den Bok, Nico. *Communicating the Most High: A Systematic Study of Person and Trinity in the Theology of Richard of St. Victor*. Paris: Brepols, 1996.

De Oliveira, Pinto. "Image de Dieu et dignité humaine." *Freiburger Zeitschrift für Philosophie und Theologie* 27 (1980): 401–36.

Derrida, Jacques. *Given Time: I, Counterfeit Money*. Chicago: University of Chicago Press, 1992.

———. *The Gift of Death*. Chicago: University of Chicago Press, 1995.

Descartes, René. "Discourse on the Method." In *The Philosophical Writings of Descartes*. Translated by John Cottingham, Robert Stoothoff, and Dugald Murdoch, 1:111–51. New York: Cambridge University Press, 1985.

———. *Treatise on Man*. In *The Philosophical Writings of Descartes*. Translated by John Cottingham, Robert Stoothoff, and Dugald Murdoch. New York: Cambridge University Press, 1985.

DeVito, Joseph. *The Interpersonal Communication Book*. New York: Harper and Row, 1986.

Dictionary of Biblical Imagery. Edited by Leland Ryken and others. Downers Grove, Ill.: InterVarsity Press, 1998.

DiNoia, Augustine, OP. "Imago Dei—Imago Christi: The Theological Foundations of Christian Humanism." *Nova et Vetera* (English edition) 2, no. 2 (2004): 267–78.

Döring, Heinrich. "Die Communio-Ekklesiologie als Grundmodell und Chance der ökumienischen Theologie." In *Communio Sanctorum: Einheit der Christen—Einheit der Kirche*, herausg. Josef Schreiner and Klaus Wittstadt, 439–70. Würzburg: Echter, 1988.

Downey, Michael. *Altogether Gift: A Trinitarian Spirituality*. Maryknoll, N.Y.: Orbis Books, 2000.

Doyle, Dennis M. *Communion Ecclesiology: Visions and Versions*. Maryknoll, N.Y.: Orbis Books, 2000.

Drumm, Joachim. "*Communio.*" In *Lexikon für Theologie und Kirche*, edited by W. Kasper, vol. 2, col. 1281–82. Freiburg: Herder, 1993–2001.

Dulles, Avery, SJ. *The Splendor of Faith: Theological Vision of John Paul II*. New York: Crossroad, 1999.

Eco, Umberto. *La Struttura assente*. Milan: Tascabili Bompiani, 1989.

Eliade, Mircea. *Myth and Reality*. New York: Harper Torchbooks, 1963.

———. *A History of Religious Ideas*. Chicago: University of Chicago Press, 1979.

Elias, Norbert. *The Civilizing Process: History of Manners*. Translated by Edmund Jephcott. New York: Urizen Books, 1978.

Emerson, Ralph Waldo. *Essays and Journals*. New York: Doubleday, 1968.

Fitzmyer, Joseph A., SJ. *Romans: A New Translation with Introduction and Commentary*. New York: Doubleday, 1993.

———. *Tobit*. Berlin: Walter de Gruyter, 2003.

Fox, Patricia A. *God as Communion. John Zizioulas, Elizabeth Johnson, and the Retrieval of the Symbol of the Triune God*. Collegeville, Minn.: Liturgical Press, 2001.

Freud, Sigmund. *The Future of an Illusion*. Translated by W. D. Robson-Scott. Garden City, N.Y.: Doubleday, 1961.
Funkenstein, Amos. *Theology and the Scientific Imagination from the Middle Ages to the Seventeenth Century*. Princeton, N.J.: Princeton University Press, 1986.
Gadamer, Hans-Georg. *Truth and Method*. Translated by Joel Weinsheimer and Donald G. Marshall. New York: Crossroad, 1990.
———. "Hermeneutyka." In Andrzej Bronk, *Zrozumieć świat współczesny*, 280–90. Lublin: Wydawnictwo Naukowe Katolickiego Uniwersytetu Lubelskiego, 1998.
Gardeil, Ambrose, OP. *The Holy Spirit in Christian Life*. St. Louis: Herder Book, 1953.
Gaudel, Auguste-Joseph. "Péché originel." In *Dictionnaire de théologie catholique contenant l'exposé des doctrines de la théologie catholique, leur preuves et leur histoire, commencé sous la direction de Jean-Michel A. Vacant*, vol. 12-1, col. 479–602. Paris: Letouzey et Ané, 1943.
Grabowski, Marian. "W stronę antropologii adekwatnej." In *O antropologii Jana Pawła II*, edited by M. Grabowski, 15–67. Toruń: Wydawnictwo UMK, 2004.
Grenz, Stanley J. *The Social God and the Relational Theology of the Imago Dei*. Louisville, Ky.: Westminster Press, 2001.
Gresham, John L., Jr. "The Social Model of the Trinity and Its Critics." *Scottish Journal of Theology* 46, no. 3 (1993): 325–43.
Grisez, Germain. "Dualism and the New Morality." In *Atti del Congresso Internazionale Tommaso d'Aquino nel Suo Settimo Centenario*, 5:323–30. Rome: Pontificia Accademia Romana di San Tommaso d'Aquino, 1977.
———. *Christian Moral Principles*. Chicago: Franciscan Herald Press, 1983.
Grundmann, Walter. "ἐγκράτεια." In *Theological Dictionary of the New Testament*, edited by Gerhard Kittel, 3:339–42. Grand Rapids, Mich.: Eerdmans, 1965.
Grygiel, Stanisław. "Czyn objawieniem osoby?" *Znak* 23, no. 2–3 (1971): 200–208.
———. "Od samotności do daru." *Znak* 34, no. 5 (1982): 363–84.
Guillet, Jacques. "God." In *Dictionary of Biblical Theology*, edited by Xavier Leon Dufour, SJ, 182–90. New York: Desclee, 1967.
Hall, Douglas John. *Imaging God: Dominion as Stewardship*. Grand Rapids, Mich.: Eerdmans, 1986.
Hall, Edward T. *The Hidden Dimension*. Garden City, N.Y.: Doubleday, 1966.
Hammer, Jerome, OP. *The Church Is a Communion*. New York: Sheed and Ward, 1964.
Harvey, Van A. "Hermeneutics." In *The Encyclopedia of Religion*, edited by M. Eliade, 6:279–86. New York, 1987.

Hauck, Friedrich. "καθαρός: Clean and Unclean in the NT." In *Theological Dictionary of the New Testament,* edited by Gerhard Kittel, 3:423–24. Grand Rapids, Mich.: Eerdmans, 1965.

———. "κοινός." In *Theological Dictionary of the New Testament,* edited by Gerhard Kittel, vol. 3, 789–809. Grand Rapids, Mich.: Eerdmans, 1965.

Hebblethwaite, Peter. *Paul VI: The First Modern Pope.* New York: Paulist Press, 1993.

Herbert, Arthur S. "The Song of Solomon." In *Peake's Commentary on the Bible,* edited by Matthew Black, 468–74. London: Thomas Nelson, 1962.

Hildebrand, Alice, and Dietrich von Hildebrand. *The Art of Living.* Manchester, N.H.: Sophia Institute Press, 1994.

Husserl, Edmund. *The Crisis of European Sciences and Transcendental Phenomenology: An Introduction to Phenomenological Philosophy.* Evanston, Ill.: Northwestern University Press, 1970.

———. *Ideas Pertaining to a Pure Phenomenology and to a Phenomenological Philosophy.* Translated by F. Kersten. Hague: Martinus Nijhoff Publishers, 1983.

Ide, Pascal. *Eh bien, dites: don. Petit éloge du don.* Paris: ed. de l'Emmanuel, 1997.

Ihde, Don. *Hermeneutic Phenomenology: The Philosophy of Paul Ricoeur.* Evanston, Ill.: Northwestern University Press, 1971.

Jacob, Edmond. *Theology of the Old Testament.* New York: Harper and Row, 1958.

Jaworski, Marian. "Teologia a antropologia: Aspekt filozoficzny." In *Teologia a antropologia: Kongres teologów polskich 21–23 IX 1971,* edited by Marian Jaworski and Adam Kubiś, 68–96. Kraków: Wydawnictwo Papieskiej Akademii Teologicznej, 1971.

Jacob, Edmond. *Theology of the Old Testament.* New York: Harper and Row, 1958.

Jeanrond, Werner G. *Theological Hermeneutics: Development and Significance.* New York: Crossroad, 1991.

Jerwell, Jacob. "Bild Gottes: biblische, frühjüdische und gnostische Auffassungen." In *Theologische Realenzyklopädie,* edited by G. Krause and G. Mähren, 6:494–98. Berlin: W. de Gruyter, 1980.

Jewett, Robert. *Paul's Anthropological Terms: A Study of Their Use in Conflict Settings.* Leiden: Brill, 1971.

John Paul II. "Homily for the Inauguration of the Pontificate. October 22, 1978." www.vatican.va.

———. *Familiaris consortio* (apostolic exhortation). November 22, 1981. www.vatican.va.

———. "Homily of January 25, 1985." www.vatican.va.

———. *Mężczyzną i niewiastą stworzył ich: Odkupienie ciała a sakramentalność małżeństwa.* Vatican City: Libreria Editrice Vaticano, 1986.

———. *Dominum et vivificantem* (encyclical). May 18, 1986. www.vatican.va.

———. *Redemptoris mater* (encyclical). March 25, 1987. www.vatican.va.

———. "Address to the Native Peoples of the Americas. September 14, 1987." www.vatican.va.

———. *Redemptoris custos* (apostolic exhortation). August 15, 1989. www.vatican.va.

———. "The Spirit as Gift: General Audience from 21 November 1990." http://www.vatican.va.

———. *Veritatis splendor* (encyclical). August 6, 1993. www.vatican.va.

———. *Crossing the Threshold of Hope.* New York: Alfred A. Knopf, 1994.

———. *Evangelium vitae* (encyclical). March 25, 1995. www.vatican.va.

———. *Letter to Families for the International Year of the Family 1994.* www.vatican.va.

———. *Vita consecrata* (apostolic exhortation). March 25, 1996. www.vatican.va.

———. *Fides et ratio* (encyclical). September 14, 1997. www.vatican.va.

———. "Address to the Participants in the International Study Week Promoted by the Pontifical Institute for Studies on Marriage and Family. August 27, 1999." www.vatican.va.

———. *Man and Woman He Created Them: A Theology of the Body.* Translation, introduction, and index by Michael Waldstein. Boston: Pauline Books and Media, 2006.

Kant, Immanuel. *Groundwork of the Metaphysics of Morals.* In Kant, *Practical Philosophy.* Translated by Mary J. Gregor. Cambridge: Cambridge University Press, 1996.

Kasper, Walter. *The God of Jesus Christ.* Translated by Matthew J. O'Connell. New York: Crossroad, 1984.

———. "The Church as Communio." *Communio—International Catholic Review* 13, no. 2 (1986): 100–118.

Kimel, Alvin F., ed. *Speaking the Christian God: The Holy Trinity and the Challenge of Feminism.* Grand Rapids, Mich.: Eerdmans, 1992.

———. *This Is My Name Forever: The Trinity and Gender Language for God.* Downers Grove, Ill.: InterVaristy, 2001.

Kirchmeyer, Jean. "Grecque (Eglise)." In *Dictionnaire de spiritualité, ascétique et mystique, doctrine et histoire, fondé par M. Viller, continué par A. Derville,* vol. 6, col. 808–72. Paris: Letouzey et Ané, 1967.

Kittel, Gerhard. "εἰκών: The Metaphorical Use of Image in the NT." In *Theological Dictionary of the New Testament,* edited by Gerhard Kittel, 2:392–97. Grand Rapids, Mich.: Eerdmans, 1964.

Knapp, Mark L., and Judith A. Hall. *Nonverbal Communication in Human Interaction*. Fort Worth, Tex.: Harcourt, 1997.

Kobler, John F. *Vatican II and Phenomenology: Reflections on the Life-World of the Church*. Dordrecht: M. Nijhoff, 1985.

Kolakowski, Leszek. *The Alienation of Reason: A History of Positivist Thought*. Translated by Norbert Guterman. Garden City, N.Y.: Doubleday, 1968.

———. *Main Currents of Marxism: Its Origins, Growth, and Dissolution*. Translated by P. S. Falla. Oxford: Oxford University Press, 1981.

Kowalczyk, Stanisław. *Zarys filozofii człowieka*. Sandomierz: Wydawnictwo Diecezjalne, 1990.

Kowalska, Faustina. *Divine Mercy in My Soul: The Diary of Sr. M. Faustina Kowalska*. Stockbridge, Mass.: Marian Press, 1987.

Krasnodębski, Zdzisław. *Rozumienie ludzkiego zachowania: Rozważania o filozoficznych podstawach nauk humanistycznych i społecznych*. Warsaw: Państwowy Instytut Wydawniczy, 1986.

Kubiś, Adam. "Preface." In Karol Wojtyła, *Sources of Renewal: The Implementation of Vatican II*, translated by P. S. Falla. San Francisco: Ignatius Press, 1980.

Kuderowicz, Zbigniew. *Dilthey*. Warsaw: Wiedza Powszechna, 1987.

Kupczak, Jarosław, OP. *Destined for Liberty: The Human Person in the Philosophy of Karol Wojtyła/John Paul II*. Washington, D.C.: The Catholic University of America Press, 2000.

———. "John Paul II and the Legacy of *Dignitatis Humanae*." *Thomist* 67, no. 4 (2003): 662–65.

———. "Komunijny wymiar obrazu Bożego w człowieku w soborowej konstytucji *Gaudium et spes*." *Studia Theologica Varsaviensia* 44, no. 1 (2006): 139–58.

Lamarche, Paul. "Image et ressemblance: Ecriture sainte." In *Dictionnaire de spiritualité, ascétique et mystique, doctrine et histoire, fondé par M. Viller, continué par A. Derville*, vol. 7-2, col. 1401–5. Paris: Letouzey et Ané, 1971.

Laun, Andreas. *Aktuelle Probleme der Moraltheologie*. Vienna: Herder Verlag, 1991.

Le Brun, Jacques, and Eulogio Pacho. "Quiétisme." In *Dictionnaire de spiritualité, ascétique et mystique, doctrine et histoire, fondé par M. Viller, continué par A. Derville*. vol. 12-2, col. 2756–842. Paris: Letouzey et Ané, 1986.

Leeuw, Gerardus van der. *Religion in Essence and Manifestation: A Study in Phenomenology*. Translated by J. E. Turner. New York: Harper and Row, 1963.

Letter to Bishops of the Catholic Church on Some Aspects of the Catholic Church Understood as Communion. Congregation for the Doctrine of the Faith, 1992. http://www.vatican.va/roman_curia/congregations/cfaith/documents.

Lewis, Clive Staples. *Four Loves.* New York: Harcourt, Brace, 1960.
Lindbeck, George A. *The Nature of Doctrine: Religion and Theology in a Post-liberal Age.* Philadelphia: Westminster Press, 1984.
———. "The Church's Mission to a Postmodern Culture." In *Postmodern Theology: Christian Faith in a Pluralist World,* edited by F. B. Burnham, 37–55. San Francisco: Harper and Row, 1989.
Luck, Ulrich. "σώφρων." In *Theological Dictionary of the New Testament,* edited by Gerhard Kittel, 7:1097–103. Grand Rapids, Mich.: Eerdmans, 1971.
MacDonald, Margaret Y. *Colossians and Ephesians.* Collegeville, Minn.: Liturgical Press, 2000.
Mallery, Garrick. "Sign Language among North American Indians Compared with That among Other Peoples and Deafmutes." *U.S. Bureau of Ethnology Report* 1 (1879–1880): 269–552.
Marion, Jean-Luc. *Being Given: Toward a Phenomenology of Givenness.* Stanford, Calif.: Stanford University Press, 2002.
———. *God without Being: hors-texte.* Chicago: University of Chicago Press, 1991.
Mauss, Marcel. *The Gift: Forms and Functions of Exchange in Archaic Societies.* Translated by Ian Cunnison. Glencoe, Ill.: Free Press, 1954.
McLeod, Frederick G., SJ. *Image of God in the Antiochene Tradition.* Washington, D.C.: The Catholic University of America Press, 1999.
Medley, Mark S. *Imago Trinitatis: Toward a Relational Understanding of Becoming Human.* Lanham, Md.: University Press of America, 2002.
Merriell, Juvenal D. *To the Image of the Trinity: A Study in the Development of Aquinas' Teaching.* Toronto: Pontifical Institute of Mediaeval Studies, 1990.
Meyer, Rudolf. "καθαρός: Clean and Unclean outside the NT: Judaism." In *Theological Dictionary of the New Testament,* edited by Gerhard Kittel, 3:418–21. Grand Rapids, Mich.: Eerdmans, 1965.
Miller, Maxwell. "In the 'Image and Likeness' of God." *Journal of Biblical Literature* 91 (1972): 289–304.
Moeller, Charles. "Pastoral Constitution on the Church in the Modern World: History of the Constitution." In *Commentary on the Documents of Vatican II,* 5:1–76. New York: Herder and Herder, 1969.
Mouroux, Jean. *The Meaning of Man,* Translated by A. H. G. Downes. New York: Sheed and Ward, 1948.
Murphy, Roland E. *The Song of Songs: A Commentary on the Book of Canticles or the Song of Songs.* Minneapolis: Fortress Press, 1990.
Mussner, Franz. *Histoire de l'herméneutique de Schleiermacher à nos jours.* Paris: Editions du Cerf, 1972.
Nachef, Antoine E. *The Mystery of the Trinity in the Theological Thought of Pope John Paul II.* New York: Peter Lang, 1999.

"Naked, nakedness." In *Dictionary of Biblical Imagery*. Edited by Leland Ryken and others, 581–82. Downers Grove, Ill.: InterVarsity Press, 1998.
Nietzsche, Friedrich. *Pisma pozostałe*. Translated by Bogdan Baran. Kraków: Inter-esse, 1994.
Nowell, Irene, OSB. "The Book of Tobit. Introduction, Commentary, and Reflections." In *The New Interpreter's Bible*, edited by L. E. Keck, 3:975–88. Nashville: Abingdon Press, 1997.
Noye, Irénée. "Piété." In *Dictionnaire de spiritualité, ascétique et mystique, doctrine et histoire, fondé par M. Viller, continué par A. Derville*, vol. 12-2, col. 1694–743. Paris: Letouzey et Ané, 1986.
O'Brien, Thomas C., OP. "Fallen Nature." In Thomas Aquinas, *Summa Theologiae: Latin Text and English Translation, Introductions, Notes, Appendices, and Glossaries*, 26:154–61. Oxford: Blackfriars, 1964–1981.
Oechslin, Raphael-Louis. "Image et ressemblance: Des mystiques rhénans au Carmel réformé." In *Dictionnaire de spiritualité, ascétique et mystique, doctrine et histoire, fondé par M. Viller, continué par A. Derville*, vol. 7-2, col. 1451–63. Paris: Letouzey et Ané, 1971.
"On the Gift: A Discussion between Jacques Derrida and Jean-Luc Marion." In *God, the Gift and Postmodernism*, edited by John D. Caputo and Michael J. Scanlon, 65–75. Bloomington: Indiana University Press, 1999.
Origen. *Homilies on Genesis and Exodus*. Translated by Ronald E. Heine. Washington D.C.: The Catholic University of America Press, 1981.
Pannenberg, Wolfhart. *Anthropology in Theological Perspective*. Philadelphia: Westminster Press, 1985.
Paul VI. *Humanae vitae* (encyclical). www.vatican.va.
Evangelii Nuntiandi (encyclical). www.vatican.va.
Pawlikowski, John T., OSM. "Theological Dimensions of an Ecological Ethics." In *The Ecological Challenge. Ethical, Liturgical, and Spiritual Responses*, edited by R. N. Fragomeni and J. T. Pawlikowski, OSM, 40–62. Collegeville, Minn.: Liturgical Press, 1994.
Perkins, Pheme. "The Letter to the Ephesians. Introduction, Commentary, and Reflections." In *The New Interpreter's Bible*, edited by L. E. Keck, 11:371–466. Nashville: Abingdon Press, 1997.
Pieper, Josef. *About Love*. Translated by Richard and Clara Winston. Chicago: Franciscan Herald Press, 1974.
Pinckaers, Servais, OP. *The Sources of Christian Ethics*. Translated by Mary Thomas Noble, OP. Washington, D.C.: The Catholic University of America Press, 1995.
Plato. *Plato in Twelve Volumes*. Translated by H. N. Fowler. Cambridge, Mass.: Harvard University Press, 1970.
Pope, Marvin H. *Song of Songs: A New Translation with Introduction and Commentary*. New York: Random House, 1977.

Prokes, Mary Timothy. *Mutuality, The Human Image of Trinitarian Love.* New York: Paulist Press, 1993.

Rad, Gerhard von. "εἰκὼν: The Divine Likeness in the OT." In *Theological Dictionary of the New Testament,* edited by Gerhard Kittel, 2:390–92. Grand Rapids, Mich.: Eerdmans, 1964.

Ramsey, Paul. *Basic Christian Ethics.* New York: Scribner, 1950.

Ratzinger, Joseph. *Death and Eternal Life.* Translated by Michael Waldstein. Washington, D.C.: The Catholic University of America Press, 1988.

———. "Concerning the Notion of Person in Theology." *Communio* 13 (1990): 438–54.

———. *Pilgrim Fellowship of Faith: The Church as Communion.* Translated by Henry Taylor. San Francisco: Ignatius Press, 2005.

Rickert, Kevin. "Wojtyła's Personalistic Norm: A Thomistic Analysis." *Nova et vetera* 7, no. 3 (2009): 653–78.

Rico, Herminio. *John Paul II and the Legacy of Dignitatis Humanae.* Washington, D.C.: The Catholic University of America Press, 2002.

Ricoeur, Paul. *Finitude et culpabilité, II. La symbolique du mal.* Paris: Editions Montaigne, 1960.

———. *The Symbolism of Evil.* Translated by Emerson Buchanan. New York: Harper and Row, 1967.

———. *The Conflict of Interpretations: Essays in Hermeneutics.* Edited by Don Ihde. Evanston, Ill.: Northwestern University Press, 1974.

———. "Myth and History." In *The Encyclopedia of Religion,* edited by Mircea Eliade, 10:273–82. New York: Macmillan, 1987.

Saier, Otto. *"Communio" in der Lehre des Zweiten Vatikanischen Konzils: Eine rechtsbegriffliche Untersuchung.* Munich: Hueber, 1973.

Saint-Jean, Raymond. "Tempérance." In *Dictionnaire de spiritualité, ascétique et mystique, doctrine et histoire, fondé par M. Viller, continué par A. Derville,* vol. 15, col. 142–49. Paris: Letouzey et Ané, 1991.

Saward, John. *Christ Is the Answer: The Christ-Centered Teaching of Pope John Paul II.* Staten Island, N.Y.: Alba House, 1995.

Scheffczyk, Leo. "Image et ressemblance: Dans la théologie et la spiritualité d'aujourd'hui." In *Dictionnaire de spiritualité, ascétique et mystique, doctrine et histoire, fondé par M. Viller, continué par A. Derville,* vol. 7-2, col. 1463–72. Paris: Letouzey et Ané 1971.

Schindler, David L. *Heart of the World, Center of the Church: Communio Ecclesiology, Liberalism and Liberation.* Grand Rapids, Mich.: Eerdmans, 1996.

———. "Norris Clarke on Person, Being and St. Thomas." *Communio* 20, no. 3 (1993): 580–92.

Schleiermacher, Friedrich. *Hermeneutics: The Handwritten Manuscripts.*

Edited by Heinz Kimmerle, and translated by James Duke and Jack Forstman. Missoula, Mont.: Scholars Press, 1977.
Schlier, Heinrich. "κεφαλη." In *Theological Dictionary of the New Testament*, edited by Gerhard Kittel, 3:680–81. Grand Rapids, Mich.: Eerdmans, 1965.
Schmitz, Kenneth L. "The Given and the Gift: Two Different Readings of the World." In *The Human Person and Philosophy in the Contemporary World: Proceedings of the Meeting of the World Union of Catholic Philosophical Societies, Cracow 23–25 August 1978*, edited by Józef Życiński, 2:260–76. Kraków: Wydawnictwo Papieskiej Akademii Teologicznej, 1980.
———. *The Gift: Creation*. Milwaukee: Marquette University Press, 1982.
———. *What Has Clio to Do with Athena? Etienne Gilson: Historian and Philosopher*. Toronto: Pontifical Institute of Mediaeval Studies, 1987.
———. *At the Center of the Human Drama: The Philosophical Anthropology of Karol Wojtyła—Pope John Paul II*. Washington, D.C.: The Catholic University of America Press, 1993.
———. "Created Receptivity and the Philosophy of the Concrete." *Thomist* 61, no. 3 (1997): 339–71.
Schnelle, Udo. *The Human Condition: Anthropology in the Teachings of Jesus, Paul and John*. Minneapolis: Fortress Press, 1996.
Schwanz, Peter. *Imago Dei als christologisch-anthropologisches Problem in der Geschichte der Alten Kirche von Paulus bis Clemens von Alexandrien*. Halle: Niemeyer, 1970.
Schu, Walter J., LC. *The Splendor of Love: John Paul II's Vision for Marriage and Family*. Hartford, Ky.: New Hope Publications, 2004.
Seebohm, Thomas M. "Hermeneutics." In *Encyclopedia of Phenomenology*, edited by Lester Ambree and others, 308–12. Dordrecht: Kluwer Academic Publishers, 1997.
Shakespeare, William. *The Complete Plays of William Shakespeare*. New York: Chatham River Press, 1984.
"Shame." In *Dictionary of Biblical Imagery*. Edited by Leland Ryken and others, 780–81. Downers Grove, Ill.: InterVarsity Press, 1998.
Shivanandan, Mary. *Crossing the Threshold of Love: A New Vision of Marriage in the Light of John Paul II's Anthropology*. Washington, D.C.: The Catholic University of America Press, 1999.
Shults, F. LeRon. *Reforming Theological Anthropology: After the Philosophical Turn to Relationality*. Grand Rapids, Mich.: Eerdmans, 2003.
Smith, Janet E. "Paul VI as Prophet." In *Why Humanae Vitae Was Right: A Reader*, edited by Janet E. Smith, 519–31. San Francisco: Ignatius Press, 1993.
Snijders, Jan. *The Early Works of Paul Ricoeur*. Nijmegen: n.p., 1982.

Spaemann, Robert. *Happiness and Benevolence.* Translated by Jeremiah Alberg, SJ. Notre Dame, Ind.: University of Notre Dame Press, 2000.
Speiser, Ephraim A. *Genesis: Introduction, Translation, and Notes.* Garden City, N.Y.: Doubleday, 1986.
Stevenson, Kenneth. *Spousal Blessing: A Study of Christian Marriage Rites.* New York: Oxford University Press, 1982.
Sullivan, John Edward. *The Image of God: The Doctrine of St. Augustine and Its Influence.* Dubuque, Iowa: Priory Press, 1963.
Synowiec, Juliusz. *Na początku: Wybrane zagadnienia Pięcioksięgu.* Warsaw: Akademia Teologii Katolickiej, 1987.
Tatarkiewicz, Władysław. *Historia filozofii.* 3 vols. Warszawa: Wydawnictwo Naukowe PWN, 2001.
Taylor, Charles. *Sources of the Self: The Making of the Modern Identity.* Cambridge, Mass.: Harvard University Press, 1989.
Thérèse of Lisieux [St.]. *The Story of a Soul: The Autobiography.* Translated by Michael Day. Westminster, Md.: Newman Press, 1952.
Torrell, Jean-Pierre, OP. *Saint Thomas Aquinas.* Translated by Robert Royal. Washington, D.C.: The Catholic University of America Press, 2003.
Vanneste, Alfred. *The Dogma of Original Sin.* Brussels: Vander, 1975.
Van Nieuwenhove, Rik. "In the Image of God: The Trinitarian Anthropology of St. Bonaventure, St. Thomas Aquinas and the Blessed Jan Van Ruysbroec." *Irish Theological Quarterly* 66 (2001): 109–23 (part 1), 227–37 (part 2).
Vawter, Bruce."Genesis." In *A New Catholic Commentary on Holy Scripture,* edited by R. C. Fuller, 176–82. Melbourne: Nelson, 1969.
———. *On Genesis: A New Reading.* Garden City, N.Y.: Doubleday, 1977.
Volf, Miroslav. *After Our Likeness: The Church as the Image of the Trinity.* Grand Rapids, Mich.: Eerdmans, 1998.
Wagner, Christian J. *Polyglotte Tobit—Synopse: Griechisch—Lateinisch—Syrisch—Hebräisch—Aramäisch.* Göttingen: Vandenhoeck and Ruprecht, 2002.
Waldstein, Michael. "Introduction." In John Paul II, *Man and Woman He Created Them: A Theology of the Body.* Translation, introduction, and index by Michael Waldstein, 1–128. Boston: Pauline Books and Media, 2006.
Weems, Renita J. "The Song of Songs: Introduction, Commentary, and Reflections." In *The New Interpreter's Bible,* edited by L. E. Keck, 5:363–434. Nashville, Tenn.: Abingdon Press, 1997.
Weigel, George. *Witness to Hope: Biography of the Pope John Paul II.* New York: Cliff Street Books, 1999.
———. "Introduction." In Walter J. Schu, LC, *The Splendor of Love: John Paul II's Vision for Marriage and Family,* 21–24. Hartford, Ky.: New Hope Publications, 2004.

Welch, Claude. *In This Name: The Doctrine of the Trinity in Contemporary Theology*. New York: Scribner, 1952.
Wenz, Günther. "Sakramente: Kirchengeschichtlich." In *Theologische Realenzyklopädie*, vol. 29, edited by G. Krause and G. Mähren, 663–84. Berlin: W. de Gruyter, 1998.
White, Charles J. "Gift Giving." In *The Encyclopedia of Religion*, edited by M. Eliade, 5:552–57. New York: Macmillan Publishing Company, 1987.
Wojtyła, Karol. "Religijne przeżywanie czystości." *Tygodnik Powszechny* 9, no. 6 (1953): 1–2.
———. "Myśli o małżeństwie." *Znak* 9, no. 7 (1957): 595–604.
———. "Propedeutyka sakramentu małżeństwa." In *Rola kobiety w Kościele*, 87–92. Lublin: Wydawnictwo Naukowe Katolickiego Uniwersytetu Lubelskiego, 1958.
———. "O znaczeniu miłości oblubieńczej." *Roczniki Filozoficzne* 22, no. 2 (1974): 162–74.
———. *Aby Chrystus się nami posługiwał*. Kraków: Znak, 1979.
———. *The Acting Person*. Translated by Andrzej Potocki. Dordrecht: D. Reidel Publishing, 1979.
———. "Instynkt, miłość, małżeństwo." In Wojtyła, *Aby Chrystus się nami posługiwał*, 36–50. Kraków: Znak, 1979.
———. *Sign of Contradiction*. New York: Seabury Press, 1979.
———. "Tajemnica i człowiek." In Wojtyła, *Aby Chrystus się nami posługiwał*, 28–35. Kraków: Znak, 1979.
———. "Wychowanie miłości." In Wojtyła, *Aby Chrystus się nami posługiwał*, 88–93. Kraków: Znak, 1979.
———. *Sources of Renewal: The Implementation of Vatican II*. Translated by P. S. Falla. San Francisco: Ignatius Press, 1980.
———. *Love and Responsibility*. Translated by H. T. Willetts. San Francisco: Ignatius Press, 1981.
———. *Wykłady lubelskie*. Lublin: Wydawnictwo Naukowe Katolickiego Uniwersytetu Lubelskiego, 1986.
———. *Collected Plays and Writings on Theater*. Translated by Bolesław Taborski. Berkeley: University of California Press, 1987.
"The Jeweler's Shop." In Wojtyła, *Collected Plays and Writings on Theater*, translated by Bolesław Taborski, 267–323. Berkeley: University of California Press, 1987.
———. "Radiation of Fatherhood." In Wojtyła, *Collected Plays and Writings on Theater*, translated by Bolesław Taborski, 323–65. Berkeley: University of California Press, 1987.
———. "Reflections on Fatherhood." In Wojtyła, *Collected Plays and Writings on Theater*, translated by Bolesław Taborski, 365–71. Berkeley: University of California Press, 1987.

———. "The Family as a Community of Persons." In Wojtyła, *Person and Community: Selected Essays*, translated by Theresa Sadok, OSM, 315–29. New York: Peter Lang, 1993.

———. "Parenthood as a Community of Persons." In Wojtyła, *Person and Community: Selected Essays*, translated by Theresa Sadok, OSM, 329–43. New York: Peter Lang, 1993.

———. "Participation or Alienation?" In Wojtyła, *Person and Community: Selected Essays*, translated by Theresa Sadok, OSM. 197–209. New York: Peter Lang, 1993.

———. *Person and Community: Selected Essays*. Translated by Theresa Sadok, OSM. New York: Peter Lang, 1993.

———. "The Person: Subject and Community." In Wojtyła, *Person and Community: Selected Essays*, translated by Theresa Sadok, OSM, 219–63. New York: Peter Lang, 1993.

———. "The Personal Structure of Self-Determination." In Wojtyła, *Person and Community: Selected Essays*, translated by Theresa Sadok, OSM, 187–97. New York: Peter Lang, 1993.

———. "Subjectivity and the Irreducible in the Human Being." In Wojtyła, *Person and Community: Selected Essays*, translated by Theresa Sadok, OSM, 209–19. New York: Peter Lang, 1993.

———. "Transcendencja osoby w czynie a autoteleologia człowieka." In Wojtyła, *Osoba i czyn oraz inne studia antropologiczne*, 477–90. Lublin: Wydawnictwo Naukowe Katolickiego Uniwersytetu Lubelskiego, 1994.

———. "Sermon at Mogila for the Triumph of the Cross: September 16, 1978." In Adam Boniecki, *The Making of the Pope of the Millennium: Kalendarium of the Life of Karol Wojtyła*, 830–31. Stockbridge, Mass.: Marian Press, 2000.

Zimbardo, Philip G. *Psychology and Life*. 9th ed. Glenview, Ill.: Scott, Foresman, 1977.

Index

Acting Person, The, 47–49, 106–7, 120–21, 183–85
adultery, 63–65
affirmation, 39, 65–66, 98, 100, 119, 144, 182, 189, 193, 204
anthropology: adequate, 5–17; dualistic, 110, 214; relational, 79, 122, 133, 135, 145, 166–67. *See also* man; reductionism
appropriation, 61
Aquinas, Thomas, St., 56, 75, 90, 95–96, 99, 101, 115–16, 122, 134, 139, 154, 166, 168, 185
Aristotelian-Thomistic tradition, 98–101, 183, 185
Aristotle, 17, 21, 47–48, 99
Augustine, St., 32–33, 59, 61, 68, 90, 96, 101, 115–16, 139, 154, 165–66, 168

baptism, 59, 87
Barth, Karl, 135, 209–10
beginning, the, 25–33, 42–53, 78, 80, 109, 121–22, 146, 152–53. *See also* creation
being, contingent, 12
Bierach, Alfred J., 177
bioethics, 13
body, 3–9; as the image of God, 164–66; as subject, 42–54; as object, 54–65; as sign of the person, 13, 57, 60; glorified, 82; in the Cartesian thought, 4–5; in biological knowledge 13. *See also* nakedness; language of the body; sex; sacramentality of the body; meaning of the body

Book of Tobit, The, 195–98
Bultmann, Rudolf, 35, 209–10

celibacy. *See* continence
child, 111–12, 124, 128–29. *See also* family; fatherhood; maternity
Christ, 165–69; Head of the Church, 84–86; the image of God, 138–40. *See also* Church; redemption
Church, 47, 83, 91; as *communio*, 97, 102–5, 134–35; as Christ's Bride, 84–88. *See also* ecclesiology; communion
Clarke, Norris, 133
communication, nonverbal, 170–78. *See also* language of the body
communio personarum. See communion of persons
communio. See communion
communion of persons, 80, 83, 93–98, 104, 110; as the image of God, 146, 149–59. *See also* imago Dei; love; Communion of Saints
Communion of Saints (*communio sanctorum*), 79, 82, 130, 165
communion, history of the term, 96–97; in the theology of Vatican II, 101–5. *See also* communion of persons; Church; Holy Trinity
concupiscence, 59–73, 80, 125–28, 151–52, 158, 209
conscience, 56–58, 201
consciousness, 6–8, 19–20, 107, 109, 117, 121–22, 125, 145, 152, 183–85. *See also* self-consciousness

227

INDEX

continence, 74, 81–83, 163
contraception, 127, 204
conversion, 113
Copleston, Frederick, SJ, 43
covenant, 197–98
creation, 186–96; of Adam, 7–9; of Eve, 117–120; as gift, 109–16; in the Yahwist account, 44–50, 142–47; in the Elohist account, 142–47. *See also* beginning, the

death, 45–46, 193–95. *See also* immortality
demythologization, 209–10
Descartes, René, 1, 3–4, 43, 67
determinism, 15, 17, 51, 57, 159
DeVito, Joseph, 174–76
dignity, 13
Dilthey, Wilhelm, 24
divinization, 78, 129, 164
domination, of husband over wife, 85, 126; over nature, 45. *See also* governance
dualism. *See* anthropology

Eco, Umberto, 171–72
Emerson, Ralph Waldo, 94
emotions, 177–82
Erasmus of Rotterdam, 173
ethos, of the Sermon on the Mount, 62–71; of the redemption of the body, 69–70
ecclesiology: Eucharistic, 97, 134
experience, 4–9, 19, 24–33, 78–81; boundary, 53, 58; essentially human, 9, 17, 20; unity of human experience, 9; original, 25, 60

faith, 32–40, 207–8
family, 105
fatherhood, 52, 111, 123. *See also* child; motherhood; family
fear: of God, 55, 84
feminism, 212. *See also* woman
Fides et ratio, 11, 34, 37–39
Fitzmyer, Joseph A., SJ, 69–70, 196
Fox, Patricia A., 135

freedom, 15, 17, 37, 44–46, 69, 106, 119–20, 141. *See* self-determination
friendship, 99, 106, 190. *See* love

Gadamer, Hans-Georg 21, 24
Galileo, 2–3
gift, 85–86, 93–131; disinterested, sincere, 106–10, 120, 132; identification of its meaning, 167; trinitarian, 96, 101; in the philosophy of Karol Wojtyła, 100, 131–36. *See also* hermeneutics of the gift; the law of the gift
God, 43–46. *See also* Christ; Holy Spirit; Holy Trinity
governance: over nature, 2. *See also* domination; self-governance
Grabowski, Marian, 10, 40, 143, 210
grace, as gift, 91, 113–14; lost, 56; of the resurrection, 59, 69, 129, 157, 162–67
Grenz, Stanley J., 135, 165–66, 169
Guillet, Jacques, 95

Hall, Edward T., 174–77
Hauck, Friedrich, 72, 96
head, 23; the husband as the head of his wife, 84–86; Christological meaning, 84–86
heart, 42, 64–66, 69–71, 82–83
Heidegger, Martin, 21, 24
hermeneutics, 18–40; of the gift, 18–19; as existential interpretation of symbols and myths, 29–40; as a method of text interpretation, 20–22; as theory of understanding, 24–29; hermeneutical circle, 24, 29–40; of suspicion, 35, 67; of the sacrament of marriage, 19
Hildebrand, Alice von, 101
Hildebrand, Dietrich von, 101
Holy Spirit, 74–75, 102–4, 113–16
Holy Trinity, 49, 79, 115, 135, 149–51, 165
Humanae vitae, 126–27, 199–203
Husserl, Edmund, 1–2, 43, 183

idealism, 182–84
image. *See imago Dei*
imago Dei, 139–69, 211; image and like-

ness, 166; the biblical view, 142–45; relational and structural, 165–69; in the history of theology, 139–42; the communal interpretation, 146–52, 157, 165, 169. *See also* Christ
immortality, 23, 155
incommunicabilias, 100, 121–22
innocence, original, 25, 27, 53–56, 60, 92, 116–20, 125–26, 156
integration, 49, 184
introspection, 4
Ireneus, St., 154, 156–57, 166–67

Jaworski, Marian, 10–11
jealousy, 193–94

Kant, Immanuel, 62
Knapp, Mark L., 172, 174–77
Kowalczyk, Stanisław, 16
Krasnodębski, Zdzisław, 4

language of the body, 170–206; true or false 175–78, 203; in the philosophy of Karol Wojtyła, 177–86, 202–6. *See also* communication
law, of the gift, 2, 108; natural, 200–3. *See also* gift, nature
Leeuw, Gerardus van der, 94
Letter to the Ephesians, 84–89, 113
Lindbeck, George A., 207–8
liturgy: marital, 197
Love and Responsibility, 14, 62, 98–101, 108–9, 180–81, 193
love, 15, 18–19; of Christ to the Church, 84–86; four types, 98–99; limitations of, 193; marital, 179–80
lust, 58–65

man (male), 152–53. *See also* woman; fatherhood
man: cosmologic definition, 17, 144, 166; personalistic definition, 17, 166; classic definition, 43–45; as the body, 4; as microcosm, 179; in search of his definition, 6–9, 46. *See also* anthropology, body, person

Manichaeism, 66, 72
Marion, Jean-Luc, 95
marriage, 80–81, 85–89; as sacrament, 18–19, 83, 88–92, 196–99, 205; after resurrection, 77, 128; of Mary and Joseph, 83; monogamy, 23, 51, 194. *See also* liturgy; love; lust; concupiscence
mask, 177–78, 187
Mauss, Marcel, 93–94
meaning of the body, 42, 125, 129–30, 153, 187; virginal, 75–83; nuptial, 81–83 parental, 42, 52, 69, 123, 187, 198
metaphysics, 3, 11, 16
Method: phenomenological-existential, 10; phenomenological-metaphysical, 6, 11; historical-critical, 22; Cartesian, 1, 3–4, 43, 67. *See also* adequate anthropology; phenomenology; hermeneutics; metaphysics
moderation, 74
motherhood, 52, 83, 110, 123, 93–94, 167–69. *See also* child; fatherhood; family
Mouroux, Jean, 101
myth, 19–24, 29–39

nakedness, original, 53–56, 118–19; after sin, 56–59, 158. *See also* shame;
nature of man, 2; as source of the language of the body, 12, 187; as source of moral norms, 200–3; its three theological ages, 20, 25, 80, 116
nature, 2–4, 7, 12, 14–15
Nietzsche, Friedrich, 16, 67–68

parenthood, 110–11, 199–200
participation, 78–79
Paul VI, 127, 199–203, 211
perichoresis, 134
person, 8, 12, 14–15. *See also* affirmation; body; man; dignity; appropriation
Personalistic Norm, 62
phenomenology, 10–11, 16, 178, 183. *See also* method
philosophical exegesis, 10, 20, 40, 56, 142, 146, 159

philosophy, 34–39. *See also* Aristotelian-Thomistic tradition; phenomenology; hermeneutics; metaphysics
Pieper, Josef, 132
piety, 75, 84, 161
Plato, 21, 170–71
Pope, Marvin H., 191
post-modernism, 208
practical imperative, 62
prayer: spousal, 196
pride, 67–68
purity, 54, 60, 70–75, 108, 128, 161, 179, 194

quietism, 132

Rad, Gerhard von, 137, 154
Ratzinger, Joseph, 79, 97, 133–34
receptivity, 122, 133
redemption, 194; of the body, 69–70; as gift, 112–14
reductionism, anthropological, 12–16, 41, 118. *See also* anthropology
Rej, Mikołaj, 172
resurrection, 75–82, 128–30, 161–64
revelation, 5, 10, 12–13, 25
Ricoeur, Paul, 21, 23, 29–39, 67, 71, 209

sacrament, 87–92. *See also* baptism; ecclesiology; marriage
sacramentality, of the body, 83–92
Scheffczyk, Leo, 140, 142, 157
Schleiermacher, Friedrich, 21–22
Seebohm, Thomas M., 20–22
self-consciousness, 8–9, 19. *See also* consciousness
self-determination, 45, 105–6, 120, 153
self-governance, 106, 120, 128–29, 132, 167. *See also* domination, governance
self-possession, 106, 110, 120, 123, 128–29, 132, 192
sensuality, 51, 59, 132, 180–81, 189, 193
sex: 50–52; as opposition, 59–63; its complementarity, 118–22. *See also* woman, man

sexual, union, 106; as cognition 93–94, 183–84; its two meanings, 277–82. *See also* marriage
shame, 52–59, 89, 118–19, 124–25, 158–59, 209
sin, 62–64, 74, 139; and *imago Dei*, 147, 151–52, 156–59; as rejection of the gift, 113; original, 25, 27, 31–33, 53–57, 59–61, 92, 119, 124–25
solitude, original, 7–9, 27, 44–51, 116–17, 144–46
Song of Songs, The, 23, 83, 186–98
Sources of Renewal, 101–4
spiritualization, 77–78, 129, 164
subjectivity of man, 7–9, 12, 14, 17, 20, 28, 41. *See also* body as the subject
symbol, 19–21, 29–39, 209–10. *See also* myth

Tatarkiewicz, Władysław, 43
Taylor, Charles, 3
Therese of Lisieux, St., 148
transcendence, 47, 57, 120, 137, 167
transcendentals, 11

utilitarianism, 35

Vatican Council II, 47, 49, 91, 140; and theology of John Paul II, 97–104, 142, 150, 160, 168, 211–12; participation of Karol Wojtyła, 105–9
visio beatifica, 78–79

Weigel, George, 211–12
Welch, Claude, 168
will, 15, 64, 66
woman, 127, 208, 212; discriminated, 50–51, 61; in the creation, 50–51. *See also* feminism; man; sex
work, 44

Zimbardo Philip G., 174–75
Zizioulas John, 135